Financial Management in the Public Sector

Bernard M. Jones

Principal Lecturer in Public Sector Management
Sheffield Business School
Sheffield Hallam University

THE McGRAW-HILL COMPANIES

London · New York · St Louis · San Francisco · Auckland · Bogotá · Caracas
Lisbon · Madrid · Mexico · Milan · Montreal · New Delhi · Panama · Paris
San Juan · São Paulo · Singapore · Sydney · Tokyo · Toronto

Published by
McGRAW-HILL Publishing Company
Shoppenhangers Road, Maidenhead, Berkshire SL6 2QL, England
Telephone 01628 23432
Facsimile 01628 770224

British Library Cataloguing in Publication Data

Jones, Bernard M.
  Financial management in the public sector
    1. Finance, Public 2. Public administration 3. Budget
  I. Title
  351.7′2

  ISBN 0-07-707888-8

Library of Congress Cataloging-in-Publication Data

Jones, Bernard
    Financial management in the public sector / Bernard Jones.
      p. cm.
    Includes bibliographical references.
    ISBN 0-07-707888-8 (alk. paper)
    1. Finance, Public. 2. Finance, Public – Accounting.
  3. Managerial accounting. I. Title.
  HJ141.J66 1996
  350.72–dc20
                                            96-15745
                                              CIP

McGraw-Hill

A Division of The McGraw·Hill Companies

1 2 3 4 5 CUP 9 9 8 7 6

Typeset by Paston Press Ltd, Loddon, Norfolk
and printed and bound in Great Britain at the University Press, Cambridge

Printed on permanent paper in compliance with ISO Standard 9706

CONTENTS

PREFACE

This book was started in 1993 and completed in 1995 with a break during 1994 while I worked on another book and a number of smaller projects. This fallow period was not wasted as it gave scope for reflecting on changes in the financial arrangements of central government and the civil service, and understanding the evolving nature of the NHS and the way in which its structures and internal market were working in practice. The pace of change in local government seems to have abated somewhat: dare we assume a period of relative stability?

READERSHIP

The book is intended to be of value to five sets of people:

1. Students on undergraduate courses (BTEC Higher or Degree) in such areas as Public Administration or Public Sector Management, where Public Finance or Public Sector Financial Management is an integral component of the curriculum. Such students know that a knowledge of the basis of public finance and the way in which financial decisions are operationalized by managers is increasingly necessary in obtaining a position in the public sector. The book is intended to cover the basic groundwork without assuming any prior knowledge or experience.
2. Students on post-experience management courses such as DMS or MBA where there is frequently scope for changing the balance of the study of finance away from the private sector towards the public sector which provides many, often the majority, of the course participants. It is hoped that the book will provide them with suitable material for enhancing their study of finance and that they will be able to bring their experience to bear in interpreting the material.
3. Students working for professional examinations, for example within the parameters of CIMA or CIPFA. The book is not aimed at any particular syllabus, but Sections A, B and D should provide useful contextual material, although the material in Section C is usually studied in far more detail by such students.
4. Teachers of all the above classes of students. Such teachers have sometimes come either from a non-financial background and thus need support with basic financial material laid out in intelligible form, or else from a technical financial background within the private sector and thus need support with understanding the idiosyncrasies of the public sector and its financial arrangements.
5. Public sector managers who need to update themselves on this central area of competence and to have a reference book which will help them understand what the financial experts within their organization are actually saying!

HOW THIS BOOK IS ORGANIZED

The organization of the book is perhaps a little different from the conventional. The first three chapters which comprise Section A are discursive in nature and are intended to provide the context in which the changing nature of public sector financial management is located. Section B, which covers terminology and concepts, is arranged as a set of encyclopaedia-style articles on various key terms and underpinning knowledge. It is deliberately non-mathematical in scope. Some of the many mathematical/numerical techniques available to decision makers are introduced in Section C with worked examples drawn predominantly from the public sector. Section D includes exercises for student working and case studies for class discussion. Finally, a set of appendices provide a glossary, an outline description of some key concepts of accounting and how they are applied in the public sector and a bibliography arranged in a format which may help students to make sensible selection of texts for further study.

This organization owes much to the experience of over fifteen years of teaching public finance to a variety of students with different needs and abilities. Most were interested in the political/governmental aspect—particularly as the fifteen years covered the whole of the Thatcher and early Major periods of government when nothing in public finance could be taken for granted. Most needed insights into the key concepts. Many struggled with the quantitative aspects and needed a far gentler treatment than was available in conventional texts aimed at numerate and relatively sophisticated accountancy students. A detailed treatment of accountancy was not necessary and in any case was beyond my competence, but an outline treatment was found useful by many in-service students who needed to establish meaningful dialogue with their finance section colleagues. Earlier versions of the glossary proved useful to several generations of students preparing for professional examinations.

ACKNOWLEDGEMENTS

It ought to be stressed that I am qualified neither as an accountant nor as an economist. My former head of department, Professor Bob Haigh, suggested that as a mathematically literate teacher I might like to take a few local government finance classes. These were soon supplemented by some NHS finance groups and almost before I knew it my main teaching and research thrusts were in this direction. I was helped in my early studies by some key figures in the Sheffield area. Terry Jennings and Trevor Gee from the Sheffield City Council Treasurer's Department were constant providers of helpful advice, information and guest lecturing. Later Terry arranged for a period of secondment. John Brassington, first in his capacity as Director of Finance of Sheffield Health Authority and latterly as Director of Finance for the Trent Region was invaluable as a source of information on the NHS. He too arranged for a period of secondment to the Sheffield DHA.

These periods of secondment were seminal. In both I was located in the relevant audit section undertaking value for money studies at a time when both local government and the NHS were coming to terms with cash limitation. There were too many helpful people at all levels from audit clerk to head of section to mention by name, but I learned a great deal of lasting value from my work with an often undervalued section which has a role to play at all levels, from the scrutiny of detailed operations to the offering of more general strategic policy advice.

More recently a number of colleagues have proved very helpful. The Director of Sheffield Business School, Professor Kevan Scholes, has helped me enormously with both encouragement and practical advice: I worked with him on preparing a couple of case studies and found his guidance as to clarity and directness of great value. My subject leader, Roger Ottewill (a CIPFA man) has made many pertinent comments on various parts of the draft manuscript as well as facilitating the workload flexibility necessary to sustaining long periods of writing. Other close colleagues who have looked at various sections of the draft include John Kingdom, Ann Wall and Clive Woodman. For some of my advice I have turned to colleagues in the School of Financial Studies and Law. Here Jane Ducker and Jim Ryan, with each of whom I have shared courses, have taught me a lot. Jim also looked at some of the draft as did John Joyce, an ex-NHS auditor now teaching management accounting, and Peter Vincent-Jones who is an expert on the role of contracts and quasi-contracts within internal markets. Outside Sheffield Hallam University I have been fortunate to obtain help from Richard Allen, Under Secretary at HM Treasury, and from Ian Yates of Fearn Yates limited, a firm of specialist auditors. None of these people is, of course, responsible for any of the errors which are bound to surface.

At McGraw-Hill my initial contact was Brendan Lambon who was very encouraging in the initial stages of draft preparation. Later Anthea Coombs took over his role and kept me going through pressures of work, illness and the varied circumstances of domestic life. I also offer thanks to Alastair Lindsay, Lynne Balfe and Karin Henderson who were involved in the editing and production of the book. Nicola Dale provided excellent secretarial support, particularly in producing a decent version of the final manuscript from my rather basic word processing.

To all the people I offer my sincere thanks. I should also like to thank my wife, Dorothy Jones, for putting up with my routine of hours at the keyboard and bouts of grumpiness when it was not going too well.

Bernard M. Jones
October 1995

DESCRIPTION AND ANALYSIS

THE STRATEGIC LEVEL OF PUBLIC SECTOR FINANCIAL MANAGEMENT

INTRODUCTION

The public sector manager working in a service department in, say, the NHS or local government has, to all intents and purposes, no control over Government financial policy. Neither, in strict terms, is it necessary for such a manager to understand Government financial policy except inasmuch as it impinges directly upon service provision. Nevertheless, the British public servant in the 1990s is expected to manage resources with an eye to economy, efficiency and effectiveness in a way undreamt of in the late 1970s when James Callaghan, who warned that public spending must be reined, and Anthony Crosland, who more graphically told us 'the party's over' were widely ignored.

Since then the notion of public sector financial management has emerged, crystallized and been disseminated. The change is mostly due to the reshaping of attitudes and policies instigated by the Conservative administrations of Mrs Thatcher from 1979 to 1983, 1983 to 1987 and 1987 to 1990 and, more recently, the administrations of Mr Major from 1990 to 1992 and 1992 to date. No manager, of whatever political persuasion, can have escaped the changes wrought by these governments; it is thus important that the main substance of this book should be located in the context of underlying history, theory and political belief.

It must, however, be made plain that just as a knowledge of the history of science does not make one a scientist nor a knowledge of science make one an engineer, so a knowledge of history or economic theory does not of itself make a manager. There are techniques of management, particularly of financial management; they may be better applied by those who know and understand the context in which they are practised.

Given this premise, it is legitimate to ask what we mean by the strategic level of public sector financial management. The easy answer is management practised by the strategists, i.e. the Government if we regard the United Kingdom as the organization in question. Such an answer is empty; we need to know why the Government feels that it has to manage, what it can manage and how it manages. The last question has two aspects: 'what tools does it have at its disposal?' and 'what outcomes have resulted?' The answer to the final question feeds into the first; the Government (any government) is pressured for positive outcomes.

Figure 1.1 summarizes the answers that will be given to these questions and thus sets both the structure and the agenda for this chapter.

Why do governments manage?
- Management involves *maintaining* what is there; history, most of it fairly recent, has created public expectations which must be largely satisfied.
- Management involves *reacting to pressures*: political parties, pressure groups and, increasingly, international bodies all create a changing climate that invites response.
- Management involves a *creative dimension* which *seeks to act*: beliefs and ideological systems arising within government can lead to radical change.

What can governments manage?
- In norman circumstances governments have direct responsibility for and have to a large extent control over *governmental income* and *governmental expenditure*.
- In normal circumstances governments have considerable, and maybe direct, control over *interest rates and currency exchange rates*.
- As a consequence of the factors instanced above it is widely, although not universally, believed that governments have at least some influence, if not control, over *inflation* and *growth*.

How do governments manage?
- The major instruments which determines government income are the *budget* and the *taxation system* which it defines.
- The major instruments which determine government spending are the *Public Expenditure Survey Processes* and their consequences.
- In the UK the Government has control of the *Bank of England* and thus direct control of the prevailing rates of interest.
- A series of *international agreements* to which governments have been more or less willing parties define the system for valuing the pound.
- Of recent years *monetary supply* has been seen as an important factor in controlling inflation and encouraging economic growth.
- Related to several of the above is the question of the level of *public sector borrowing* which affects *annual debt servicing charges*, *interest rates* and the *total level of national debt*.

Figure 1.1   The 'Why', 'What' and 'How' of governmental financial management

WHY GOVERNMENTS MANAGE

The tasks of management

Managers maintain, react and initiate. That general statement can be applied to governments. In democratic states where, however crudely, the public will is voiced at intervals, governments are aware that they will be judged on their performance in meeting expectations. Those public expectations arise:

- partly from history: the public has grown used to a level of provision of certain goods and there will usually be discontent if that level is not maintained;
- partly from relatively informed opinion: nothing is static and there will always be opinion leaders criticizing or praising governments for reacting to change unwisely or sensibly;
- partly from relatively informed opinion: sometimes a government initiates changes rather than reacts to circumstance, and there will always be opinion leaders criticizing or praising as above.

In any organization maintenance is usually seen as the job of lower level managers, initiation as the role of senior managers and reaction as the task of managers at an intermediate level. To an extent this is true of national governments. The routine tasks of maintenance are usually delegated away from the central and political to the peripheral and the administrative. They are brought back towards the centre if major reaction or initiation come on to the political agenda.

Nevertheless, maintenance requires finance and thus governments, in working at the strategic level of allocating financial resources and determining structures, are playing a maintenance role. It is worth looking, albeit sketchily, at the British public sector to see how past initiations and reactions have changed the scope of maintenance.

The basic tasks of government

The classic justification for state activity in liberal democracies is the 'preservation of the realm' (defence) and the 'safety of person and property' (law and order). It is interesting to note that these criteria are also the ones used in international affairs in determining whether or not a new state will be recognized by existing states. Such activity gives rise to a minimal state having a public sector concerned only with policing and defence matters. Interestingly, different states define the boundaries between policing and defence in different ways and in emergent or troubled states there is usually no difference at all!

Such state activity might historically be supplemented by a religious dimension involving a state religion and/or state licensing of religious leaders. The 'establishment' of the Church of England is a relic of this phase and the central role of Islam in some Middle Eastern states is a current manifestation of this phenomenon. It is worth nothing that religion has usually taken a leading role in supporting education, health and 'charity'; all of which are now aspects of state provision in Britain. It is also worth noting that, because of its 'security' aspect, the postal service has almost invariably been a primary state enterprise.

The growth of government ownership of the infrastructure

From the early nineteenth to the mid twentieth century in Britain there was a considerable growth in the extent of state enterprise. The industrial revolution created towns and cities which needed water and drainage. The drains were almost invariably municipal, the water provided by a mixture of municipal and private enterprise. The same was true of roads and, later on, gas and electricity. Telephone services were mainly state run with some local authority and private schemes. International air services and the BBC were national enterprises from their inception, but internal air services were in private, often railway, hands as was passenger shipping. By 1951 all the infrastructure services just listed, along with coal mines, the steel industry and the road haulage industry were in state hands. They were either nationally or locally run, but (with odd exceptions such as some local waterworks and certain toll roads/bridges) they were part of the provision of the state and their maintenance and funding were the responsibility of government.

W. H. Greenleaf[1] showed that in the years from 1792 to 1950 central and local government expenditure grew from 11 per cent to 39 per cent of gross national product (GNP). The bulk of this growth was concentrated in the 40 years from 1910 to 1950 (a period embracing two world wars) when it tripled from 13 per cent to 39 per cent. In employment terms, and including the public corporations, the public sector grew from 2.4 per cent of the workforce to 26 per cent of the workforce in the century from 1851 to 1951.

Such growth over a period of more than a century was not steady. Indeed much was quite tightly focused into periods of stress, particularly following major wars. The Attlee governments of 1945–50 and 1950–51, for example, were responsible for much of the tidying up of the infrastructure including the nationalization of the railways and the mines. The railways had effectively been nationalized from 1914 to 1921 (during and just after the First World War) and had been restructured from 1923 by government fiat. The Second World War brought about another effective nationalization, but this time, in 1948, the railways were not returned to private hands but kept as part of the suite of nationally owned enterprises. Their management had thus become a maintenance task for Government, but the nationalization was in part a reaction (to circumstance and pressure) and in part an initiative taken in the light of certain ideological considerations current in the post-war Labour party.

The mining industry was also nationalized for similar reasons. The need for coal was intense. There was little or no private capital available for the necessary complete overhaul of an industry in which profits had not been great for many years. The same mixture of reaction and initiative brought the coal mines into public ownership and imposed a duty of maintenance upon the Government. On the other hand, the nationalization of road transport and the steel industry were stimulated much more by initiative than by reaction. There were no intense external pressures on Government to make the change, but there were internal pressures of an ideological nature and thus the Government may be said to have initiated change. Be that as it may, the results were an enlarged public sector and an enlarged task of maintenance management.

The growth of the welfare state

The same period also saw an enormous extension in governmental provision of welfare. The concept was not new. The Poor Law Act of 1601 had made public, albeit rudimentary, provision for some sections of the sick and poor. The intervening centuries had seen occasional ad hoc state intervention, but in the years from about 1870 (Education Act) to 1948 (NHS Act) the major arms of the welfare state were initiated, often by charity, developed, often in partnership with government, and at last integrated, for the most part, into the state system. It has to be said that a strong private sector remained in many fields (e.g. education and health) and also that without voluntary provision in some fields (e.g. the care of children and the elderly) the welfare state could not have worked.

A full list of welfare services would be too long for this bird's eye view. It could, however, be divided into infrastructural services (e.g. the NHS, the education services, the family and community support services and public health monitoring) and income support payments (e.g. child allowances, pensions, unemployment and sickness benefits and various allowances for housing). It is a debatable point whether housing itself should be considered a part of the welfare state or a part of the economic infrastructure. Be that as it may the provision and upgrading of housing has been seen as a major role of Government (local and/or central) for over sixty years.

Table 1.1 indicates some key acts and reports in the periods from 1834 to 1946.

The Attlee Governments of 1945–50 and 1950–51 usually receive much of the credit for the formation of the welfare state, and certainly the major legislation which implemented the recommendations of the Beveridge Report was due to Attlee and his team. It should be remembered, however, that the welfare state did not just happen: it grew piecemeal in response to pressures over a long period and both Liberal and Conservative governments passed legislation in earlier years without which the welfare state would have been an impossibility.

It is worth, once again, drawing attention to war as a catalyst for change. Poor physique in Boer War recruits, for example, led to action intended to improve the health of the lower classes. The Second World War swept away many of the attitudinal and institutional objectives to rationalization of the diverse provisions for welfare that had existed until 1945.

Be that as it may, by 1951 the welfare state was a reality and its maintenance a duty which the public expected Government to undertake.

Table 1.1 Key dates in the growth of the welfare state

Year	Key feature
1834	Poor Law Act—established Poor Law Boards
1848	Public Health Act (Russell) enabled establishment of local Health Committee (administrated by Edwin Chadwick)
1868/1875	Artizans' and Labourers' Dwellings Acts (enabling legislation)
1870	Education Act (Forster) 'education for all'
1875	Public Health Act (Disraeli/Cross)—sanitary districts, Medical Officers of Health
1908	Old Age Pensions (Asquith/Lloyd George)—'five bob a week ... Lloyd George gave me' (old song)
1911	National Insurance Act (Lloyd George/Winston Churchill)—contributory scheme for sickness and unemployment
1918	Education Act (Fisher)—'free and compulsory education to 14'
1919	Housing Act (Addison)—'homes fit for heroes'
1934	Unemployment Act—Unemployment Assistance Boards: 'the means test'
1942	Beveridge Report—'to defeat ... the five giants ... want, disease, squalor, ignorance, idleness'
1944	Education Act (Butler)—'secondary education for all'
1946	National Health Service Act (Bevan)—'treatment free at point of delivery'
1948	National Assistance Act—consolidating legislation

The help of my colleagues John Kingdom and Ann Wall in compiling this table is gratefully acknowledged.

Financial and economic stability

Over a long period of history the British economy had been relatively strong. True, there had been bad times in the nineteenth century and depression in the 1920s and 1930s, but by the mid-1960s the predominant picture was of economic growth, albeit slow, with relatively low inflation and consequently relatively low interest rates. Theoretical work, such as that by J.M. Keynes in the inter-war period, had made Government 'intervention' in economic matters acceptable and it seemed that Government had taken on board a task of maintaining growth and consequently full employment. By the mid-1960s there was a general feeling of security—the years of Harold Macmillan's alleged 'our people have never had it so good' quote.

Greenleaf[1] shows how GNP, reduced to 1900 prices, grew from £154m in 1792 to £6,223m in 1970. By 1990 this figure had grown to £9,656m. This growth, divided into a number of periods each approximately 20 years long, shows an average annual increase ranging from a minimum of £2.7m p.a. to a maximum of £171.6m p.a. or, in percentage terms an annual growth rate ranging from 0.7 per cent to 5.2 per cent. Overall the annual growth for the period averages rather less than 3 per cent.

Important, however, to any government's calculations, is the value of the currency; the rate at which it can be traded against other currencies, for example the US dollar, the Japanese yen or the German mark. The exchange rate is primarily a measure of how much confidence the money market places in the British economy. The science is imprecise and over a period of years there are temporary and often short-lived ups and downs for no obvious reason. There has also been since

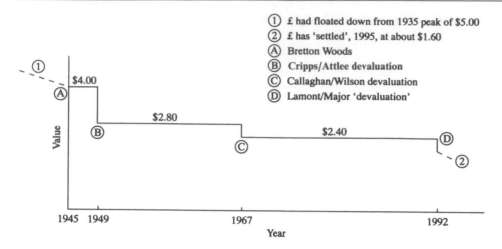

Figure 1.2   Value of £ since 1945

1945 a general downward drift of sterling against the currencies mentioned which has from time to time led to a step change in the value of the pound (Figure 1.2). These step changes (devaluations) have been resisted by the governments concerned because, although they can bring short-term benefits in terms of interest rates and making it easier to export, the psychology of the situation is such that the Government is perceived to have 'failed' in some way in its task of maintaining national standing and prestige.

The Governments from the mid-1960s to the late 1970s (Wilson 1964–66 and 1966–70, Heath 1970–74, Wilson again 1974–74–76 and Callaghan 1976–79) all had to struggle in various ways with pressures on the pound. By the end of James Callaghan's (Labour) administration it was beginning to be understood that, rightly or wrongly, the external valuation of the pound depended, among other factors, upon how outsiders saw the effectiveness of the government in controlling public spending. One obvious factor was the willingness of the Government to borrow, another its willingness to 'print money': both seen as inflationary factors. Inflation of its own is not necessarily a bad thing: indeed it is likely that growth will be accompanied by the corresponding inflation. Problems arise when inflation markedly outstrips growth, and this was a severe problem throughout the period mentioned.

It must also be mentioned that during this period (in 1973) the United Kingdom joined the European Economic Community (now termed European Union) and thus came under the closer influence and scrutiny of major actors on the world economic scene. This joining with Europe has clearly affected the way in which the UK government can manage finance.

Three post-war phases

If we look at the management aspect of government, i.e. concentrate on the basic tasks of management, we find that the post-war period may be divided into three phases.

The Attlee governments of 1945–51 reacted to post-war circumstances but took their chance to create new organizations by rearranging industry and service provision so that the private sector was reduced in size and the voluntary sector was incorporated into state provision through either local or central government. These six years are usually seen as crucial in building the welfare state and the large nationalized industries.

The various *Conservative and Labour governments from 1951 to 1979* had to maintain these creations which had, in the case of the welfare state, engendered public support and affection. There was, of course, much reaction to circumstance, particularly difficulties with exchange rates and balance of trade figures. There were also some creative moves, e.g. the immediate partial denationalization of steel and road haulage, the deliberate and fairly controlled break up of the British Empire (with consequent economic and financial effects) and the entry into Europe which was both positively bipartisan (Harold Wilson supported by Edward Heath) and opposed by factions within both the major parties (e.g. by Enoch Powell (C) and Tony Benn (L)). Although this period saw the European entry which may prove to be the most significant strategic development in British economic history, the overriding impression of a period of nearly thirty years is of government without the desire to do other than maintain and react.

The Thatcher governments of 1979 to 1990, however, were clearly driven by creative (some would say 'destructive'!) urges. The answers to various problems posed by international and demographic trends were seen as lying, at least in part, in a radical restructuring of the public sector rather than in a series of ad hoc reactive measures. Thus, whereas the Attlee governments had taken a semi-public sector and rearranged it into a much enlarged public sector, the Thatcher governments did precisely the reverse.

A much enlarged semi-public sector has been created, comprising for example housing associations, and infrastructure utilities with their corresponding regulatory bodies. Furthermore, devices such as internal markets and competition for tenders have been introduced as means of increasing the cost effectiveness of the public sector. It is in this changed environment that the public sector manager of today works and which forms the major focus of this book, but the object of the current argument is to draw attention to the motive for the Thatcher management; it was creative, and in that respect was more similar to the governments of Attlee than to the string of Governments, both Conservative and Labour, between 1951 and 1979. Of course Margaret Thatcher had maintenance tasks to perform, but the burden of her argument was that, unless there was a radical restructuring, external pressures on the system would render maintenance increasingly expensive and ad hoc reaction continually less effective. 'The frontiers of the State' had to be 'rolled back'. There was 'no alternative'.

Table 1.2 lists the major changes to the public sector during the Thatcher phase.

Summary

It has been argued in this section that the major tasks of management are maintenance, reaction and creation. It has also been argued that the post-war governments have maintained, reacted and created in different proportions and for different reasons. The public sector manager currently operates in an environment deliberately created in strategic response to long-term pressures. The period since 1979 has been crucial; not least because Thatcher, whether rightly or wrongly, was prepared to be innovative in her approach in a way that compares to the innovation of Attlee, although, of course, the outcomes were radically different.

This historical account has been deliberately superficial, as the focus of the book is on techniques in the current environment. Nevertheless, the historical dimension is a necessary prerequisite to understanding the answers to the questions 'what' and 'how' governments manage.

Table 1.2 Major changes in the public sector during the Thatcher years

Organization	Key change
General	Performance indicators/targets/'charters'
	Competitive tendering/internal markets/cost control
	Value for money—economy, efficiency, effectiveness
NHS	1982 abolition of area health authorities
	Griffiths Report on managerialism (1983)
	Korner Reports on collection and use of information (1981–84)
	White Paper: NHS Trusts and 'internal markets' (1989)
	Act extending Audit Commission's remit to NHS (1990)
Local	Compulsory sale of council dwellings (1980 Act)
government	Requirement for DLOs to make profits (1980 Act)
	Establishment of Audit Commission (1982 Act)
	Rate capping (1984)
	1985 Abolition of the GLC and Metropolitan County Councils
	'Poll tax' (1988 Act) (but n.b. subsequent repeal)
Education	Local (financial) management of schools (from 1988)
programme	Grant-maintained schools (from 1991)
	'Incorporation' of polytechnics 1989
	Abolition of university/polytechnic distinction 1992
	FE colleges moved out of LA control 1993
Civil	Rayner Scrutinies (1979–83)
service	Financial management initiative from 1982 onwards
	'Next Steps' (1988)
	Agencies created from 1988 onwards
Public	Sale of major industries and infrastructure utilities to private sector, e.g. British
corporations	Aerospace, British Telecom, British Gas, water and electricity from early 1980s.

WHAT GOVERNMENTS MANAGE

Direct and indirect management

There is a fundamental distinction between those aspects of the economy which it may be claimed are, in normal circumstances, directly controlled by government and those which are controlled only indirectly:

- The former category, direct control, includes the income and expenditure of government, the prevailing rate of interest on borrowing and the underlying value of the currency.
- The latter category, indirect control, includes the rate of inflation, the rate of economic growth, the level of employment and the balance of trade.

Three important caveats must be registered.

The phrase 'normal circumstances' is significant. Perhaps circumstances are never completely 'normal', but there are clearly times when circumstances are abnormal. At such times, perhaps a war or a radical restructuring of international relationships, individual state governments seem sometimes to be at the mercy of events rather than to be controlling them. For example:

1. at the time of the various oil crises in the 1970s governments all over the world had problems in coping with the effects of rapidly rising oil prices on many aspects of both public and private economies;
2. the problems which the German Chancellor Kohl faced with the rapid and unexpected collapse of Communism in Eastern Europe and the consequent re-integration of the two German states;
3. the pressures—some at governmental level, some arising in the private sector—on various European governments in 1992 caused by the strength of the German currency in relation to various previously agreed rates of exchange.

A second caveat concerns the extent of the control. It is possible to argue that even in normal circumstances governments do not have complete control over, say, government income or expenditure:

- The former arises mostly from taxation and will thus, other things being equal, be higher in a thriving economy than in a depressed economy. Since governments do not directly control the level of economic activity, then, by inference, governments do not control the level of their income.
- The latter includes many transfer payments to individual needy recipients (unemployment benefits for example). Since governments do not directly control the level of employment, then, by inference, they do not control the level of their expenditure.

The third caveat is the argument that the category of indirectly controlled economic functions is actually better regarded as a set of indicators. The government does not control them, as such, either directly or indirectly. What actually happens is that both government and opinion formers use them to indicate success/failure and potential success/failure:

- High unemployment is seen as an indicator of government failure by critics who force governments on to the defensive unless the public can be persuaded that unemployment is a necessary evil.
- Similarly, the achievement of low inflation is usually represented as a major step forward by governments, and critics are forced to bring other indicators into the picture and represent them as being of more significance.

The position adopted in this book will be that governments do genuinely have considerable control over the first (direct) category, and that the second category, while more loosely controlled, is sufficiently under the influence of government to warrant the use of the term 'control'. It is also sensible to think of the second category as 'indicators' since that is the way in which they are used. But, again, so too are rates of exchange and interest.

Directly controlled factors

The details of how these are controlled will be discussed in the next section. For introductory purposes, however, we need some definitions.

By far the most substantial block of government income is taxes of one sort or another. But, in addition to taxes, government also receives money from sales of assets, from borrowing, from fines and penalties and, believe it or not, from voluntary bequests! Of this list, the only items of significance are taxes, sales and borrowings. Taxes far outweigh the other two items.

Government expenditure is primarily on various services, such as health or education, which are funded mainly from the public purse. In addition, government makes many transfer payments (pensions, benefits), services a national debt, makes capital investments and maintains its own bureaucracy. Service provision and transfer payments are the most significant items.

Interest rates are, in theory, arrived at by 'the market' and it is true that the market determines levels within bands. Reduced interest rates are available to borrowers regarded as low risk and who borrow large amounts. High-risk borrowers of smaller amounts are usually charged much more for the privilege. The market, however, operates under constraints, the main one being that the Bank of England is the banker's bank and that it controls the primary lending rate—the 'base rate'—upon which all other interest rates ultimately depend.

Currency exchange rates are determined by both longer term international agreements and shorter term market pressures. Governments have direct control over the international agreements.

From day to day they may resist or even instigate market pressures by buying or selling currency. When market pressures become too great for the longer term valuation to remain stable, then a government decision changes the underlying value of a currency. In Britain's case these step changes in valuation have of recent years been downwards—'devaluation'. The German currency, the mark, has effectively been revalued upwardly several times in the post-war period.

Indirectly controlled factors

The indirectly controlled factors which, as we have seen, may be regarded as indicators are as follows:

1. Inflation is the rate of change of the value of money over time. It is conventionally expressed in terms of percentage points per year (for example 3.6 per cent p.a.). The opposite, which is very rare indeed, is deflation. In general terms British inflation has kept approximate step with growth over a long period, but there have been periods when inflation has been well ahead of economic growth and these periods have been seen as representing problems for the government of the day. Inflation is usually advantageous to borrowers as, unless interest rates rocket, 'good money' is borrowed and 'bad money' repaid! Britain has never experienced the rates in excess of 100 per cent undergone in recent years by Iceland and Israel. Neither have we had the 'hyper-inflation' of inter-war Germany.
2. Economic growth is the rate of change of the size of the economy in cash terms expressed in terms of percentage points per year. The standard measure of size of economy is the gross national product (GNP) although there are other measures such as the gross domestic product (GDP) which may be more appropriate in certain circumstances. British growth over nearly two centuries has been of the order of 3 per cent, although there have been periods well in excess of this. Growth and inflation are linked in the sense that there seem to be no adverse effects if the rates are similar, whereas inflation significantly higher than growth is seen as a problem.
3. Unemployment is seen as an indicator of governmental success partly because governments have consciously aimed to eliminate it and partly because it occurs when the economy is not doing as well as it might. All unemployment figures from whatever source should be treated with suspicion until the basis on which they are calculated is made plain. The real indicator of the health of an economy is the employment rate—how many people are actually in work—

and again such figures must be treated with caution. It is usually considered that there are three sorts of unemployment: frictional, people between jobs; cyclical, due to normal trade cycle; and structural, due to fundamental changes in an economy. Britain's present unemployment is predominantly a mixture of the structural and cyclical varieties, and there is no easy way of telling what the proportions are.

4. The balance of trade is the difference in cash between a state's exports and its imports. The equation is not just about 'visibles' (for example cars and weapons out, electronics and coffee in), but also about 'invisibles' (for example tourists in and out and financial services such as banking and insurance which, in Britain's case, usually tilt the balance in our favour. The rate of exchange is very much linked to the balance of trade as a weaker pound favours exports, but makes imports dearer. Traditionally, the balance of trade figures, issued monthly, have been seen as an indicator of government success.

Summary

The above account is very basic. In the next section we turn to the matter of how governments manage, a question which has both descriptive and evaluation dimensions.

HOW GOVERNMENTS MANAGE

The twofold meaning of this question

It has already been suggested that a 'how' question can have at least two different sorts of answer. If I were asked, 'How do you manage your desk?' I might reply in terms of allocating time to different aspects of my job—teaching, research, administration, management and so on—and in terms of prioritizing my efforts within those categories. Such a reply would be descriptive. I might also reply, according to my mood, 'Very badly; I always seem to be behindhand!' or, 'Really well; I am on top of things.' Such replies would be evaluative. The same is true of questions asked in far more serious contexts, such as the performance of governments.

The 'how?' question can be answered as a series of descriptions of what tools are used by governments. It can also be answered as an overall evaluation or series of evaluations, rather like a school report. In this section both sorts of answers will be attempted, but it should be noted that the descriptions will be relatively uncontentious, that is they will probably be about right and agreed upon by informed readers. The evaluations, on the other hand, are contestable. They will depend upon a host of political preconceptions and prior dispositions.

One more philosophical point: the present set of tools has evolved over many years and has thus been subject to generations of prior evaluative criticism. There is a link between the two sorts of answers we have been discussing. The link is usually termed 'feedback', a word borrowed by communications experts and management theorists from cybernetics—an important branch of engineering. And this reference to engineering is not casual; engineers have to make things work, often on the basis of incomplete data and challengeable theory. Governments work like that. They must be seen to deliver. There is a further analogy. What counts as 'making things work' changes with time. A crude railway engine or a stick-and-string aircraft amazed the Victorians and the Edwardians. We have come to expect rather more from our engineers: to an extent they are the victims of their own success.

Government income: the budget and taxation

British government, in any year, derives its spending power from several sources. The main one, by far and without any doubt, is the sum of the various taxes which are collected from individuals and organizations. In addition to taxes, the Government from time to time sells assets, borrows more than it repays, collects interest and dividends on various investments and even has money given to it, sometimes to avoid duties, sometimes more altruistically! Figure 1.3 shows the main sources of government revenues for 1995–96.

Part (a) approximates closely to the Government's own classification of its income. It shows clearly the traditional distinction between those taxes collected by the Inland Revenue and those collected by the Customs and Excise. It also demonstrates some confusion over the classification of social security receipts, which are mostly, and to all intents and purposes, taxes on income. There is also an interesting distinction in classification between business rate shown under the third Government heading and council tax receipts, which are shown under the fourth Government heading, although they are both local taxes.

Part (b) rationalizes these confusions to some extent, although it still leaves social security receipts as a separate item. It demonstrates the overwhelming preponderance of taxation as the

(a) The weightings of various types of tax

Inland Revenue (mainly income tax and corporation tax)		£96.5bn	
Customs and Excise (mainly VAT and various duties)		£77.0bn	
Miscellaneous taxes (including business rates)		£52.4bn	
Other income (mainly NI and 'council tax')		£52.9bn	
	Subtotal	£278.8bn	
	Borrowing for revenue purposes	£21.5bn	
	Total	£300.3bn	

(b) The predominance of taxation

Total of taxes, duties, royalties and rates	£214.3bn	
Social security receipts (i.e. NI etc.)	£44.5bn	
Interest, dividends, trading surpluses, 'other'	£20.0bn (estimated)	
Borrowing	£21.5bn	
Total (as above but differently formatted)	£300.3bn	

(c) Revenue from 'six main sources' and the rest

Income tax	£70.1bn	23%
VAT	£49.0bn	16%
Social security receipts	£44.5bn	15%
Taxes/duties on petrol/tobacco/alcohol	£35.0bn	12%
Local taxes (i.e. nndr (national non-domestic rate)) and council tax	£30.0bn	10%
Corporation tax	£26.4bn	9%
Borrowing	£21.5bn	7%
All other sorces (14 items)	£23.8bn	8%
Total as above but differently formatted	£300.3bn	100%

Figure 1.3 1994 budget forecast of government revenues 1995–96. (Figures (rounded) calculated from a variety of government sources.)
(a) The weightings of various types of tax
(b) The predominance of taxation
(c) Revenue from 'six main sources' and the rest

major source of Government income. Eighty-six per cent of Government income comes from the first two headings which between them cover every aspect of tax.

Part (c) demonstrates the domination of the tax system by six main sources which between them contribute six-sevenths (roughly 85 per cent) of Government revenues. The other 15 per cent is made up of borrowing and 14 separate items. Change to the proportion of borrowing would, of course, be very important. Changes to the 14 minor items, although they might be of great significance to individuals, would make little difference to governmental income. Changes, even relatively small, to the six major items imply significant change to that income. It is not surprising therefore that the eyes of the public at budget time are focused on the Chancellor's words, especially concerning these items.

The 'budget' itself is a financial statement which reflects the political judgements of the Chancellor of the Exchequer in response to needs for maintenance, reaction to short- and long-term trends and any creative urges. It is therefore quite clearly an instrument of strategic management. It is, of course, the primary source of the authorization of income needed by government for its purposes.

It would be a mistake, however, to regard the budget as solely an instrument for raising money.

- It reflects all manner of balances, for example the balance between corporate and personal taxation or the balance between direct and indirect taxes.
- It reflects political factors. For example, the independence of local government depends upon the level of local taxation which can be 'capped' effectively from within the budget. Thus pressure can be brought on local government by central government through consideration of the profile of government revenues.
- It reflects international commitments and pressures. The rate of VAT, for example, is moving towards harmonization with VAT rates in other EU countries. The world oil price rises of the 1970s have proved a significant factor in subsequent changes to the rate of duty on petrol and diesel.
- It reflects policy decisions of Government. For example, privatization policies pursued in the 1980s brought significant cash income from the sale of nationalized industries. This enabled taxes to be held down and minimized public borrowing, but the policy itself was about balance of power and not government income as such.
- It reflects internal pressures. The level of taxation on tobacco, for example, reflects a pressure from anti-smoking groups (the argument that smoking is inherently harmful) and a realization that the health costs of smoking (significant in NHS financial terms) could and maybe ought at least to some extent be borne by smokers.
- It has public appeal potential. A 'good' budget (as interpreted by financial experts) can bring popularity to a government, sometimes at electorally significant times.

These are all significant factors which affect the pattern of taxation. They are not primarily to do with mere maintenance of government income. Since 1993 the 'budget' has changed its timing from March to November and, more significantly, has changed its emphasis from receipts to a global consideration of receipts and expenditure. The 'unified budget' as it is now known has become a potent economic tool and a much better focus for government planning than the two, previously separate, budgeting and expenditure processes.

Government expenditure: the PESC processes and programmes

The minister responsible for public expenditure is the Chief Secretary to the Treasury, a Cabinet Minister who liaises closely with the Chancellor of the Exchequer and the Prime Minister. Ultimate responsibility for spending lies with Parliament itself, which through a 'supply process' authorizes all government expenditure. The reality is, however, that the details of spending are decided within individual government departments and the principal decisions are made by the Cabinet which plays the role of umpire in an annual review known as the Public Expenditure Survey, or PESC if the PES Committee is considered.

The details are less important than the principle which is that on a rolling basis those items of expenditure which are within the purview of central government are considered, prioritized and cash limited. Items which are not so easily controlled, such as debt interest, are estimated and added on to give a total picture of public expenditure.

- The rolling basis consists of a consideration of recent past performance which gives empirical guidance as to the reality of a three-year projection of desired future trends.
- The consideration is done initially within government departments which produce their individual spending plans.
- The prioritization is done in a series of bilateral discussions between individual departments and the Treasury. Where agreement cannot be reached, the 'Star Chamber' (a Cabinet committee) adjudicates. Difficult cases may be decided by the Cabinet itself and all unresolved issues are arbitrated.
- The November Statement, now part of the unified budget, sets out the spending plans for the next three years along with other relevant financial data. This statement used be followed by a January White Paper, but from 1991 a series of detailed departmental spending plan papers are issued. These papers reflect, of course, any re-prioritization done by the relevant department in the light of any cash limitation less than its own plans: an entirely normal situation!

A combination of the government policy and pressures on government have seen a sharpening of the process over the years since 1982. The 'Star Chamber' was invoked with increasing frequency and thus the Cabinet became more involved. It is fair to say that the process is now more overtly recognized as competitive than before. It has thus perforce become more politicized.

The actual outcomes of the process may be presented in several different ways, for example by department, by function or by economic category. See Fig. 1.4.

A few words of explanation are necessary since it seems at first sight that the figures do not always square up. This is because a given 'function', for example 'education and science', is not necessarily delivered by what seems to be the obvious department. In the case of 'education and science', or 'health' for example, the Offices for Scotland, Wales and Northern Ireland are responsible for spending some of the money. Most of the spending of the Department of the Environment is channelled through local government.

On the other hand, there is a close linkage between the spending on social security or defence with the relevant department. At this point it should be mentioned that local government spends just over a quarter of general government expenditure, some raised through its own taxes (business rates and council tax) and some through grants.

The breakdown by economic category has some interesting features, notably the transfer payments ('grants to persons' in government phraseology) such as sickness benefit, unemployment benefit and pensions:

(a) Government expenditure by department, 1995–96

Department of Social Security	28%
Department of the Environment	15%
Department of Health	13%
Scotland, Wales and Northern Ireland	11%
Ministry of Defence	9%
All other departments	20%
Local government self-financed expenditure	4%

(b) Public expenditure by function, 1995–96

Social security	29%
Health services	11%
Defence	7%
Local government	24%
Other spending	20%
Debt interest	8%

(c) Public expenditure by economic category, 1995–96

Provision of services	48%
Transfer payments to persons	31%
Debt interest	7%
Capital transactions	10%
Other/adjustments	4%

Figure 1.4   Patterns of government expenditure ((a) based on November 1993 *Red Book* figures for 'New Control Total'; (b) based on HM Treasury, *The Budget in Brief*, November 1994; (c) calculated from a variety of sources. All figures rounded.)

- The level of pension provision represents a continuing and growing problem in terms of the increasing proportion of elderly persons.
- The level of unemployment benefit is clearly inversely related to the health of the economy, and draws attention to the paradox that when the economy is most buoyant, the need for high taxation is least; when the economy is sluggish, the need for high taxation is greatest.
- Finally, it is sometimes alleged that the ready availability of sickness benefit, at least in the short term, is damaging to the economy in terms of unnecessarily lost days of work. Whether this is so or not, the perception is clearly of political significance.

The Bank of England and interest rates

The Bank of England was nationalized in 1948 and became an adjunct of the Treasury. Its underlying function is to preserve the confidence which is necessary in any system of monetary exchange. The expression 'safe as the Bank of England' draws attention to this confidence aspect. The guarantee on banknotes, 'I promise to pay to bearer on demand ...', is meaningless unless one has confidence in the value of the currency that the Bank underwrites.

There are several ways of looking at the value of a currency. One is to do with how other trading centres regard it; its value on the international market. This is considered next. Another is how it is preserved over a period of time relative to the overall economy of the state. This too is considered.

One of the tools, however, available to government in regard to regulating both of these aspects, is the base rate of interest. In crude terms, if interest rates are relatively high then overseas investors will buy pounds in order to take advantage of this situation. If, on the other hand, interest rates are relatively low then British industry can afford investment more easily, maybe leading to economic growth. Consumers can also afford to borrow more easily, and can thus buy more: this may contribute to inflation.

A government will wish to preserve a balance between these factors of growth and inflation and will thus have a notion of what is the appropriate interest rate on these fronts. This notional figure may not be the same as the rate which would be optimum to contribute to preserving the value of the pound on the international markets.

It should be remarked that the confidence factor which underpins the value of a currency is also intimately linked to the willingness of both domestic and overseas investors to risk their money in supporting British business growth. Ultimately, it is confidence which supports a government and lack of confidence which brings it down. It is thus a key concept in understanding why governments pay such attention to the Bank of England and its role in defining interest rates.

The Bank of England is not independent of government. It is closely linked to the Treasury and ultimately has to do what the government of the day instructs it, although its Governor has never been a passive recipient of orders but has always played a part in advising government.

This close link between government and national bank is not universal. The Deutsche Bundesbank ('BuBa', the German Federal Bank), for example, is separated by constitutional provision from the German government and can, in theory, operate independently. There are doubts about whether this constitutional freedom is always a reality! In September 1992, for example, there was clear evidence that the German bank was acting on German government instructions in the events which surrounded the realignment of several currencies, including the pound.

The US Federal Bank (the 'Fed'), is also independent of the US Federal government. Here it is more easy to see its independence. There are strong economic arguments for separating the Bank of England from the British government, along the lines of the models discussed. The problem would seem to be, however, that a 'free' Bank of England would in reality operate more like the Bundesbank and less like the 'Fed'.

The value of the pound

The value of the pound on the international markets is, as discussed, of crucial importance. Not only does it affect the willingness of investors to invest in Britain, but it also affects the relative ease with which Britain can import and export and thus the balance of payments. A stronger pound means that it is easier to import but harder to export. A weaker pound has the opposite effect.

Two major factors affect the value of the pound:

1. The nominal level which at any given time is set by the government within the context of a set of international agreements. The chief of these is the Bretton Woods Conference (1944) which set the post-war stage for international finance and, through 'the World Bank', had played a major part in keeping confidence relatively high and currencies relatively stable. More recently the various aspects of an economically and monetarily united Europe have come to play a dominant role.
2. The pressure, upwards or downwards, which exists because of 'market factors'. Operators in the international monetary markets, for whatever reason, determine to buy sterling, thus

raising the value. Persistent and continuous pressure on the pound can interact with the first major factor discussed.

The government is a major player. Obviously it has been a party to the various international agreements. It also plays a role in supporting the pound, when the pressure is downward, i.e. when sterling is losing its value. It does this both by adjusting interest rates, as discussed above, and by using its reserves of foreign currency to buy sterling and thus keep up its value. The problem is that it can do this for only so long: it does not have inexhaustible reserves and in any case it may be that the markets are sensing that the pound is actually valued wrongly. By this we mean that the basic underlying rate of exchange, as determined by government in the light of international agreement, is wrong, not in detail but in principle.

When this happens, as for example in 1967 or in 1992, the government of the day is forced to 'devalue', either openly as by the 1967 Wilson (Labour) Government, or less openly as by the 1992 Major (Conservative) Government which allowed the pound to 'float' to a new level:

- The Wilson devaluation (from $2.80 to $2.40) was fought strenuously with sustained purchase of sterling by the Government. The European issue was at that time largely irrelevant.
- The Major 'devaluation' (from DM2,80 to about DM2,60) was again fought strenuously, using weapons of both interest rate variation and sterling purchase. The European issue was by no means irrelevant. The whole business was conducted within a framework of concern over the future of Europe, over economic and monetary union and over Britain's continuing participation in the exchange rate mechanism (ERM). It is also interesting to note that the whole episode was described in terms of the value of the pound against the mark, the dollar being largely irrelevant on this occasion.

Figure 1.2, earlier, showed the value of the pound against the currency of United States (to 1992).

Money supply and inflation

An avowed aim of the Thatcher Governments from 1979 onwards was to reduce the rate of annual inflation which had reached a peak of over 25 per cent in 1975. This aim was continued under John Major and Norman Lamont, as Chancellor of the Exchequer, was using the success of the policy (a figure of around 3.5 per cent had been achieved) as justification for continuance of much criticized policies as late as October 1992.

The mainspring for the policies was monetarist theory in various guises. The central tenet of such theory is that the amount of money in circulation affects inflation, and that if too much is allowed to circulate, then inflation will follow. The Conservatives therefore followed a deliberate policy of cooling inflation by reducing the money supply through such measures as cutting public borrowing (see next section) and keeping interest rates high.

Both these factors have had a considerable effect on the public sector as a whole. Local government in particular has had to reconsider its spending priorities very carefully. The main reason for this has been the effect of the lower borrowing ceiling which has meant reduced ability to make capital investment. Where local authorities borrowed, legitimately or otherwise, to meet revenue expenses, the high interest rates and low inflation have combined to maximize the impact of servicing accumulated debt, and reduced revenue freedom considerably.

In this connection the point should be made that inflation, provided that interest rates are not too high, acts to assist the borrower. In crude terms 'good money' is borrowed and 'bad money' is repaid. It is probable that large local authorities which borrowed heavily in the early 1980s were reckoning on inflation continuing at a high rate so that servicing the debt would not bear too heavily on them!

It should also be mentioned that inflation of itself is not a bad thing provided that it is reasonably in step with growth. Greenleaf showed that, taking twenty-year periods over two centuries, only once had the underlying rate of growth exceeded 5 per cent, and that in the 1950 to 1970 period when post-war changes were being consolidated.

Public sector borrowing and the national debt

Government and its agencies (central, local and public corporations) borrow considerable amounts of money. The total amount of unrepaid central government debt is known as the national debt. It is similar, but not identical, to the total indebtedness of the public sector.

The main reasons for government borrowing are as follows:

1. to finance wars, which normally cost well beyond the limits of possible immediate taxation;
2. to finance public works of various sorts, which may be undertaken not only for their intrinsic merit but to reduce unemployment and to stimulate the economy;
3. to finance any real growth in the infrastructure of the welfare state such as schools or hospitals;
4. to compensate shareholders in industries such as railways, mines and steel when they were nationalized;
5. to finance year on year budget deficits whether such deficits are caused by unintentional overspend/revenue shortfall or by deliberately engineered public borrowing;
6. to finance balance of payments shortfalls by borrowing abroad.

The main effects of public borrowing are as follows:

1. the government has more money available to it for either current spending or capital investment;
2. less money is available for investment in and by the private sector;
3. the growing debt requires higher taxation to service it—indeed borrowing may be seen as deferred taxation;
4. the balance of payments situation will be distorted if the borrowing is substantially from abroad;
5. it is possible that inflation will result from the increased public spending—a point made by James Callaghan (Labour) well before Margaret Thatcher became Prime Minister and made it one of her central tenets.

Figure 1.5 shows the growth in national debt over two periods. The first is from its origin in 1694 (when the new Bank of England lent the government £1.2 million) to 1945 (the end of the Second World War). The second is from 1900 to date at ten-year intervals. The repayment of the national debt ceased to be a practical proposition by about the beginning of the Second World War, although up to that time it was given serious consideration.

The national debt now stands at around £2,500 per head of population and is not excessively high in relation to other western countries. It is, for example, only about one-third of the corresponding figure for Belgium.

(a)

		National debt (£ million)
1694	Bank of England created	1
1727	Accession of George II	52
1784	End of American War of Independence	243
1815	End of wars with France	861
1918	End of First World War	5,821
1945	End of Second World War	27,773

(b)

1900	Turn of the century	c.1,000
1910	Before First World War	c.2,000
1920	After First World War	c.9,000
1930	During inter-war depression	c.8,000
1940	During Second World War	n/a
1950	After Second World War, near end of Attlee administration	c.25,000
1960	Relative prosperity	c.27,000
1970	Relative prosperity	c.30,000
1980	Beginning of Thatcher administration	c.95,000
1990	End of Thatcher administration	c.190,000

Figure 1.5   National debt. (a) 1694–1945 (taken from D.I. Trotman-Dickenson (1983) Heinemann. *Public Sector Economics Made Simple*); (b) 1900–90 (from a variety of sources, including *National Statistics* (various issues), Central Statistical Office).

Evaluation

A key question in any discussion of evaluation is 'Who is doing the evaluation?' When one considers the evaluation of the strategic financial management of the Government or of a series of governments the question must be answered.

Quite clearly the whole business is at the centre of the political arena. Evaluation is thus an ongoing process with criticism invariably coming from the opposition parties and, quite frequently, from 'rebels' on the government's own parliamentary back benches. This has been true whether Labour or Conservative parties have been in office. The core question of Britain's relationship with the rest of Europe, upon which a good number of policies since 1973 have depended, has not really been a party matter.

Pressure groups have formed another significant source of criticism with the Confederation of British Industry and the Institute of Directors speaking up frequently and by no means always supporting Conservative policies. The trade union movement has made its voice heard through both concerted action via the TUC and as individual unions. It has normally been pro-Labour, certainly in the sense of being anti-Conservative, but has not in the past been averse to criticizing Labour governments and, indeed, it has been claimed that 'the winter of discontent' (concerted union action against a Labour-inspired public sector pay-freeze) brought down the Callaghan government in 1979.

Over the last decade the NHS has in various ways espoused criticism of Conservative Governments. The ways in which the NHS has been restructured, reorganized and redefined have met with criticism from the workforce (professional, managerial, administrative and manual) and pressure for both more resources and less interference.

Local government of all political complexions, and at both politician and officer level, has resisted change and criticized the Government severely for the way in which it has handled both taxation and resource allocation. It has also been vocal, particularly through the manual and administrative unions (formerly NUPE and NALGO, now UNISON) in supporting NHS resistance to such devices as competitive tendering and contracting out. These devices are all part of the Government's operationalizing of its strategy of producing a leaner public sector.

The press plays its role in both support and criticism and the media more generally play an important role in forming public opinion. 'Expert opinion' now forms a regular part of the TV newscasts and, although there is an effort to achieve balance, there is never any difficulty in finding expert voices critical of the Government and sceptical of its strategies and their realization.

With all these sources of criticism what can we say, in general terms, of how our strategic financial management has succeeded?

- On the one hand, the United Kingdom is clearly a prosperous and important state. It is still a member of G7, the group of the world's most important economies. It is a major player in Europe, with several positive performance indicators such as a low rate of annual inflation and low ratio of national debt to GNP.
- On the other hand, the decline in manufacturing industry and the change to a service economy has not inspired support and confidence either at home or abroad. It is possible to argue that the weakness of the pound endemic in the early 1990s reflected this lack of confidence.

It may be that there can be no objective answer given to the question for several years to come— because of lack of evidence, shortness of timescale and involvement of key critics and commentators in the processes themselves. This involvement leads to a lack of that objectivity necessary for balanced judgement.

It is also possible to ask whether the actions of government are really that significant. The forces that change the world may be so strong and complex that Government makes little difference on the great stage and in the long run! In the short run, however, and on the smaller stage of the United Kingdom, clearly government makes a good deal of difference. The style of strategic financial management practised since 1979 has meant a different way of working for managers throughout the public sector. It is to the financial implications of these new ways of managing that this book now turns.

NOTE

1. W. H. Greenleaf. (1983) *The British Political Tradition*, Vol. 1, Table 1, p. 33, Methuen, London.

WHERE WE ARE NOW

INTRODUCTION

In 1994–95 the British government planned to spend just under £300bn. Of this, rather more than £250bn would come from taxation and other revenue receipts while the difference of just less than £50bn would be borrowed or financed from privatization receipts[1]. It was the Government's avowed intention to reduce the level of public borrowing to zero by the end of the century and this, since there was little scope for further major privatizations, implied a planned reduction in public expenditure of the order of £50bn[2], that is about 18 per cent.

Such a change (3 per cent per year for about 6 years) was not marginal. If implemented successfully it would have profound effects upon the whole of the British economy, let alone the public sector. In order to answer the question implied by the title of the chapter we need to discuss a complex set of interrelated topics. These include:

- The current pattern of spending and how is it related to current needs
- The major environmental factors which affect government thinking about trends of change in this pattern
- The major institutions of state which actually spend the money and how they are adapting to the implied changes
- The interrelationship of capital and revenue finance at both macro and micro levels

This chapter attempts to deal with these topics, at first in isolation, and then, in a section of discussion, to make some synthesis. The main aim of the chapter is to complement Chapter 1, concerned with governmental strategy, by discussing how that strategy is operationalized. The objectives include preparation for later discussion, which is to be more focused on practical financial management, by providing a bridge between the level of strategic discussion to the level of, often uncomfortable, management by pointing up the reasons for some of that discomfort.

THE CURRENT PATTERN OF SPENDING

By department

The main spending departments are as follows:

- The Department of Social Security, currently responsible for about 28 per cent of Government expenditure
- The Department of the Environment which, because it is responsible for the majority of local government grants in England, spends about 13 per cent

- The Department of Health which, predominantly through the NHS, spends about 11 per cent
- The Ministry of Defence which spends about 8 per cent

The interest on debt amounts to about 8 per cent of the total and the remaining 32 per cent covers the work of the Offices for Scotland, Wales and Northern Ireland (about 9 per cent), the self-financed portion of local government expenditure, i.e. council tax and local fees and charges (about 8 per cent) and the work of all other central government departments (about 15 per cent).

It is clear that the current major spender is the Department of Social Security. Its money is mainly spent on various transfer payments[3] to individuals, but, of course, there is a necessary bureaucracy to be maintained.

The Offices for Scotland, Wales and Northern Ireland are responsible, among other things, for local government and the operation of the health services in their parts of the United Kingdom, and so the proportions of government spending on these items are actually higher than indicated, as will be seen.

By function

When the complications arising from the different ways of funding the health services and local government are resolved it is possible to illustrate the spending pattern graphically. Figure 2.1 shows in piechart form the functional allocation of public money for 1994–95. The financial significance of the expenditure on both social security and local government is immediately apparent.

By economic category

The main categories used by government are:

- Expenditure incurred in the provision of services
- Transfer payments

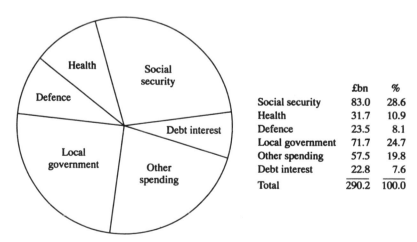

	£bn	%
Social security	83.0	28.6
Health	31.7	10.9
Defence	23.5	8.1
Local government	71.7	24.7
Other spending	57.5	19.8
Debt interest	22.8	7.6
Total	290.2	100.0

Figure 2.1 1994–95 public expenditure (by function) (taken from HM Treasury, *The Budget in Brief*, November 1993. Figures are subject to small rounding errors.)

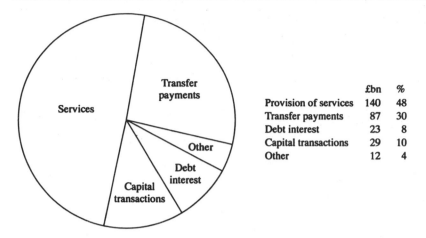

	£bn	%
Provision of services	140	48
Transfer payments	87	30
Debt interest	23	8
Capital transactions	29	10
Other	12	4

Figure 2.2   1994–95 public expenditure (by economic category) (figures are approximated and calculated from a variety of sources)

- Capital transactions
- Debt interest

The figures for 1994–95 under these headings are shown in Fig. 2.2.

What is immediately apparent is the high value for transfer payments. The bulk of such payments are pensions and various forms of Social Security payments. The Government reckons[4] that approximately £16bn (i.e. around 5 per cent of total spending) is 'cyclical social security expenditure', i.e. dependent upon the level of economic activity. This still leaves about £70bn of non-cyclical expenditure.

Capital transactions have for many years formed about 10 per cent of total spending. The debt interest is inescapable, being the result of a national debt built up over many years and subject to a rate of interest which, because of its method of financing, follows the longer term trends while ironing out shorter term variations.

It is clear that expenditure on services will be to some extent caught in a pincer between these blocks of spending.

THE MAJOR ENVIRONMENTAL FACTORS

Demography

There are two major phenomena which are totally outside of the direct control of the Government but which have direct and immediate impact upon the pattern of state spending:

1. The population is ageing in the sense that people are living longer and therefore older people are forming a higher proportion of the whole.
2. The population of younger people is declining in proportionate terms (younger people form a lower proportion of the population as a whole).

Table 2.1 has two components. Part (a) gives the 1991 composition of the population on the basis of firm existing figures. Part (b) is, of course, a prediction based on current trends but one which is

Table 2.1 Population statistics

(a) 1991 age profile of UK

Age (years)	Population (millions)	
0–4	3.9	
5–9	3.7	
10–14	3.5	
15–19	3.7	
20–24	4.5	
25–29	4.7	
30–34	4.2	
35–39	3.8	
40–44	4.1	
45–49	3.5	
50–54	3.1	
55–59	2.9	
	Male	*Female*
60–64	1.4	1.5
65–69	1.3	1.5
70–74	1.0	1.3
75–79	0.7	1.1
80–84	0.4	0.8
85+	0.2	0.7
Totals		
0–19	14.8	
20–59/64	32.3	
60/65+	10.5	
Population	57.5	

(b) Median age (UK)

Year	Median age (years)
1995	36.1
2005	38.9
2015	41.2

Source: (a) HMSO, *1991 Annual Abstract of Statistics*, Table 2.5. (b) OECD figures. *Note*: These figures are predictions but are likely to be accurate.

likely to be very accurate. It shows that the median age[5] of the population is likely to rise by 5.1 years over the period 1995–2015.

The prediction is based on two other predictions:

- An increase in longevity due to a decline in the death rate
- A decrease in the young population due to a stabilization of the birth rate at a relatively low figure

These predictions are, as is the case with all predictions, subject to a degree of uncertainty. It is possible that a massive epidemic afflicting elderly people could totally change the pattern. It is possible, indeed perhaps more likely, that the pattern of births could change. In Sweden, for example, a birth rate of 1.6 children per couple, which is not sufficient to sustain a population in the long term, was turned to a birth rate of 2.1 children per couple within a matter of a few years.

Table 2.2 shows the predicted population composition for two years 1996 and 2021. Two important figures which can be calculated from this table are known as 'dependency ratios':

1. The 'child dependency ratio' is the number of children aged between 0 and 14 expressed as a percentage of the population aged between 15 and 64. For 1996 this figure is estimated to be 31 per cent while by 2021 it is estimated to have moved to 29 per cent[6], a reduction of 2 per cent.
2. The 'aged dependency ratio' is the number of people aged 65+ expressed as a percentage of the population aged between 15 and 64. For 1996 this figure is estimated to be over 24 per cent while by 2021 it is estimated to have moved to nearly 29 per cent, an increase of over 4 per cent.

Table 2.2 Age distribution of resident population (projections)[a]

Age range	1996 (000s)	2021 (000s)	%age change
0–4	4019	3783	−5.87
5–9	3879	3679	−5.16
10–14	3677	3617	−1.63
15–19	3517	3748	+6.57
20–24	3752	3995	+6.48
25–29	4457	4045	−9.24
30–34	4698	3863	−17.77
35–39	4182	3629	−13.22
40–44	3750	3422	−8.75
45–49	4088	3584	−12.33
50–54	3462	4239	+22.44
55–59	2991	4378	+45.37
60–64	2765	3732	+34.97
65–69	2618	3107	+18.68
70–74	2381	3014	+26.59
75–79	1818	2152	+18.37
80–84	1306	1407	+7.73
85+	1054	1351	+28.18

[a]The projections are calculated by the Actuary General and Registrars for births and deaths.

The figures for the population in the 0–24 age range are estimates based on a known population of women aged 15–44 and a predicted fertility rate.

For the population aged 25 and over the people concerned are already born. The projections are based on predicted death rates.

Source: The first three columns from HMSO, *1993 Annual Abstract of Statistics*, Table 2.5. The final percentage change column is calculated.

Table 2.3   United Kingdom birth data[a]

Year/three-year range	Annual average (000s)	Crude birth rate (/000)	General fertility rate
1900–02	1,095	28.6	115.1
1910–12	1,037	24.6	99.4
1920–22	1,018	23.1	93.0
1930–32	750	16.3	66.5
1940–42	723	15.0	n/a
1950–52	803	16.0	73.7
1960–62	946	17.9	90.3
1970–72	880	15.8	82.5
1980–82	735	13.0	62.5
1991	793	13.8	63.8

[a]The crude birth rate is births/population in 1,000s.

The general fertility rate is based on women aged between 15 and 44 and is expressed per 1,000 of that population.

Source: HMSO, *1993 Annual Abstract of Statistics*, Table 2.16.

Since the ratios are expressed to the same base it is possible to add them to make a total ratio. This would be 55 per cent for 1996 and 57 per cent for 2021, an increase of 2 per cent. Since it is also possible to argue that the child dependency ratio should be based on young people aged 0–19 rather than 0–14 (to cater for the increased length of education/training) it is clear that any UK government has a serious long-term problem with the ratio of dependants to productive population.

Table 2.3 shows various measures of birth data over a period of nearly a century.

In interpreting this table it should be remembered that the number of births in a year is dependent upon two factors:

- The number of women capable of giving birth, which is officially regarded as the female population aged between 15 and 44
- The rate at which this population does, in fact, give birth

The first factor is known very accurately. The second factor is affected by a number of subfactors, for example 'cultural' (e.g. the desire to reproduce), 'bio-medical' (e.g. the availability and use of reliable contraception) or 'economic' (e.g. the possibility of making secure provision for offspring).

As an added complication, it is possible that there could be differing patterns within different sections of the population. This might, in the long term, add a dimension of change in pattern of need due to circumstance as well as to numbers. Whether or not this is the case, it is clear that even if the economy were to pick up, the probable upward effect on the birth rate would be moderated by the relatively low numbers of fertile women. In any case the child dependency rate would increase for 15 years (19 would be a better figure) before the additional cohort numbers swelled the ranks of the productive.

Economic activity and patterns of employment/unemployment

There are four main factors with regard to employment which have a bearing on public sector finance:

- The gross number of persons seeking benefit from the state for unemployment and any trends in that number
- The pattern of such employment in terms of jobs available and any implications that this may have for government support of industry
- The probable future shape of employment and any implications that this may have for the funding of training/retraining
- The demographic pattern of employment in terms of both geographical location and distribution as between age and gender

The first factor, linked directly to the volume of transfer payments funded from taxation, is of immediate concern to any government. The second factor raises the political question as to what extent, if at all, government should support industry through any form of subsidy or selective purchasing. The third factor is of direct importance to both the volume and shape of the funding of education/training. The fourth factor raises potentially serious questions regarding, for example, regional support policies, the age of retirement and the financial implications of casualization and part-time working.

Table 2.4, covering the years 1989 to 1993 (a period in which the Government claims that the United Kingdom was rising out of the recession), shows a reduction in the proportion of the workforce actually in employment over the period. This reduction was from about 94 per cent in 1989 to about 89 per cent in 1993. It was accompanied by an increase in the ratio of women to men employees (0.89 to 0.97 over the same period). Table 2.5, which is entirely derived from Table 2.4, shows a considerable increase in the number of those claiming benefit and a reduction of those on directly funded government training schemes. It must be stated clearly, however, that the number of those in training or education paid for by the FE or HE funding councils (as distinct from those on government training schemes) rose considerably. The pool of those people not employed and not claiming any benefit remained constant at about 4 million.

Table 2.4   Employment statistics[a]

Year	Workforce	Workforce in employment	Employed males	Employed females	Employed total	Self-employed	Forces
1989	28,427	26,684	11,992	10,668	22,661	3,253	308
1990	28,498	26,943	12,046	10,872	22,918	3,298	303
1991	28,296	26,055	11,530	10,731	22,262	3,143	297
1992	28,149	25,470	11,207	10,646	21,853	2,990	290
1993	27,794	24,929	10,864	10,485	21,350	2,989	271

[a]The workforce is reckoned to be made up of employed people + unemployed claimants. Figures in 1,000s.

Employed people are reckoned to be composed of employees, the self-employed, HM forces and (since 1989) those people on government training programmes.

Source: HMSO, *The Monthly Digest of Statistics*, March 1994 (No. 579), Table 3.1.

Table 2.5   Composition of workforce

Year	Workforce (millions)	Claiming benefit (millions)	On training schemes
1989	28.427	1.743	462,000
1990	28.498	1.555	424,000
1991	28.296	2.241	353,000
1992	28.149	2.629	337,000
1993	27.794	2.865	319,000

Note: Claiming benefit = workforce − workforce in employment

On training schemes = Workforce in employment − employed total − self employed − HM forces

Entries to further education (16–19+) and higher education (18+) rose significantly during the period in question.

There is a pool of about 4 million people who are not employed and not claiming any benefit. This pool has several subcomponents including, for example, 'housewives', 'comfortably-off persons', 'early retirements', prisoners, students.

THE MAJOR INSTITUTIONS OF STATE

Local government

Local authorities in Britain are responsible for delivering the greater part of the services of the state. A very high proportion of local government spending is directed towards service provision. The current spending pattern places the emphasis firmly on major provision such as school education and social services, together with a variety of less costly services such as cleansing, environmental care, libraries and recreation facilities. The provision of council housing is a major local authority service which (although large in volume terms) is effectively revenue neutral (i.e. expenditure on local authority housing is balanced, by law, with the income from rents). Local authorities also process various transfer payments such as housing benefits or student maintenance grants, but these form a small proportion of the whole.

Local authorities vary in detail, but a generally accepted approximation is that up to about three-quarters of the net expenditure of an authority providing education and social services currently goes on that provision. Within Britain there are currently two main types of local authority[7].

1. Unitary authorities, for example the London boroughs (e.g. Harringay or Croydon) and the metropolitan districts (e.g. Solihull or Wigan), effectively provide a full range of locally delivered services[8].
2. Two-tier authorities, for example the so-called 'shire counties' (e.g. Nottinghamshire or Hampshire) and the non-metropolitan districts within their boundaries (e.g. Bassetlaw or Portsmouth) provide between them complementary services.

Wales has counties and districts (all shire/non-metropolitan). Scotland has regions (e.g. Strathclyde) within which are districts. Again the model is non-metropolitan in type. There is effectively no local government in Northern Ireland. For England it is worth noting that 18 million people are served by the 32 London boroughs and 36 metropolitan districts, while 30 million people are served by the combination of 39 shire counties and the 296 non-metropolitan districts within their boundaries.

The structure of local government was in late 1995 the subject of both a Government Commission and an expression of Government will. The Commission had reported in stages and, in general, had recommended a unitary structure of local government for England and Wales. This implied the abolition of counties and many shire districts as administrative units and their replacement by unitary authorities made up of groups of smaller districts or, in some cases, the reinstatement of previous county boroughs. Derbyshire, for example, would have six authorities including the City of Derby and five groups of existing districts.

Although the Government had stressed that it wished this pattern to be uniform across non-metropolitan areas (the metropolitan authorities were already uniform) the Law Lords had held that the terms of reference of the Commission precluded Government insistence that this pattern should be continued and, in any case, the Commission itself had not always gone down that path.

By late 1995 the position was not clear. There seemed to be a general acceptance that with a few possible exceptions unitary local authorities were more sensible than a two-tier framework. There was also renewed interest in a regional tier of government. Since there was some uncertainty about the party of government following a general election in 1996 or 1997, local government was given a breathing space. Change of some sort seemed almost inevitable in the late 1990s.

The future pattern of local government is financially significant in two ways. First, it will affect the shape of service delivery and therefore, possibly, its overall cost effectiveness. Second, the Government hopes that there will be genuine savings on overheads by stripping out redundancies and duplications in the town and county halls.

In common with other aspects of the public sector, local government changed significantly during the 1980s and early 1990s. The four main thrusts of the changes may be summarized as follows:

1. A series of financial pressures (for example, changes in the formulae for the allocation of grants, changes in the basis of local taxation, limitations on both revenue and capital spending and 'capping' of rates/community charge/council tax) had the effect of reducing the cash resource available to local authorities for service delivery.

2. A series of measures designed to increase the economy, efficiency and effectiveness of service provision, which began in 1980 with a limited requirement for direct labour organizations to show an annual profit and a requirement for all local authorities to publish a range of performance indicators. The establishment of the Audit Commission[9], specifically charged to oversee the search for value for money in local government, accentuated this trend.

3. The emergence of a developing philosophy which may be summed up in the phrase 'the enabling authority'. This philosophy argues that there is no need for a public authority to provide a service itself: the service may be provided by the private sector with the public sector providing the finance and monitoring the quality. For local government several 'rounds' of competitive tendering for services both external to and internal to authorities have considerably reduced direct service provision and enhanced the 'enabling' role.

4. Worth recording as a separate thrust because of the volume of resource involved, is the considerable reduction in local government control over the provision of education. The polytechnics, colleges of higher education and further education colleges were removed from local authority control in the late 1980s and early 1990s[10]. More significant was the erosion of local education authority control over schools through the provisions for 'Local Management

of Schools'[11]. Later the development of 'grant-maintained schools' gave the option for schools to leave the local authority framework completely, receiving their income directly from central government and spending it, within reason, at their discretion.

Despite these significant changes local government is still an important factor in the public sector with a key financial role to play. As at the fourth quarter of 1993 local authority staffing in Great Britain[12] totalled 2,602,600 FTEs[13]. It can be seen that this figure is approximately 8 per cent of the employed workforce. Since the figure includes many part-time workers, the actual proportion of the workforce employed by local authorities is, of course, higher.

In financial terms total local authority spending for 1995–96 is planned to be £73.4 billion out of a government planned spending total of £300.4 billion[14].

The National Health Service

The NHS is responsible for delivering the great majority of health care in the United Kingdom, although there is a growing private sector funded predominantly from insurance schemes and interest in some quarters of government in developing a dual public/private service. For the time being, however, the future of the NHS as the major deliverer of health care looks certain.

The NHS is the main activity of the Department of Health which is responsible for the great bulk of its cash resources, with a small proportion coming from bequests, donations, charities and some service sales to the private medical sector. Currently, there are three layers of organization: the regions, the districts and the various trusts/units. This pattern is in the process of evolution. The last great stimulus to structural change was the Government White Paper, 'Working for Patients', 1989. As a result of action following this paper the following changes have taken/are taking place:

1. There were once 14 regions but these were grouped into 8 regions or consortia of regions which corresponded to the regional offices of the NHS executive. Their planning and co-ordination powers were considerably reduced. Their main function in late 1995 was the planning/co-ordination of major capital activity. From 31 March 1996 regions were abolished with their functions, offices and staff being taken over by the NHS executive.
2. The districts, of which there are about 130[15], once operated as a very clear planning and control layer for the financing of the service delivery units within their charge. The function has now changed to being the major 'purchaser' of services from the various 'providers' available to them. In theory, these providers include the private sector and units/trusts from outside their district boundaries, but in practice the great majority of purchases are made from within the traditional boundaries. Since the purchases are predominantly made in blocks and the shape of the purchases is to a large extent dependent upon historical patterns, the purchasing exercise results in the providers ending up with reasonably stable and predictable budgets.

The main thrusts of financial change (which have been concomitant with the structural changes described) have been the move towards an internal market, the pressure on health authorities to make 'efficiency savings' and the stimuli, which come from a number of directions, to move away from roll-forward budgeting. The earliest attempts, dating from the early 1980s, to achieve efficiencies consisted in cash-limiting authorities to a gross budget which took account of inflation and planned service change but permitted growth only if savings (typically of the order of 1 per cent per annum) were made. Over a period of about seven years, such savings amounted to around 7 per cent, but were, for political reasons, often presented as 'the cuts'. Once districts appreciated that the Government was serious in its attempt to seek cost effectiveness in health care delivery, an effort was made to reconsider baseline budgets and to make more radical changes. It was, however, 'too little and too late' and the creation of an internal market with the consequent reduction in the power of both regions and districts was the Government's response. The internal market is not operating fully: the term 'quasi-market' is often used to describe the relationship between the district purchasers and the trust providers.

Demography plays an important part in planning for change within the NHS. The ageing of the population clearly suggests that an increasing proportion of resource will be directed towards elderly people. The change is not, however, directly proportional since historically elderly people have been more demanding on resources since they are more prone to illnesses and less tractable in treatment. The proportionate consequences of demographic change are thus compounded by this factor. Equitable treatment of elderly people is a matter for public concern. It is a moral issue: they have rights and have paid their taxes in their time. It is a financial issue: resource use has to be kept within limits—even if those limits are higher than currently perceived. It is a socio-medical issue: much expenditure is on 'patients' who are not so much ill as elderly and for whom medical treatment as such may be inappropriate. It is a fiscal issue: the aged dependency ratio, previously described, has implications for the pattern of taxation. It could be a cultural and religious issue: there are very sensitive overtones to some of the possible solutions. It is an electoral issue: elderly people have votes.

Discussion of the possible direction of future change is to some extent speculative. It may, perhaps, best be characterized in terms of three possible shifts in balance. First, a shift in balance from curative medicine towards preventive medicine. Second, a shift in balance from secondary (hospitalized) provision towards primary (GP and community) services. Third, a shift in balance from predominant state funding towards a more mixed economy combining state and private funding. The first shift is facilitated by the coincidence of a change in professional views concerning health models with the economic imperatives: preventive health care is cheaper! The second shift is facilitated by the growth of integrated practices in purpose-built accommodation having facilities for minor surgery and effective liaison between GPs and community services. The third shift is unproblematic in financial terms: it makes sense to government, to private health care providers and insurers and to the increasing proportion of comfortably-off citizens. It is, however, problematic in political terms: no government could be seen as having presided over the demise of the NHS.

The Audit Commission, originally set up to stimulate the search for value for money in local government, had its remit extended in 1990 to cover the NHS. Since then it has published major reports, to be discussed in Articles B5 and B6, which have discussed basic questions of delivery rather than marginal questions to do with economy and efficiency. In other words, the question of effectiveness has been raised. The possible trends as discussed in the previous paragraph are about effectiveness patterns at a very high strategic level. The possible moves towards more effectiveness as so far discussed by the Audit Commission (e.g. use of beds in acute hospitals, use of the time of trained nurses) are at a lower level. Nevertheless, they are at a higher strategic level than saving pence on the price of bandages or increasing productivity in the rostering of ambulance drivers.

Despite these important changes which have mostly taken place over the years since 1989 and which may well continue, the NHS remains a very important factor in the perceptions of the British people, in the thinking of government and in the economy. It is often characterized as the largest single employer in Britain, but since being broken down into trusts the monolithic nature is fast disappearing and in volume terms local government has at least an equal claim. Nevertheless, the NHS employed a total of 1,027,863[16] people in 1991 (a reduction of 20,000 over the ten years since 1981). Over the same period the number of medical staff had increased from 44,706 to 52,828 (up 18 per cent) and the number of nurses had increased from 474,497 to 483,493 (up 2 per cent). Whether monolithic or not the NHS is clearly a large employer!

The civil service

The civil service has not been immune to the winds of change which have swept through the public sector. Figure 2.3[17] shows that in the years from 1979 there have been six major initiatives which have affected the size, structure and quality of service delivery of the civil service. A White Paper on the civil service (Cm 2626, July 1994) and a Green Paper on resource accounting and budgeting (Cm 2627, July 1994) in combination have implications for the resourcing, budgetary control and accounting aspects.

The 'milestones' identified by Allen fall into three types. The establishment of the Efficiency Unit (1979), the Financial Management Initiative (1982) and Next Steps (1988) were mainly concerned with increasing value for money in the delivery of public services by providing a framework for tighter overall budgetary control and decentralized management. The Citizen's Charter (1991) and Competing for Quality (1992) created a framework for improving the quality of public services and for encouraging competition—in some cases by the setting up of internal markets—in the provision of such services. The Open Government (1994) initiative was intended to make the delivery of public services—and the performance of public servants—more accessible to public scrutiny. The proposals in the civil service White Paper and the Green Paper on resource accounting and budgeting will take these reforms still further and, in addition, will change the arrangements for managing the senior civil service.

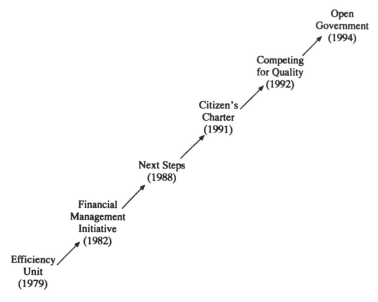

Figure 2.3 Civil service management reform: milestones

1. The Efficiency Unit, reporting to the Cabinet Office and thus to the Prime Minister, was responsible for a series of departmental studies, the so-called 'Rayner scrutinies', which were mainly concerned with the economy and efficiency end of the value for money spectrum.
2. The Financial Management Initiative was intended to give managers three things:
   (a) a clear view of their objectives with, wherever possible, measured outputs of relevant performance;
   (b) well-defined responsibility for making the best use of the resources, especially with regard to value for money;
   (c) appropriate information, training and advice to enable them to exercise these responsibilities effectively.
3. The Ibbs Report (Next Steps) made three main recommendations:
   (a) the work of each department should be organized in such a way as to allow managers to focus on the effective delivery of policies and services;
   (b) the management should ensure that their staff had appropriate experience and skills to perform the required tasks;
   (c) there should be genuine pressure on and within each department leading to improvement in value for money.
4. The Citizen's Charter White Paper set out seven principles of public service. These embraced: putting the customer first, setting standards, information and openness, choice and consultation, courtesy and helpfulness, putting things right and value for money. Many branches of the public sector have published charters based on this initiative.
5. Competing for Quality required an analysis at three yearly intervals of several options for service delivery prior to a decision on how such service was to be delivered. The options included questions regarding the abolition, privatization, contracting out or market testing of a service. The 1994 White Paper suggested that five years might be a more appropriate time period. Executive agencies and trading funds are required to publish their main targets, and performance against them, in their annual reports. The Green Paper proposed that a similar approach should be considered for government departments as a whole. The objective of this proposal was to encourage departments to focus attention on the outputs they delivered and to relate these to the resources consumed.
6. The April 1994 Code of Practice on Access to Government Information laid down three principles. There were to be:
   (a) a clear presumption of disclosure of information (within specified limits);
   (b) a right to independent review by the Parliamentary Commissioner (Ombudsman);
   (c) a statutory right of access to personal records and so on. This would require legislation.

Of the various reforms, the ones which have had the most obvious impact on the service as a whole have been Next Steps and market testing and contracting out of services under the Competing for Quality initiative. The service has to a very large extent already been changed to an agency basis and the numbers of civil servants have been trimmed significantly. Figure 2.4[18] shows a clear downward trend in the overall numbers of civil service staff.

Figure 2.5 shows that by April 1993 nearly two-thirds of civil servants worked in executive agencies while a further 20 per cent approximately were either definite or possible candidates for being moved to such agencies. It is reasonable to suppose that by the turn of the century nearly 80 per cent of the civil service will work in agencies on a much more decentralized basis with greater managerial flexibility and greater potential for genuine financial management and control. Only some 20 per cent of the service will remain in its traditional mode of employment and operation,

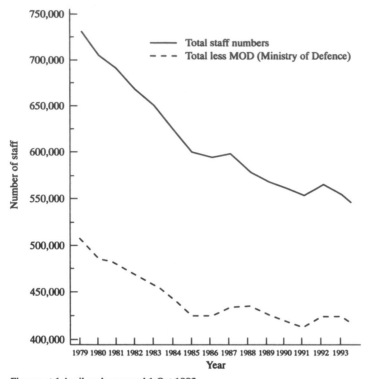

Figures at 1 April each year and 1 Oct 1993

Figure 2.4 Trends in civil service staff numbers, 1979–93

i.e. at the centre of departments: perhaps half of this remaining central function will be devoted to traditional activities such as policy advice, finance and personnel, and half to executive type activities (e.g. the immigration service) which are not deemed to be suitable for executive agency status, regulatory work, etc.

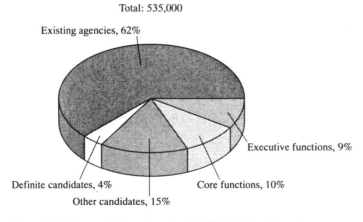

Figure 2.5 Home civil service (April 1994 staffing figures)

THE INTERRELATIONSHIP OF CAPITAL AND REVENUE EXPENDITURE

The principles of the distinction

The word 'capital' has gained a technical meaning within the context of financial management and, while it is a relatively easy concept to understand, it is worth looking briefly at some of its antecedents. A common-sense view of 'capital' as some large sum of money which, because of its size, is worth extra consideration before spending or investing is not far off the mark. The literature of the nineteenth and early twentieth centuries is full of reference to 'property' or 'capital' as the means of ensuring a comfortable existence (and considerable power/respect), not by spending it but by investing it wisely.

More precisely, nineteenth-century economists, notably Karl Marx, regarded capital as the means of preserving a major class distinction. Capitalists invested their money (at a risk to themselves) in providing opportunities (e.g. factories) for labour to produce goods which could be sold at a profit. Capitalists paid wages to the labour force but at a rate which enabled them to keep a proportion of the profits and thus live off their investments. The 'surplus value', i.e. in Marxian terms the proportion of the profits earned by the labour force which was not paid to them, was 'alienated' from them by the capitalists. The concept of 'surplus value' contributed to economic theory: by the time Marx and his successors had finished with it 'alienation' had become a sociological and political concept.

Such considerations may help us to understand why capital is seen as central to the private sector of the economy and its proper use as increasingly important to the public sector. They may also help us to understand why there is suspicion in some parts of the public sector concerning more business-oriented approaches to financial management.

In order to clarify the distinction between capital and revenue, it is necessary to distinguish also between sources of finance, i.e. where the money is coming from, and expenditure, i.e. to what purpose the money is applied.

Capital expenditure   In principle, this refers to monies spent on major items which have a life of longer than the standard accountancy period, usually one year. Obvious examples are land, buildings, vehicles and plant of various sorts. It is customary to draw an arbitrary limit at some figure, usually a few thousand pounds, below which expenditure counts as revenue even though the items purchased may last for some time[19].

Revenue expenditure   In principle, this refers to expenditure on goods and services which are to be consumed within the standard accountancy period, usually one year. Obvious examples are wages and salaries, consumables such as stationery or drugs, and services bought in such as cleaning or training. The provisos referred to directly above and in the accompanying note should be noted.

Capital finance   This refers to the sources of finance for capital expenditure. These will be discussed in detail later, but the main source of public sector capital finance is borrowing. Such borrowing necessarily incurs capital charges (e.g. interest) for the borrower and the proper method of accounting for such capital charges is a major feature of current debate within the public sector.

Revenue income   This refers to the income required to finance revenue expenditure. For the British public sector the great majority of this is derived from central or local taxation, although an increasing proportion is coming from charges to consumers for at least a part of the goods and services which they consume (council house rents or NHS prescription charges provide examples)[20].

It is becoming more widely perceived within the sector that capital expenditure should be seen to contribute in some way to the effectiveness of the use of the revenue budget, and it is to this topic that we now turn.

The necessary connections between capital expenditure and revenue budgets

Every item of capital expenditure implies change to the associated revenue budget:

1. The chances are that the capital finance was borrowed, in which case the revenue budget must bear the annual cost of servicing the debt, i.e. paying interest charges and making provision for paying back the borrowed money.
2. The item bought will probably depreciate[21], i.e. lose its resale value on a year-by-year basis over a period of time, and this depreciation should be shown in appropriate accounts of the organization concerned[22].
3. The item concerned will usually require maintenance in order to keep its utility.
4. The item concerned is intended to be used and so will require staff time and materials, e.g. a van will require a driver and fuel.
5. The item concerned may yield an income which contributes to the totality of revenue income, e.g. a leisure centre will attract a considerable income from charges to users.

Not all these considerations may apply in every case but, but at least one and probably three or more will apply. There is no exception to the rule that capital spending affects the revenue budget. The NHS has a special phrase, 'revenue consequences of capital schemes' (RCCS), and, although this phrase is not used anywhere else in the sector, the concept is: if a capital purchase is made the revenue budget must alter in some way.

The place of capital controls in managing a public sector

The British public sector has played and continues to play a major part in capital formation, i.e. spending on relatively permanent assets. There is direct ownership of a significant proportion of the housing stock either by district councils or semi-public housing associations. Schools, colleges and universities all have substantial buildings and, in the form of equipment ranging from personal computers to elaborate scientific apparatus, a good deal of expensive capital assets. The hospital stock of the NHS together with associated land, as well as technical and medical equipment, is another focus. Add to this the fleets of vehicles, ranging from street cleaners to buses, owned by the public sector and throw in the installations, equipment and weaponry owned by the military forces and the value of the directly owned assets, although unquantifiable with precision, can clearly be seen to be enormous.

Indirectly, the purchase of these assets has assisted the capital formation of a significant proportion of the private sector. There is no data available from which a precise figure can be derived, but it is clear that substantial industries, with all their invested capital in the form of factories and equipment, exist in order to provide, say, the vehicles and the technical equipment referred to above. The construction industry, from the volume house builder to the major civil engineer, together with the secondary industries such as brickmaking or concrete production, are closely dependent on the investment of the public sector in housing and engineering projects.

It is thus apparent that for any government a set of tensions exist on the matter of public sector capital formation.

On the one hand, it is clear that major public works can act as a stimulus to the economy. The 'New Deal' of Roosevelt in the 1930s USA and the autobahn construction and militarization of Hitler's 1930s Germany are both pre-war examples of conscious decisions to revitalize economies through massive public capital expenditure. The 1960s boom which enabled Harold Macmillan to claim, in 1963, that the people of Britain had 'never had it so good' was to a large extent based on the capital investment in the post-war reconstruction of the public sector. Thus there is a drive, which can be based on the economic theory of Keynes[23], to invest in the public sector in order to stimulate economic recovery and growth.

On the other hand, it can be argued that the capital borrowed by governments for public sector investment is not available for investment in the private sector which, it has been argued, makes better use of its capital assets. It is therefore better in the long term to allow the private sector to develop without artificial stimulation. This argument is logically separate from (although often run together with) the idea that if an economy is revitalized at too great a rate then inflationary pressures build up which have unfortunate effects on the value of the currency and make for difficulty in exporting and consequent negative effects upon the balance of payments. The 'Thatcherite' ideas of the Conservative Governments from 1979 onwards owe much to such theories associated with the term 'monetarism'[24].

Governments can control public capital expenditure in a number of ways:

1. Where the expenditure is directly funded by government, as for example on the military or the NHS, then direct capital control is possible. The expenditure (and its associated borrowing by government) is negotiated as part of the PESC process (see Chapter 1).
2. Where the expenditure is incurred by a quasi-autonomous authority such as local government, then central government can control gross spending, by a series of authorizations, perhaps organized by 'programme', for example education, housing or transport.
3. Alternatively to this control of spending, government could control the source of capital finance, by setting limits to the amount of borrowing either from the government itself[25] or directly from the capital market[26].
4. More dramatically, government can reduce the size of the public sector by privatizing enterprises. At a stroke, new borrowing by, say, water authorities ceases to be public sector borrowing[27].

As a matter of fact, all such control possibilities have been and continue to be used by government in relation to public authorities. It is becoming much harder to incur capital expenditure, those wishing to do so having to demonstrate need and/or potential for saving/income generation. Additionally, other methods of financing the expenditure, e.g. by savings or by sale of existing assets, have to be considered before borrowing is sanctioned.

AN ATTEMPT AT SYNTHESIS

The totality of public sector spending may in essence be reduced to four constituents:

1. Very much the largest is expenditure on the provision of services. This has capital and revenue aspects and accounts for over half of total public expenditure. The services may be delivered either by public sector employees or by private sector contractors. The main service deliverers

are civil servants (including the staff of agencies), local government employees (including those of the police and fire services), NHS employees and armed services personnel.

2. The second largest is expenditure on transfer payments such as benefits and pensions. Such payments are almost entirely administered by civil servants/agency staff and local government officers. The level of funding is decided, with only the most minor of exceptions (e.g. local authority discretionary grants) by central government. When the entitlement to benefit is high, e.g. at times of high unemployment, governments have resorted to borrowing as an alternative to taxation, but in principle such payments are usually funded directly from taxation.

3. Significant and inescapable is the servicing of past debts. Britain's per capita national debt is not particularly high in comparison with those of other states, developed or undeveloped, but nevertheless costs around £25bn annually to service (comparable to total expenditure on the NHS). The level of the cost of debt servicing is dependent upon longer term trends in interest rates rather than short-term fluctuations. Apart from a short period towards the end of the 1980s, there has been no serious attempt made in recent times to pay off the national debt, but nevertheless governments would not wish to see it rise significantly because of the constraining effects of the servicing.

4. Much smaller, but necessary, is expenditure in supporting the apparatus of state itself. This includes expenditure on democracy, e.g. supporting Parliament and local councillors with associated electoral expenditure, and the expenditure on those who advise the decision makers, e.g. the senior grades of the civil service and those local government officers who occupy comparable positions in relation to the executive groups of councils.

One major factor, which looks to be relatively permanent, has a considerable bearing on the balance of these blocks of expenditure. The demographic trend towards longer life implies the need for higher expenditure on the pensions aspect of transfer payments. There is also a pressure for higher expenditure on those services which cater for the increasing proportion of elderly people. This long-term factor is currently exacerbated by the relatively high level of unemployment which has an effect on both the level of transfer payments (benefits) and the call for certain services (mostly social services administered by local government). It also has the effect of reducing the tax income available to government. This government has a long-term problem (demography) and a problem (unemployment) which is seen as relatively short term.

Since the expenditure on debt servicing is inescapable and the costs of support for the state apparatus are relatively small, it is clear that both the longer and shorter term problems must be dealt with by a combination of rebalancing the expenditure on services in relation to transfer payments and/or by alterations to the balance of taxation and borrowing.

The governmental choice since the late 1970s has been to try to keep the level of taxation down by borrowing, by using the proceeds of privatization and by seeking considerable gains in the cost-effectiveness of public services. The techniques for achieving the last have included serious scrutinies by the Audit Commission and the (Rayner) Efficiency Unit, together with a set of structural changes which may be characterized as the creation of a series of bodies authorized to spend money either within or outside the public sector on purchasing the provision of services. The competitive tendering procedures and the concept of the enabling authority for local government, the internal market for the NHS and the agencies within the civil service are all aspects of the same phenomenon.

As a result of these changes there has been a considerable reduction in the total number of public employees with a consequent reduction in the gross amount spent directly on public services. The real increase in public expenditure over the period described has been due to increases in the real value of transfer payments. As a by-product of the changes described it is now relatively easy to define public expenditure and it is relatively easy to describe the services available to the public. It is less easy to define with precision exactly who is a public servant!

The relationship between expenditure on capital and revenue budgets is not a casual one. At the macro level there are important connections of great political (one might almost say 'ideological') significance. At the micro level there are potential trade-offs between capital and revenue which, in a culture that encourages devolution of responsibility for financial management, could lead to important changes in patterns of service delivery and public employment.

One such change has happened: capital investment in housing has been directed away from local government and into housing associations. One such change is happening: the provision of education, including control of capital provision, is moving away from local education authorities and towards quasi-autonomous bodies comparable in some ways to NHS trusts. A longer term change may lie in the pattern of acute hospital provision where it is possible to discern a trend towards fewer, much larger, acute hospitals serving greater catchment populations[28]. The importance of sensible capital expenditure in the context of long-term strategic planning cannot be overstated.

SUMMARY

Chapter 1 discussed the main macro-economic environment in which the British government manages its finances. This chapter has summarized the way in which the governments of the last 15–20 years have pressurized the public sector towards more effective and more cost-effective service delivery. The major factor of demographic change, which has potential impact on all aspects of service delivery and is of considerable political significance, has been inescapable and has impinged directly on the NHS and on local government. The basis for the financial pressures has been found in a set of beliefs regarding the desirability of relatively low taxation, low (or zero) public borrowing and low inflation. These beliefs have impinged upon the civil service as well as local government and the NHS.

(Budgetary) devolution as a managerial device has obvious harmonies with a desire to break up big organizations with central authority structures into smaller units with (quasi) internal market mechanisms. This, in turn, has sat quite easily with the idea of tendering, compulsory or otherwise, and the fruitful coexistence of public and private sectors in facilitating (enabling) service delivery. A small step from this position leads to the possibility of a more private sector view of capital utility, which in turn accords with the governmental desire to reduce public sector borrowing.

In the simplest possible terms, the Government would like to maintain annual public expenditure at or around the £300bn mark (certainly no more), but with a reduction in both unemployment-related transfer payments and public sector borrowing. It pins its faith to some extent on a continuing recovery of the economy which will increase tax income without increasing tax levels. It believes that there are still considerable effectiveness/cost-effectiveness savings to be made, and that these can be directed towards solving the problems of demography.

It is my opinion that any government in the relatively near future based on the Labour or Social Democratic parties (singly or in combination) might well differ from the Conservatives in details (such as the alleviation of the short-term distress caused by some unemployment and changes in employment structure). There might also be a re-presentation of the role of education in the move towards changing the economic structure of Britain, but the main thrusts of the Conservative arguments of the years since 1979 had their roots in changes perceived by the pre-

1979 Labour administration, and perceived even more clearly now by both alternative parties. The details of Thatcherism may well be amended: the principles have gained a considerable acceptance.

It is in this environment that today's public sector managers must manage finance. They must look for economy and efficiency savings. They must look for effectiveness gains. They must be prepared to tender cheaply and with outcomes defined in terms of volume and quality in a market situation. They must be prepared to take more personal responsibility for budgetary decisions and learn to deliver to a stated price. They will have more say in defining and using constructively the interface between revenue and capital expenditure. It is to these practical themes that the book now turns.

NOTES

1. *Economic Briefing No. 6*, February 1994, HM Treasury. Figures are contained in Table 1 of the article 'The public sector borrowing requirement'.
2. The same article (note 1) contains a clear statement of such policy in the initial paragraph and a subsequent diagram (Chart 2) illustrating this.
3. A transfer payment is money which passes from an individual or organization to another individual or organization which is not a payment for services. Thus a child benefit, a pension or a student grant are examples of transfer payments, because nothing is expected in return, while a rent or a fee/charge are not transfer payments because something is received in return.
4. Table 1 of article 'Public spending in the UK' in HM Treasury, *Economic Briefing No. 5*, August 1993.
5. The 'median' is one of several statistical concepts used to typify the diversity of groups. It is the 'centre point'. In this case it means that in 2005 a person aged 38.9 years will have as many people younger than him or her as there are older. The fact that the median age is increasing clearly indicates an ageing population.
6. The calculations for the two dependency ratios for the two years in question have been calculated from the data in the tables and are rounded to the nearest whole number for convenience.
7. Additionally, there are 'parishes' which can be found both within unitary and two-tier authorities. Although a handful of these offer such services as swimming pools, the total volume of expenditure is minuscule and for all practical purposes can be neglected.
8. Police, fire services and some transport co-ordination were in late 1995 provided by special authorities (e.g. the Metropolitan Police) or by the remains of the old GLC or metropolitan county councils.
9. The Audit Commission for Local Government was established by the 1982 Local Government Finances Act. It began its VFM work in 1983. Its remit was enlarged in 1990 to include responsibility for auditing the NHS. Its full title in current form is The Audit Commission for Local Government in England and Wales and the National Health Service.
10. The removal of the polytechnics and higher education colleges, 'incorporation', was more of a blow to prestige than to finances since the founding had been predominantly through central government grants for many years. The incorporation of the FE colleges was more significant to LEAs because it reduced freedom of financial action for provision for post-16 students. The changes were inevitable given that an increasing proportion of the income for FE colleges was arising from work undertaken for various government training schemes.
11. Local Management of Schools, first introduced through the Education Reform Act of 1988, required local authorities to fund schools according to a formula based predominantly on capitation. In principle 'money was to follow pupils'. Initially, all secondary schools and primary schools with over 200 children were to be included. Within a very short time most local education authorities extended the formula funding to all schools.
12. Great Britain comprises England, Wales and Scotland. The United Kingdom includes Northern Ireland as well. The full title is thus 'The United Kingdom of Great Britain and Northern Ireland'.
13. This figure is taken from *Monthly Digest of Statistics*, No. 580, April 1994. The figures include those for law and order (i.e. police and magistrates courts' staff) and agency staff. FTE stands for full-time equivalent. The figures do not include the 97,000 lecturers and other staff in FE colleges which were removed from local authority control in April 1993.
14. HM Treasury, *The Budget in Brief*, 29 November 1994.

15. In 1991 there were 190. By late 1993 the figure had fallen to 140. The main reason for this reduction was the combination of districts in an attempt to secure purchasing power. The number may well have fallen to fewer than 100 by 1995.
16. The figures are taken from HMSO, *1993 Annual Abstract of Statistics.*
17. Figure 2.3 is based, with his permission, on an OHP used by Richard Allen, Under Secretary at HM Treasury, in his lecture to the Public Finance Foundation on 7 June 1994. Much of the substance and structure of the section is derived from other parts of the same lecture. I am very grateful to him for permitting me to use this material and also for making constructive comments and suggestions on a draft of this section. Any errors of fact or interpretation are, of course, due to me and not to him.
18. Figures 2.4 and 2.5 are taken, with permission, from Richard Allen's PFF lecture referred to previously.
19. It should be noted that some branches of the public sector have oddities of expenditure that counts as capital even though it is in all respects revenue: the NHS for example counts as capital expenditure the salaries of those people employed as capital administrators and planners. It is worth noting that central government has only recently begun to use the distinction at all in its own planning and accounting and that the public sector usage is to some extent at variance with the conventions of private sector accounting. Public sector 'revenue' is comparable to the private sector's 'working capital', while public sector 'capital expenditure' is comparable in large part to the private sector's 'expenditure on fixed assets'.
20. It is, of course, possible (and some would say desirable in certain circumstances) to fund at least some revenue expenditure by borrowing. A proportion of the currently high level of social security payments is funded from borrowing which in 1993–94 ran at about £50bn, or one-sixth of general government income.
21. There are exceptions to this rule which provide accountants with a few problems. Land and buildings, for example, may 'appreciate', i.e. gain in resale value, and this appreciation may or may not be at a rate faster than the basic rate of inflation. This problem should not be seen out of proportion. Depreciating assets are far more common.
22. Appendix 2 gives a basic understanding of some of the key terms of accountancy. The exact way in which public bodies do their capital accounting is currently under review in a period of change
23. John Maynard Keynes, the British economic theorist whose ideas directly and indirectly influenced post-war British governments up to the late 1970s. In essence he argued that the investment of capital monies produced a 'multiplier effect' the extent of which depended on the 'marginal propensity to save' and which resulted in every pound of public investment being spent several times over with a consequent beneficial stimulus to the economy.
24. 'Monetarism', strictly speaking, relates to control of economies by controlling the money supply, i.e. how much money there is in circulation. It is thus a relatively narrow concept. It has become, however, associated with a whole set of arguments such as those outlined in this paragraph, which are associated with the economist Milton Friedman. Any modern textbook of economics deals in far more depth with these topics, as well as Keynesianism (see note 23). Beware, however, that there is much political baggage carried with the economic theories and that even academic writers are not always strictly objective!
25. The Public Sector Loans Board (PSLB) borrows from the capital market on behalf of the central authorities and re-lends to public sector bodies, predominantly local authorities.
26. Many public sector bodies, historically including local government and more recently including NHS trusts, have authority to borrow directly from the capital market: banks, insurance funds, investment trusts and individual members of the public.
27. It is, of course, possible for government to assist private sector organizations by capital subsidies of some kind. Such subsidies, if borrowed, would count as part of the total of public sector borrowing.
28. A figure of 26 such hospitals for mainland Britain was quoted (albeit speculatively) by a senior officer of the Health Service Management Executive at a talk to an invited audience at Sheffield Business School in early 1994.

THREE

THE BUDGETARY CYCLE

INTRODUCTION

The idea of an annual 'revenue budget' is central to all public sector organizations—indeed it is significant in all organizations, public and private sector. There is one necessary prerequisite to any such budget: there must be a fair predictability of at least a substantial proportion of annual income. It is also helpful, although not strictly necessary, if there is a fair stability, over a period, of the required outcomes. There is an important question implicit in this point: is 'budgeting' in its traditional form appropriate in an internal market situation?

Any budget is a plan (usually in financial terms). It is also a document which, provided it is available to and understood by all personnel who have to manage finance, can be used to control the cash flows (income as well as expenditure) by informing such personnel—the budget holders—when deviations from the plan appear, thus affording to the organization the chance to take suitable corrective action. The dynamics of the current public sector financial situation are such that it is possible that the budgets were incorrectly constructed in the first place and that therefore the corrections may be to the budgets and not to the actual income/expenditure patterns.

There is no doubt that a long-term financial strategy, discussed in the previous chapters, exists at governmental level and is reflected with varying degrees of acceptance at top levels within public sector organizations. There is equally no doubt that at the lower levels of organizations where services are delivered there is considerable resistance to changing the current pattern of work required to deliver the service. There is thus a tension, and an important one, between strategy and service delivery. The 'budget', both expressed in overall organizational terms and in the form of a budget holder's spending authorization (and/or income generation expectations), is a key link in resolving this tension.

This chapter discusses these points in the context of the traditional incremental annual revenue budget and the possibilities which exist for change. The impact on the planning and control processes is also considered. It does not deal with capital budgeting, project budgeting, non-financial budgeting or with business planning (which may be seen as encompassing budgeting) as these topics are dealt with in later articles.

Static and dynamic elements of budgeting

It may be helpful in explaining the significance of this distinction to contrast two very different operations: a 1960s local authority and a 'one-person business', say a jobbing decorator. The financial aspect of a local authority in the 1960s was very predictable. Income was substantially from rates and government grants which were relatively generous and related to actual spending, and not (on the whole) to some estimate by government of what 'ought' to be spent. There were also charges, but these were mainly left to the discretion of the authority which in many cases exercised such discretion towards token charges. Expenditure was easily increased in line with inflation (which was relatively low) and any upward or downward changes in the level of service provision were visible and the bases of negotiation were clear. Budgeting was thus almost invariably 'incremental' and cash flow was eminently predictable. The same story would have been true for a health authority: predictable income, predictable expenditure, roll-forward budgeting.

The 'one-person business', by contrast, has considerable elements of uncertainty on both income and expenditure side. The income depends upon the ability of the decorator to find work, with five days' work a week and, say, £60 a day clear. These hopes are not always realized. A bad week may have only two or three days' work. Job times may be poorly estimated and the daily rate drop to £35 or £40. Customers may not pay promptly. A hoped-for annual income of £15,000 may in reality yield only £10,000. On the expenditure side calculations based on domestic expenses (i.e. what the decorator takes out of the business), savings for retirement, major expenses such as the vehicle which may serve for both business and domestic use and the possibility of holidays, can be completely thrown out by a series of bad weeks. Bank loans taken out to ease cash-flow problems can add to them by the necessity to prioritize interest payments. Cash flow is not predictable: budgeting has no certain base. It is still, however, necessary!

All organizational finance falls somewhere between the extremes of the eminently stable, predictable and 'static' 1960s public authority and the unstable, unpredictable and volatile one-person business. Large organizations, public and private, tend to resemble the more static end of the spectrum, but the recent fortunes of IBM or Woolworth, which have had to effect considerable financial improvisation in recent years, might serve to counterbalance this view. Smaller organizations, manufacturing, service or retail, tend to resemble the less stable end of the spectrum, but again some small organizations grow rapidly and the volatility may be the result of success.

In public sector organizations there is still an overwhelming budgetary stability. Several factors, however, as discussed in the first two chapters, have contributed towards increasing dynamism. In particular, a smaller proportion of income is assured, and a smaller proportion of call for services is certain. The inflation of the 1970s and early 1980s, the appreciation by government of the significance of demographic change, the structural changes in Britain's economy and associated difficulties, together with ideologically based beliefs about the role, structure and management of the public sector have led to a reappraisal of the role of budgeting.

It would be a serious mistake to believe that the changes brought about since 1979 have removed the basic stability. It is equally a mistake to deny the import of the budgetary dynamism brought about over the same period. Authorities must now acknowledge and cope with continual change on both income and expenditure sides.

The budget as a planning document v. the budget as a control document

The budget serves two purposes:

1. As a statement of the intended pattern of income and anticipated expenditure it serves to authorize both the general pattern of transactions and the individual transactions which fall within its ambit. Where a political dimension is involved, e.g. in local government, its

publication serves to legitimize a part of the political process, by providing voters with information which, in principle, may help to decide their electoral choice.
2. Once authorized, and in the form of documents more detailed than those generally available to the public, the budget—by now a set of sub-budgets—serves as a control device. All spending must in principle be within the limits of authorization and thus budget holders must see their sub-budget as important. If their spending (or income generated) differs from the authorized pattern then periodic checks will reveal the extent of such differences (variances) and changes can be made to bring actual and plan back into harmony.

In an incremental budgeting system there is a third purpose which unites these two aspects. On a macroscale the extent of difference between plan and actual is a most useful input to the process of planning future budgets. The pattern of actual budget implementation is a control for future budgetary planning.

Figures 3.1 and 3.2 may be helpful in understanding the difference between the planning and control aspects of budgeting. They are each based on the false assumption that the budgetary process is zero-based, i.e. started anew each year. The reason for this apparently unhelpful assumption is to separate clearly the theoretical differences between the concepts of planning and control. As will be shown later, the differences in practice are much less clear and the diagrams can be helpfully combined in a number of ways.

Figure 3.1 shows that an annual budget is constructed in the light of financial constraints, desired goals and environmental factors. These are shown as independent whereas in fact they are interrelated and also related to the budget for the previous year. The point that is being made,

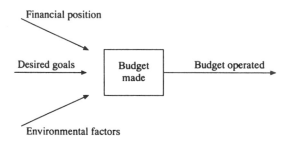

Figure 3.1   Budgetary planning (non-loop)

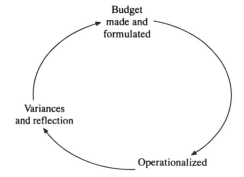

Figure 3.2   Budgetary control (loop)

however, is that in principle the budgetary planning process takes place in advance of the budget period.

Figure 3.2 shows that once the budget has been made and formulated in such a way that each budget operator knows the limits of his or her spending authority and discretion, the actual operation is subject to a continual comparison of outcomes with plans. This is usually restricted to a comparison of financial outcomes with financial plans, but there is no reason whatever why there should not be a comparison of achieved outputs/outcomes[1] with planned outputs/outcomes.

Any differences between financial outcomes (actuals) and plans (budget) are known as 'variances' and are often termed 'overspends' or 'underspends'. It is always a matter of judgement as to whether any particular variance is serious enough to warrant corrective action.

Figure 3.2 is shown as if the operation for one year is independent of the budget for the next year: in fact there is usually a strong degree of dependence of the budget for one year on the outcome of the control of the previous year. The point being made, however, is that in principle the budgetary control process should take place while the budget is being run.

The tension between strategic planning and short-term budgetary operationalization

At the heart of many managerial dilemmas lies the tension between the long-term goals of an organization and the current position in terms of staffing, resources, attitudes and culture. This often shows up, in financial terms, when a manager is asked to deliver a service using fewer resources than previously. In most branches of the public sector this means either a significantly reduced staffing budget or an expectation that the current staff will deliver more in the form of increased outputs/outcomes.

In such circumstances there will almost inevitably arise occasions when the service just cannot be delivered by the existing staff working in their accustomed ways and the response of senior management, 'the staff will have to change' is inappropriate in view of a perceived need for urgency of service delivery. At such times devices such as overtime or the use of temporary or agency staff to relieve pressure are probably justified. A number of practical manifestations of the tension then appear:

- How far should authority to cope with such problems be delegated? If it is delegated too far then it may be used too readily as a device to slow down necessary change. If it is held centrally then it may be too slow and clumsy to react to genuine problems.
- How should training for change, which itself demands resources, be prioritized in view of its financial costs and the opportunity costs[2] of the training time of the service deliverers?
- How can the uncertain potential long-term benefits of change be presented most effectively to staff and to consumers when there are sometimes obvious and immediate current losses in quality that are visible to both?

INCREMENTAL BUDGETING

Linear and helical understandings of the process

We have already seen that the budgetary process has both planning and control dimensions. The real difference between the two is that the *planning* process takes place *before* the budget is implemented while the *control* process takes place *while* the budget is being worked.

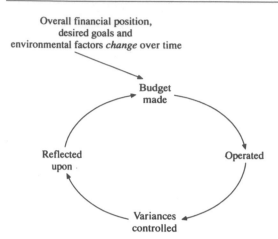

Figure 3.3 Combined planning and control model for budgets

In most public sector organizations, however, there is, as has been indicated, a strong connection between the budgets for successive years and hence the control aspect with its outcomes for one year is a factor, some would argue a determining factor, in the planning process for the next year's budget. Figures 3.3 and 3.4 may help to illustrate this.

Figure 3.3 shows that, in an incremental system, the budget for any particular year is made in the light of consideration of the operation of budgets for previous years:

1. The budget is made and then operated.
2. Reflection takes place in the light of how the operation has worked, such reflection taking place both during and immediately after the period of operation.
3. The budget for the next year is then made, ideally in the light of full knowledge of the out-turn for the previous year, but in practice with only partial knowledge of how things have gone.

This model is, of necessity, presented on a flat sheet of paper. It may be helpful, however, to think of the model as a helix (corkscrew), since there is always a progression between the years (Fig. 3.4).

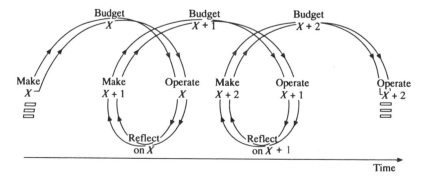

Figure 3.4 Helical model of the budgetary cycle

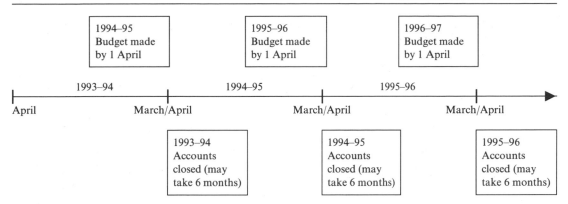

Figure 3.5 The sequence of reporting and budgeting

There is a complication which must be discussed even when very straightforward incremental budgeting is being considered. This complication has to do with the fact that the 'tidying up' of the out-turns for one year is never completed in time for the making of the budget for the next year. This has two important effects:

- The 'starting point' is not known accurately, i.e. the 'carry forwards' of balances either surplus or deficit.
- Proper consideration cannot be given to any trends which should be included somehow in making the new budget.

The sequence in this case is best shown in Fig. 3.5. This shows that even when the budget is made as late as possible and accounts are closed as early as possible, the relevant outcomes cannot be fed into the new budget in full.

In practice, the first draft of the budget is made starting in December or even November, and the accounts may not be closed until July or even August. There may thus be a mismatch of nearly a year between two key events, one of which is meant to happen before the other. The growth of client–contractor (local government) and purchaser–provider (NHS) relationships and the need to define cost and service levels in good time has imposed even tighter time constraints at a period of greater budgetary complexity.

In practice, incomplete out-turns (which may be quite accurate[3]) are used and adjustments made during the course of the operation of the budget. Given the circumstances, this is inevitable, but it is not easy for anyone concerned.

The role of the budget in the internal market

It has already been indicated that as the structure of the public sector changes to that of a genuine internal market with services being bought and sold within that market at agreed levels and prices, then both the nature of budgeting and its role within the organization may change. Budgeting, however, possibly in a modified form, remains necessary.

At the extreme the public sector turns into a set of jobbing decorators, to use our previous example, each competing for trade with others in a market made up of independent and discerning purchasers. If that is the case then the concept of an annual roll-forward budget may not be as helpful as a set of 'project budgets'[4] within a financial business plan.

There are a number of reasons why such a model is not helpful:

1. There is a steady and predictable demand for a great number of services. The NHS, for example, can predict with fair certainty the level of demand for most of its treatments. The number of children requiring education is known four or five years in advance.
2. Jobbing decorators are an extreme case in themselves. Most private sector organizations are larger and do in practice have budgetary procedures, albeit probably more capable of flexing in response to change than those of the public sector.
3. The purchasers of public services are mostly relatively constrained geographically. A purchaser in urban Barnsley might well turn to Sheffield or Wakefield for a provider but a purchaser in rural Cornwall or Cumbria has usually little choice.
4. The main elements of discernment are usually held to be price, quality and availability. As yet there is no real evidence of accurate pricing of services because the necessary associated costing systems are neither yet fully in place nor fully understood. There is also little evidence of choice on the basis of quality[5]. Availability has some influence on the pattern of demand for services[6].

Thus the market which might render budgets unnecessary is by no means perfect and thus budgeting, in some form, is likely to continue. What is likely is that the form of budgeting will change over time and that increased flexibility will be introduced within budgets to facilitate speedy response to changes in demand and negotiated price.

The way in which such changes may be facilitated will form one of the major themes of this book. It must, however, be stated clearly that for the foreseeable future annual budgeting is likely to remain an important feature and that annual budgets will continue to be recognizable descendants of existing arrangements for some time to come.

NON-INCREMENTAL BUDGETING

Zero-based budgeting

Zero-based budgeting (ZBB) is the most radical alternative to incremental budgeting. It had its origins in the United States of America where, under President Carter's administration, it was applied in the mid-1970s to the spending of central government. It was abandoned as unworkable. Its principle is clear: a budget is made for one year and at the end of that year a new budget is made with every heading being examined from scratch, i.e. with a zero base.

If it were applied in Britain, each manager with budgetary responsibility would be required to detail what resources, in cash terms, were necessary to deliver required outputs/outcomes. The requirements would be prioritized by the next layer of management, consolidated at executive level and finally funds (i.e. authorization to spend) would be allocated.

The important point which marks off a strict ZBB from all alternatives is that no project or service is guaranteed funds for more than the current year. The rolling nature of incremental budgeting, the dimension of continuity, has been removed. It has been replaced by a dimension of uncertainty and change which may match up to a fast-changing world but which may also lead to the inefficiencies of stress and muddle. In practice, where ZBB has been tried it has been on a department-by-department basis and the budgets so constructed have been used (incrementally modified) for several years.

The process looks rational, and indeed the idea should be commended for its insistence on taking nothing for granted and re-examining on a regular basis the resources needed, the service outputs and the methods of delivering these service outputs/outcomes. It neglects, however, the political dimensions associated with all resource allocation. In all organizations there is a mini-political system, based among other factors on departmentalism, which places limits on rationality and change. In public sector organizations there is also a limit to the changes which can be accepted by the people, who in one sense are the customers served by the organization and in another sense are the electorate to whom the government is responsible.

Planning, programming and budgeting systems

Another way of tackling the issue of the lack of co-ordination which incremental budgeting can lead to is the use of a planning, programming and budgeting (PPB) system. Such systems allow for both continuity and departmentalism, and are thus more realistic in concept, but are intended to look at budgets across whole organizations. The idea originated in the US Defense Department and it is still used there although its use has not been continued elsewhere in US government. The key principle is that the organization, rather than the individual departments, defines desired outcomes.

In a PBB system the goals are defined and possible alternative ways of achieving those goals outlined. It is then possible to estimate the costs and benefits of each and thus determine priorities and allocate resources. Predetermined performance indicators are an integral part of the system and the budget can be revised on the basis of effectiveness of output as measured against these indicators.

The idea, if not the label, has found some use within the British public sector. Central government uses the idea of programmes but is not wedded to the idea that these programmes must necessarily be delivered by traditional departments in traditional ways. The move of the responsibility for the care of the elderly from the NHS to local government, or the move of much of education from the control/influence of the Department for Education to a variety of departments and quangos may be cited here. Within local government the relatively recent internal reorganizations of departments into programme groups owe much to the thinking of the Bains Report in 1972 with its emphasis on 'corporate management'. In the NHS the combination of clinical audit and the internal market may in time change the emphasis of what medical services are provided for whom and by whom as power passes from the departmentally organized, clinically based providers to the purchasing authorities which, in theory at least, have an overview.

ZBB and PPB in practice

Since both these American techniques have been rejected as such in Britain and since PPB survives only in one US department, it is legitimate to ask what lessons, if any, can be learned from them. There are four key points:

1. ZBB teaches us the need to take nothing for granted. We may not redraw the budget from scratch each year, but we should periodically, perhaps on a rolling basis, scrutinize each cost centre as if from a zero base.
2. PPB teaches us the need to look at the organization as a whole so as to eliminate duplications and redundancies and to check that nothing is being left out. Organizationally, we need to

check whether the structures, including budgetary structures, which served us well yesterday continue to serve us today and will continue to be adequate tomorrow.

3. PPB also teaches us the need to consider how the effectiveness of spending is to be monitored and brings predetermined performance indicators into focus. This reinforces the idea of an output budget as well as the more traditional input resource budget.

4. Both ZBB and PPB highlight the notion of prioritization on a rational and considered basis both within organizational units and across the organization as a whole.

TECHNIQUES FOR PRIORITIZATION

This emphasis on the need for prioritization leads us to consider two techniques which can be applied in a climate of limited resources. The first, marginal opportunity analysis, can be used within a department or across an organization. The second, priority-based budgeting, is usually applied to an organization as a whole.

Marginal opportunity analysis (MOA)

The principle of MOA is straightforward. Two sections/departments are paired and an appropriate sum of money, say £50,000, is nominated. The two sections/departments are then asked the same two questions:

1. What extra service would you provide with an extra £50,000?
2. What service, if any, would you cut if £50,000 were removed from your budget?

The four answers to these questions can be arranged in a two-by-two matrix and a judgement of the worthiness of supporting one departmental/sectional development at the expense of another departmental/sectional cut can be made with clarity.

The apparent simplicity of the technique is deceptive!

- It is neither easy nor necessarily fair to twin sections/departments in this way.
- Different sized departments are sensitive to different amounts of financial resource. In local government, for example, an education department with a budget of several hundred million pounds can more readily absorb a £1,000,000 cut than a cleansing department where a £25,000 cut might have similar significance.
- In times of resource constraint, it may be that the gains have to be less than the cuts, so that the figure used in the two questions would not be the same.
- Some departments have inefficiencies within them which would enable them to absorb a reduction of financial resource without a concomitant cut in service delivery.

Despite these difficulties MOA, if sensitively and selectively applied, can be used with good effect.

Priority-based budgeting (PBB)

A technique used in local government in the 1950s and 1960s, then known as 'rate rationing', can be applied more generally across any organization where the gross financial resource is fixed. Departments are asked to rank their various activities (with costings) in order of priority. This gives them a degree of ownership of the process. The activities are then drawn out in tabular form

Section Activity	A	B	C	D	E	
1	A1	B1	C1	D1	E1	
2	A2	B2	C2	D2	E2	
3	A3	B3	C3	D3	E3	
4	A4	B4	C4	D4	E4	Funded
5	A5	B5	C5	D5	E5	
6	A6	B6	C6	D6	E6	
7	A7	B7	C7	D7	E7	
						Cut-off line
8	A8	B8	C8	D8	E8	
9	A9	B9	C9	D9	E9	Not funded
10	A10	B10	C10	D10	E10	

Figure 3.6 Priority-based budgeting matrix

with a cut-off line drawn across the whole at the point which can be afforded. Activities above the line are funded: activities below the line are not. See Fig. 3.6.

The advantages of this technique include the seeming openness and fairness: it looks transparent and equitable. On the other hand, particularly in local government, departmental heads can, often with justification, plead that their activities are statutorily required and that therefore they must be above the line. It is also possible to argue that the apparent simplicity of the method is deceptive. In reality the cut-off line would be proportionately much lower and only a handful of activities would be up for consideration. If this were the case then each would have to be considered on its merits and not dealt with in some arbitrary way.

CONTROL

The concept of 'control' has its origins in the idea of steersmanship. The Greek word for a steersman (*kybernetikos*) leads via Latin (*gubernator*) to the English word 'governor' which has both political and administrative senses and is obviously linked to the idea of government. It also has an engineering sense: a 'governor' was a device fitted to steam engines to keep their speed within pre-set limits.

If we pursue the nautical analogy a little further we can visualize the perils of a situation where no-one was at the helm; the ship's wheel being free to spin in any direction. We can also envisage the perils of a wheel lashed so as to prevent its movement; the ship would be at the mercy of the wind and waves and the crew unable to respond speedily to a hazard looming ahead.

The notion of control avoids these extremes: it has within it a dimension of flexibility. A controlled situation is one where the operator has freedom, within understood limits, to respond to changing circumstances. In terms of budgetary control the extreme positions described above would correspond to total licence on the one hand and total inflexibility on the other. A budget holder who made no attempt to check whether spending conformed to budget could not be said to be in control. Nor, for the opposite reason, would a budget holder who had absolutely no freedom; every item being prescribed in detail in advance.

On this account, budgetary control can be practised properly only by managers who have a degree of autonomy and who have the information to enable them to make sensible decisions. It is worth considering both the dimension of autonomy and the nature of the information:

Stores department   January (month 10)

Item	Annual	Monthly	Expenditure	Variance
1 Salaries	£60,000	£5,000	£5,250	(£250)
2 Heating	£2,400	£200	£500	(£300)
72 Stationery	£600	£50	£500	(£450)

Figure 3.7   Example of a simple budgetary report

- A typical budget holder will have a degree of delegated authority. It is the extent of this delegation which is a measure of autonomy. Typically, a revenue budget will have both pay and non-pay aspects. Very few public sector managers have much freedom over their core pay budgets although matters of overtime, temporary/casual staff and maybe bonuses can fall within their remit. The non-pay budgets are typically much smaller, but managers normally have more discretion, although for many routine items there are arrangements for central purchasing which should be adhered to. Operational managers rarely have any control over major capital items, although they may have a 'non-recurrent' budget head for less expensive durable items, which may or may not count as capital.
- The information that a budget holder receives is normally through the medium of a regular budgetary statement, usually monthly but conceivably weekly, which sums up annual and period budgetary authorization, actual and cumulative expenditure and the variance between the cumulative authorization and the cumulative actual. Figure 3.7 shows an example of a monthly report which, for simplicity, omits the cumulative columns.

The key information is in the column of variances. It could be said that the art of successful budgetary control lies in knowing when a variance should cause concern and having a range of techniques at one's disposal in order to deal with those variances which are significant. The more a budget holder is in the position of making the judgement of significance and the more freedom that budget holder has in sorting out any problems within limits, the more he or she can be said to exercise budgetary control.

Variances and the need for 'profiling'

If we consider the simple statement exemplified in Fig. 3.7 we can see that there are relatively small unfavourable variances[7] on all three items. This is not necessarily a cause for worry. Inspection of the monthly budget column reveals that in each case the monthly budget is the yearly budget divided by 12. No attempt has been made to profile the budget in any way.

- For the salaries budget in a department such as stores, this is probably a sensible way of dealing with the situation. There is likely to be a relatively large core of permanent staff drawing salaries on a regular basis.
- For heating, such lack of profiling is likely to be misleading. January is known to be a cold month: it might be expected that heating would cost more in the winter months. Perhaps there is only background heating at a very cheap rate in the months from April to September.
- For stationery, which is not a large budget in any case there may well be an explanation for why virtually the whole budget is spent in one month. Perhaps there are post-Christmas sales

which a prudent manager has waited for, perhaps there is a bulk discount available on one order of £500 which would not be available on several orders of £50. If this sort of thing is known about in advance, then the budget can be constructed differently to reflect peaks and troughs in anticipated expenditure.

It is clear then that the three budgetary items each have a different status with regard to the way in which the permitted annual spending is divided between the various months:

- Salaries, being a very steady expenditure in a stores department, is almost certainly profiled correctly. It is probably right to have the year divided into 12 even monthly instalments.
- Heating, being an expenditure subject to seasonal ups and downs, is almost certainly profiled incorrectly. It would have been better to have allowed smaller expenditure in the warmer months than in the colder months.
- Stationery might or might not be profiled correctly. The explanations offered above were only speculations. Any explanation provided by the manager which was along those lines, however, would support case for future profiling.

It is clear that one of the variances (that for heating) is probably due to the absence of profiling. If profiling had been undertaken, then the spending of £500 might not have seemed so large in relation to the budget.

Another of the variances (that for stationery) might well not be a problem. If either or both of the possible explanations offered above were correct, then a profiled budget would have shown that the £500 expenditure was not out of line with the budget.

The only one that looks serious is the unfavourable variance under the salaries item. If repeated on a month-by-month basis it would lead to an annual overspend of £3,000, which on a £60,000 base works out at 5 per cent.

We must now turn our attention to another aspect missing from this simple example. There is no record of spending in previous months. We do not know whether the general level of spending in months 1 to 9 has been below, at or above the budget. The headings missing are thus, 'Cumulative budget', 'Cumulative expenditure' and 'Cumulative variance'. Figure 3.8 shows the same basic budgetary statement as Fig. 3.7 but expanded by the appropriate columns, and making assumptions about profiling along the lines indicated above.

It can be seen that, as expected, the serious worry is with salaries. There should be a small concern over heating and there is no apparent cause for concern over stationery.

Stores department   January (month 10)

Item	Annual budget	Monthly budget (profiled)	Cumulative budget	Monthly expenditure	Cumulative expenditure	Monthly variance	Cumulative variance
1 Salaries	£60,000	£5,000	£50,000	£5,250	£52,500	(£250)	(£2,500)
2 Heating	£2,400	£350	£1,800	£500	£1,900	(£150)	(£100)
72 Stationery	£600	£500	£600	£500	£600	(zero)	(zero)

Figure 3.8 Example of a more complex budgetary report

Timeliness of information

Budgetary information/control statements such as the example discussed above are sent out regularly throughout the public sector in a format which varies only in minor matters of detail from the example. 'Regularly', however, does not necessarily imply 'promptly', and yet it is a matter of considerable importance to budget managers that the information they receive is both accurate and timely. Suppose that, as a matter of course, the statements are received six weeks after the end of the control period (month) to which they refer. Thus the April statement (month 1) would arrive in mid-June, and the January statement (month 10) would arrive in mid-March. If any expenditure problem showed up in month 1, the manager would still have more than nine months to correct it. If any problem, however, showed up in month 10, then only two weeks would be available for taking corrective action. Good management demands up-to-date information: a six-week delay is not acceptable.

Until comparatively recently, however, a six-week delay was entirely typical of budgetary information throughout local government and health authorities and in some departments of central government. The typical delay has now been reduced[8] to about three weeks. This is more acceptable. An ideal situation would produce the statements within a few days of the month end as is the practice within the private sector, but in my experience there are no public authorities delivering their information with such timeliness.

One other factor which can be mentioned in this connection is the need for managers to know not just what they have spent but what they have promised to spend, i.e. their commitments. Many managers keep their own records of such commitments, especially where they are relatively few, but there are compelling reasons why such commitments should be known centrally. Suppose, for example, a manager has been deliberately underspending a training budget on a monthly basis so that there will be money available in March for a staff development day. In a time of crisis, say if some other section were overspending, the apparent underspending might be 'clawed back' in some way. It would have been helpful to the prudent manager if the commitment to spend in March could have been registered earlier so as to protect the plans. If the March staff development day were to be a regular feature, then, of course, the budget could be profiled to reflect it.

Techniques of budgetary control

Staff slippage   In normal circumstances the most common source of serious overspend in the public sector is on staffing. The basic expenditure—routine salaries and wages—which falls under this heading is, in fact, usually completely outside the manager's control. The most common way of dealing with such overspending is to allow slippage. This means that if a person leaves, a replacement is not sought immediately. If a six-month delay is achieved, then half a salary is saved. If staff turnover is at 5 per cent (i.e. 1 out of 20 leaves each year), then a 2.5 per cent annual saving in salaries is achieved simply by delaying the replacements by 6 months in each case.

Staff slippage obviously imposes an additional load on colleagues who have to do the work on a temporary basis of the non-replaced staff. It therefore demands a lot of goodwill and can cause considerable stress. On the positive side, each vacancy and each period of slippage affords an opportunity for management to consider whether any particular job should be replaced or whether, perhaps, the budget could better be applied elsewhere. Vacancies can provide opportunities for restructuring services and/or redefining workloads. Such a consideration reminds us that the links between managing finance and managing people are very strong.

Temporary staff One technique which is being used with increasing frequency is using temporary staff to fill a vacancy, at least in the first instance. Such temporary staff are often employed on relatively low hourly rates as compared with the salaries of permanent staff. There are no annual increments and also fewer staff-related overheads to consider. Use of short-term temporary staff may be seen as little more than 'holding the fort'.

There is, however, a more serious longer term move towards the casualization of staff taking place in the public sector. This reflects a move which has already taken place in the private sector. In essence, an organization has a core of tenured or established staff paid on a weekly or monthly basis, and a periphery of non-tenured staff working under various forms of temporary contract. Financially, this makes a good deal of sense, especially in the short term: the basic salary costs are lowered and associated on-costs are also reduced. There are, however, associated problems including demotivation of both sets of staff and possibly increased costs of training and/or error correction.

On a positive note, there are non-financial gains to the employer in terms of increased organizational flexibility. It is also possible to treat the non-tenured staff as on some sort of 'probation' with the possibility of offering tenure if they prove effective in their roles.

Bonuses and overtime These factors occur more frequently when dealing with weekly waged staff than with salaried staff. Bonuses represent a way of rewarding staff for effective work, either performed well or performed within specified time limits. Overtime is payment for work additional to the normal weekly hours: it is normally paid at a rate of, say 'time and a quarter' or 'time and a half'. Both bonus systems and overtime can present managers with problems. Bonuses have sometimes become so generous that they are very easy to earn and therefore have become regarded by the workforce as part of the basic pay. Overtime, which should be an occasional feature used to cover short-lived demand peaks or emergencies, has often become institutionalized: in effect, it has become an expected part of the job and the payments an expected part of the wage.

The reduction of expenditure under both these subheadings can be an effective way of reducing overspends on weekly staff pay. To effect such reduction, however, demands more than financial management skills: the manager who seeks such reductions is in effect asking people to work harder for their basic pay and also faster if the usual output is to be achieved without recourse to overtime. A manager who requests this is not likely to be popular!

The use of overtime, even where the workload is genuine, may not be the most cost-effective way of delivering a service from management's point of view. If a section is regularly and needfully working, say, 40 hours' overtime a week, then this will be costing 50 hours' pay (at 'time and a quarter'). Such payment might better be spent on employing an additional member of staff, possibly on a temporary contract.

Stock reduction and control Short-term savings can sometimes be achieved by cutting down on the volume of stock held in storage. Money is clearly saved on a one-off basis. Less obviously, money can be saved on wastage, unauthorized usage and deterioration. The costs of storage can also be reduced. Attitudes of staff towards stock usage may also be changed, at least in the short term.

In the longer term, reduction of stock can play only a minor part in effecting significant overall savings. Any financial problems of the NHS or the education services will not be solved by reducing the number of bandages or pencils. Although it is true that every saving helps and there are almost certainly a host of relatively minor savings that can be made in any organization, it remains true that serious expenditure problems can be solved only by reappraisal of staffing policies.

Virement

Virement is the moving of spending authority from one expenditure head to another. If spare monies under the stationery budget are transferred for spending on heating, then the manager has 'vired' between stationery and heating. If authorized to do so, then the manager is said to have the power to vire, at least between such heads as these. Virement is clearly a device which can bring some degree of flexibility to the management of finance. For this reason it is popular with budget holders. It is, however, usually restricted in scope.

Virement in the public sector can normally be one of two types:

- Virement between revenue heads, e.g. between 'stationery' and 'heating' as above
- Virement between revenue and capital or vice versa

The first of these is quite widely practised, although there are usually severe restrictions placed upon any virement between staffing and non-staffing heads. The reason for such restrictions is clearly to prevent any local temporary arrangement becoming institutionalized.

The second of these is usually not available as an option to local government managers since the restrictions on capital spending preclude there being much spare capital around to vire to revenue. Likewise, the pressures on revenue budgets preclude transfers the other way. When such virement does take place it is normally authorized at a very senior level within an authority. Within the NHS, virement between these heads has been institutionalized to some extent. Under the funding arrangements current up to the early 1990s, a virement within districts of up to 10 per cent of capital to revenue or 1 per cent from revenue to capital was permitted by regions and this power was usually then passed on to units. Under the current purchaser–provider arrangements the roles of regions and districts are less clear in this respect, but the tradition of the power to vire within these limits seems to have been retained. Whether it will last, however, is a different matter. One factor which seems relevant is the growing importance of capital matters within the NHS now that capital is no longer a 'free good', i.e. granted by government without the need to pay interest charges, etc.

'One-line budget'

This phrase came into prominence in the late 1980s and early 1990s as indicating the ultimate in genuine managerial autonomy. In principle, a manager would be given a gross spending authority and told to 'get on with it'. How the permitted expenditure was allocated between heads or vired between those heads was up to the manager in question. In practice, there have been severe restrictions placed on managers with 'one-line budgets'. These restrictions are of two types.

The first is a requirement to consult with more senior managers and to have the one-line budget and any subsequent departures from it approved. This, of course, although it may seem reasonable, is a complete negation of the principle! All that has happened is a change in emphasis on who initiates the shaping of particular budgets. If the consultation requirement is accompanied by a power of veto, then the so-called change is non-existent. If the consultation is part of a process of training, education and experience gaining (on both sides), it is quite understandable.

The second restriction is a set of mechanisms to do with business plans, personnel policies and power to spend outside the organization:

1. Business planning processes can be used to ensure that managers working within an organization have thought seriously about a range of issues and, where necessary, have consulted widely within their section/department. It is reasonable to expect one-line budgets to reflect priorities as stated in business plans. Business plans normally include staffing profiles and plans and also statements of expected outputs/outcomes. Where the staffing element has already been largely determined by history, the one-line budget is a misnomer. At best it is a weak instrument of delegation: at worst it is misleading terminology.
2. Organization-wide staffing policies, e.g. 'no redundancy' or 'all vacancies to be filled from inside the organization' or 'no structural changes to be made without the sanction of the head of personnel', all place severe restrictions on senior managers trying to change the way their departments operate, and think that they have delegated budgetary authority with which to implement the changes. Within the public sector such authority has rarely if ever been granted.
3. Finally, many public sector organizations have in house-services for such matters as training, finance, computing, personnel and legal affairs. These are often perceived as costly by departmental managers who would rather spend their budgets outside the organization than within it. In principle, a 'one-line budget' should allow this. In practice, the amount of free money which can actually be spent ('real money') as opposed to being involved in an in-house paper transaction ('funny money') is very limited. Pressures are, however, being brought to bear on such services, e.g. within local government through compulsory competitive tendering for professional services.

It is essential to realize that there is a close connection between the staffing levels of the whole organization and its cost structures. If a departmental manager spends real money outside the organization in purchasing, say, training then the cost of training to other departments will rise. The only way to counteract this tendency is to reduce the organization's expenditure on training staff.

Genuine cost-effectiveness of service can be achieved only by slimming down staffing levels and this may be a significant outcome of the desire by managers to use their one-line budgetary powers.

SUMMARY

This chapter has analysed the budgetary process as related to both organizational planning and managerial control. Public sector budgets, which are mostly for relatively large and stable organizations, are constructed in the light of a fair degree of certainty of both income and future trends. This does not prevent that tension between strategic planning and short-term budgetary operationalization which is endemic in a situation of change.

The basic public sector budgetary model has been that of the incremental budget, but there are practical difficulties in controlling such budgets owing to imperfect operation of the financial information systems designed to support budget holders. There is also a conceptual difficulty in regard to the application of the incremental budgeting tradition to the evolving internal market which removes some of the certainties of both income and output, particularly for providers.

The analysis of the planning aspect of budgeting drew attention to deficiencies of incremental budgeting in coping with change. These were discussed in the light of certain alternatives, such as zero-based budgeting and planning, programming and budgeting systems. Techniques such as marginal opportunity analysis and priority-based budgeting were seen as helpful in providing rationales for amending incrementally derived budgets without the upheaval of full-scale change. The notion of business planning, to be dealt with more fully in Article B8, was introduced.

The analysis of the control aspect of budgeting stressed the need for timeliness and accuracy of information and discussed some techniques for ascertaining whether any particular variance was worrying and for dealing with such variances, possibly within the context of the one-line budget.

NOTES

1. A much fuller treatment of the terms 'output' and 'outcome' will be developed when 'value for money' is discussed. For the time being, however, an 'output' may be regarded as a quantity of work achieved—30 students taught, 1,000 acres of grass mowed, 250 tonsillectomies performed—while outcome has dimensions of both quality and appropriateness.
2. An 'opportunity cost' is the cost of the loss of something which is not done because something else is done instead. If a chiropodist attends a management course for an afternoon then a number of clients will not be treated. If the chiropodist's trust is paid on the basis of number of clients seen, then there is a real and immediate cost to course participation which has to be weighed against potential future savings because of enhanced effectiveness.
3. A senior member of the Treasury of a large local authority informed me privately that the November forecast of out-turn was usually within 0.5 per cent of the final out-turn figure, four months later. While this is commendable, it should be realized that 0.5 per cent of £1 million is £5,000 and that even a small public sector organization will probably have a budget of several millions.
4. A 'project budget' is a concept used in certain types of organizations, for example civil engineering firms, where workload is uneven and to some extent unpredictable. Any particular project is costed (i.e. its cost is predicted in advance) and priced on the basis of that cost. The difference between price and cost is the 'contribution' that the particular project makes to the basic costs of the firm and to its overall profits. The project manager has a limit—the projected cost—which must in principle, be adhered to. This limit is, in effect, a budget.
5. An exception to this remark is provided by cross local authority boundary demand for education from certain schools and the more·recent explicit governmental hopes that demand for some schools will either close or force up the standards of others.
6. Short waiting lists may be used by fund-holding GPs to discriminate between hospitals or even individual consultants. The NHS has for many years bought services from the private sector when its own resources have been inadequate to provide a timely service.
7. An unfavourable variance in one which is adverse from the budget manager's point of view. Conventionally these variances, overspends or underachievements on income targets are shown in parentheses, e.g. (£450).
8. The reasons for the improvement include better communication between finance departments and computer sections, better applications programmes to produce the statements, better systems for inputting the data and more commitment to the figures consequent upon managers realizing their significance.

SECTION

B

TERMINOLOGY AND CONCEPTS

WHAT THIS SECTION IS ABOUT

The context

The key financial document for public sector organizations has, without doubt, been the annual budget. In Chapter 3, budgeting as a cyclical process was discussed and attention was drawn to its dynamic nature. What was not discussed in detail was how the manager operates a budget. This is one of the themes of this section.

The public sector has changed considerably since 1980: the Local Government Planning and Land Act of that year being something of a landmark. It indicated the beginning of a phase in which financial administration gave way to financial management, and administrators became managers. The key ideas which governed the 1980s, and are of course still important, were those concerned with 'value for money'. This was the decade of the Audit Commission.

By 1995, as this book was being written, that phase was nearing completion and one of the marks of the new era is a new understanding of the role of the budget and indeed a querying as to whether the budget, as such, is the key financial document for much of the sector. Business plans, service-level agreements, contracts and tenders occupy at least as much of the time of many managers as do budgeting and budget statements.

The key concepts

There are three main groups of concepts covered in this section:

1. *Budgeting*—Articles B1 to B3 cover the questions of how the budget appears to a manager, budgetary reports and how to deal with variances.
2. A set of issues which, in various ways, provide techniques of *looking critically at expenditure*. Traditional internal audit considers the legality of expenditure and its conformity to the rules of the organization. External audit as a legal requirement has provided a certification that the accounts of the organization can be believed. More recently, for example through the work of the Audit Commission, the emphasis has switched from legality, conformity and accuracy towards the question of value for money and its components, economy, efficiency and effectiveness. These topics occupy Articles B4 to B6.
3. Topics concerned with the *new public sector* in financial terms. The internal market is now widespread within the sector and has brought to prominence such topics as costing, pricing and service-level agreements. Business planning, operating as an adjunct to budgeting, and contracting with its apparatus of tenders and tendering are discussed in Articles B7 to B9.

HOW TO USE THIS SECTION

The substance of this section consists of nine articles on topics which are relevant to the public sector manager and which can be treated non-mathematically. The articles fall into three groups, the first concerned with budgetary matters, the second concerned with aspects of audit and the third concerned with issues brought into prominence by the internal market.

Each article follows a format which includes discussion of:

- The context in which the topic is relevant (this may give clues as to other articles which can be read)
- The key concepts

In addition, other material may be included. In all cases subheadings should give prominence to the material likely to be of use to the reader.

There are clear relations to the contextual material dealt with in Section A and links to the quantitative material to be dealt with in Section C. These are indicated where they are especially important.

It is possible to treat the articles in one of several different ways:

- Each article is relatively self-contained and can therefore be used like an article in an encyclopaedia. This may appeal to practising managers who need to make reference in order to fill a gap in their knowledge.
- Because the articles come in three groups, each group could be used as a 'chapter' in its own right. Thus there would be chapters on 'budgeting and budgetary control', 'criticism of expenditure' and 'the new financial arrangements'. Reading chapters in this way may prove of use to students who need a grounding in matters of which they have, as yet, no direct practical experience.
- It is also possible to read the section at one go as a somewhat disjointed account of the transition from the administration of budgets to the management of business plans. This treatment may be of value to teachers. The transition has taken place over a defined and key period in public sector history and, for many managers who have lived through it, has proved a traumatic experience. The younger student may wonder what all the fuss was about! The teacher may come into contact with both the manager (on in-service courses) and the student (on BTEC or undergraduate courses). It is hoped that the section may help the teacher to develop both these sets of people in appropriate ways.

THE BUDGET AS IT APPEARS TO A MANAGER

THE CONTEXT

For any public sector organization 'the budget' is an important document:

- At a very minimum, it is a legally required framework set at organizational level which defines the overall spending pattern of the organization and therefore the authorized budgetary limits of managers who work within different sections of the organization.
- In reality it is much more: it is broken down into a hierarchy of budgets each of which can be operated by individual managers who are given authorization to spend within certain limits under a number of headings which will differ from manager to manager.

There have been certain trends and changes in attitude over recent years:

1. The growth in importance of the 'business plan'. Although a major change has not yet taken place, the business plan, as it gains in financial content, must eventually undermine the budget's claim to primacy as the key financial document.
2. The growth, at least so far as discussion is concerned, in the importance of the so-called 'one-line budget', the notion that a manager is given an overall spending authorization for a period and may work within that authorization how he or she wishes.
3. The growing tendency towards involving budget managers in the design of their budgets on the grounds that they are more likely to conform to a plan which they have helped to draft.
4. The idea of the strictly cash limited budget and the twin notions that any underspends (savings) can be carried forward to the next budgetary period and that any overspends must be compensated for by savings in the next budgetary period.
5. Possibly the most important is the growing understanding by managers that their budget is not just another piece of paper to be ignored, but a very important document which must be referred to regularly.
6. Closely related to the concept of business planning is income generation. In this article it is not considered, except by allusion. It will be considered in detail in the business planning article (B8).

THE KEY CONCEPTS

The concepts to be explored in this article fall under two headings. First, there are those concerned with different *perceptions of the budget* at different levels of the organization. Second, there are those concerned with the actual *format of the budget* as presented to an individual manager and the rules within which the manager must work.

Perceptions of the budget: strategic, departmental and operational

Strategic level   For strategic managers the budget is a macro statement designed to enable more junior managers to operationalize the strategic vision within limits. These limits, nowadays, are some sort of compromise between sets of pressures arising both inside and outside the organization. The main external pressures arise from cash limitations set in one form or another by central government and from public demand, usually articulated through pressure groups. The main internal pressures arise from groups of professionals articulating the perceived needs of their clients and from the resistance to change which is endemic in large organizations, public and private.

For many public sector organizations strategic managers are given more or less carte blanche to manage within their cash limit and thus are effectively given a 'one-line budget'. They will not see it this way because both the pattern of their organization and the pattern of previous commitments impose in the short term an overall shape to the budget heads and the approximate level of resource allocation.

At the strategic level, where the budget is likely to total several tens or hundreds of millions of pounds, the initial resource allocation is coarse. Departmental heads will be given global allocations that will enable them to meet the great bulk of their commitments. There will be a retention of resource at the centre in order to meet contingencies. That there will be contingencies is certain. What these contingencies will be is less certain. There may be a large pay rise to fund. There may be an emergency which places severe pressures on the resources of a particular department. There may be a shortfall on planned receipts from income-generating activities. All these possible contingencies, and others, mean that a balance has to be struck in the global resource allocation pattern between funding virtual certainties, funding probabilities and funding possibilities. On top of this, the strategic manager has to design the budget to facilitate change in the directions implied by the overall organizational plan or vision.

It follows from this that, although the budget as approved by whatever board is entrusted with its approval may look detailed, with many departmental subheadings, most attention will have been given to the overall shape and not to the line-by-line detail.

Departmental/directorate[1] level   For departmental/directorate managers the budget is more detailed. Their share of the global budget and their responsibility for any income generation are negotiated with the senior management team, theoretically in co-operation with their fellow directors, but, in reality, often in a competitive situation. The budget they receive may look like a one-line budget, but in reality it is quite tightly pre-allocated to various sections or functions, partly because they exist and have to be funded to deliver a service, and partly because the bargaining processes which have helped to shape the budget have made their own imprint on the underlying pattern. One cannot get away for long with arguing for a substantial resource and then, when it is allocated, using it for something else! There may well be an indication—in line with the departmental business plans—of how much income is expected to be generated.

Thus by the time the global resource has been allocated to departments both the overall shape and a degree of detail are imposed. There has to be flexibility within departments, however, both to meet contingencies and to cope with change, and it is one of the responsibilities of the departmental head to ensure that the departmental budget balances these needs with the immediate and pressing needs of the operational managers.

There will almost certainly therefore be some retention of resource for contingency and change. The bargaining process includes negotiation over both these aspects: how much change is funded from the centre and how much is expected from the department; what sort of contingencies will be dealt with by the centre and what sort must be taken on board by the department.

Just as the director lobbied at strategic level for a share of the resource, so the director is being lobbied from within the department by the various operational managers. The shape of the departmental budget is therefore a product of prior commitment, deliberate strategically generated change, coping with past and allowing for future contingencies, and internally operationally generated change. There is one other factor which is of great importance. The organization's budget will almost certainly have been arrived at on the assumption that a certain level of efficiency savings will be achieved. The requirement to make these savings will have been passed down to the departments, and the way in which the requirement is allocated to operational managers is clearly an important part of the budgetary process.

By the time the departmental budget is constructed it will be quite a detailed document in which a number of people will have had a hand. It will be passed on to the sectional/operational managers as appropriate for them to make it work.

Sectional/operational[2] level   For operational managers the budget is both much more detailed and much less flexible. There may be no room at all for retention for change or contingency. The only freedom given may be in terms of limited virement between certain budget heads and, perhaps, an encouragement to work within budget by permitting a degree of carry forward under certain headings.

In an organization with satisfactory budget practices the operational manager will have been involved, at least to some extent, in forming the budget and will therefore have a degree of identification with it. It is, however, the operational manger who will be most involved in making the efficiency savings and there may be a degree of bewilderment (how can I cope?) or frustration (this is beyond me) involved.

For the operational manager the budget is clearly a device more geared towards control than planning, and this may be a source of resentment. There are messages here for senior managers in the way in which they educate/train, inform/involve and support/encourage their staff.

The format of budgets: lines, columns and virement

All budgets, by the time they are issued to the managers who have to operate them, are split up into *lines*. Each line is effectively the authorization to spend up to an agreed limit on a certain item. Many budgets also have *columns*—probably on a monthly basis—which split the authorization up into time periods and reflect the anticipated profile of expenditure throughout the year. Some budgets are issued to the managers with clear statements of what, if any, *virement* is allowed: i.e. how much can be transferred by the manager from one budget head to another while remaining within overall limits.

Lines   A typical public sector revenue budget will be divided into pay and non-pay items of which the pay will usually be the greater part, while non-pay (which is usually where there is easier scope for flexibility) is often considerably smaller.

Pay items At strategic level the lines for pay may correspond to gross totals for pay for permanent staff, temporary staff and hourly contracted/agency staff with allowances for anticipated pay rises, performance-related pay, contraction of staffing base and even contributions towards redundancy or early retirement payments. Thus a university with a staff of 500 academics of various sorts, 500 clerical and admin staff and another 500 domestic and manual workers may have a total pay budget of around £25m based on existing patterns of employment. At strategic level there may well be a plan to change, and the institutional budget must reflect this perhaps with about £2.5m set aside to fund such changes. The deans of the various faculties and the heads of the various support services will receive their budgets in a form which allows them to move towards the desired institutional goals in accordance with their own priorities—possibly expressed in their business plans.

By the time the budget reaches the operational manager the lines for pay will be much more detailed. The ward manager in a typical trust will know how many full-time equivalent (FTE) staff are to be managed, what grades they are on, how much overtime may be authorized, how many agency hours can be purchased, what vacancies there are, which, if any, can be filled and, importantly, when. The manager will also be aware of whether the staff are near the top of their grades, thus creating a situation of relatively stable expense, or whether they are near the bottom, thus being relatively cheap but on a regular and predictable upwards incremental drift.

Non-pay items These include capital charges, the purchase of all goods and services from outside the organization, the payment of expenses of various sorts to staff and various 'non-recurrent items' which, in reality, are items which should fall under one of the above headings but are presented under a different name.

At strategic level the capital charges are usually of great significance. Assuming, as is the case with the greater part of the sector, that there is a distinction to be drawn between capital and revenue and assuming again that major capital is mostly borrowed, then capital charges, i.e. interest payments and loan repayment/debt redemption, are both significant and predictable. Unless the capital has been raised on fixed interest terms, they are also sensitive to changes in the prevailing interest rates. The meshing together of capital planning with revenue budgeting is an important part of the strategic manager's task. It has always been thus in the private sector: it is increasingly so in the public sector.

At strategic level the lines for goods and services are likely to reflect the pattern of previous years with changes to take account of strategic change, inflation, any growth or decline and any required economy or efficiency savings. Thus a university which wished to reduce the student–staff contact time might deliberately invest in enhancing its library and computer-based learning facilities and, if it were believed that 'the age of the book was over' might favour the computer-based learning over the library and encourage the librarian to access journals electronically rather than through the printed page.

At operational level the significance of the various items has changed. There may be a notional figure for capital charges, but it is completely outside the control of the budget manager and is there primarily for costing purposes. Most operational mangers do have some control over minor capital expense, but often in the form of relatively small items, such as furniture which, while technically capital, may be presented as non-recurrent items under a revenue heading.

Goods and services of various descriptions are important. The ward manager, for example, may well have a 'supplies' subheading which could include drugs, dressings and maybe toilet rolls, floor polish, etc. The manager may also have a training and development budget which can be used for staff development purposes. Such a budget can be used to illustrate an important distinction. If the money is spent outside the trust, for example on sending staff to a conference or hiring consultants to run an 'away day', then real money is leaving the trust to pay for these services. If, on the other hand, the money is notional and is used to 'purchase' services from the trust's own training department, then it is not real money (directly) leaving the trust but is part of a resource allocation process—ensuring that all wards have equitable access to internal training—and justification process—ensuring that the training department is broadly satisfying the training needs of the trust in both quantity and shape.

Columns: profiling   So far the discussion has been in terms of a yearly allocation of authority to spend resource or requirement to generate income. In operating a budget there is also a need to pay attention to the shape of income and expenditure over a year. Budgets are thus 'profiled', i.e. presented in such a way that the peaks and troughs of income and expenditure are indicated. Such profiling has two purposes: it can be used to assist with managing cash flow and it can be used to facilitate controlling budgets.

Cash flow   At strategic level the major significance is in cash flow terms. Cash flow has not in the past normally been a problem for public sector organizations. The bulk of expenditure has been on weekly waged or monthly salaried staff and the bulk of the income has come in weekly or monthly instalments from central government or, in the case of local government, from local taxation. Now, however, changing patterns of employment may mean the increasing casualization of staff and therefore peaks and troughs in payments. An increasing proportion of income may be self-generated and that too may have seasonal variation. If to this are added those items which are genuinely seasonal, such as energy bills or anything associated with grounds maintenance, there is a potential for temporal mismatch between resource and expenditure. This temporal mismatch (i.e. a difference in the timed phasing of income and expenditure) must be planned for in global terms and this is clearly a matter for the strategic level. If the cash resource leads (is ahead of) the expenditure, then there is a potential for income generation through investment. If the cash resource lags (is behind) the expenditure, then there will be a need to borrow, short term, and an associated expense.

Budgetary control   At operational level, the emphasis is much more on budgetary control. This is dealt with in more detail in Article B2, but in principle the purpose of profiling is to remove one anticipated source of apparent variance from budgetary statements and thus give managers one less thing to worry about! If a heating budget is divided into 12 equal instalments then there will be apparent overspends in the winter months and apparent underspends in the summer months. Profiling avoids this.

Virement   Virement is the moving of funds from one heading to another. The flexibility it gives is a major tool in the kit of any financial manager. It is dealt with in more detail in Article B3, but in principle a budget may be given to a manager with more or less virement built in. The so-called 'one-line budget' is, in theory, a mandate for unlimited virement. At the other extreme no virement at all may be permitted. The NHS for many years sanctioned a virement from revenue to capital and vice versa. The virement which many managers would find most useful, between pay and non-pay, is frequently not permitted at all.

   At strategic level there has to be freedom for virement. Budgets are, at least in part, merely indicative and the contingencies which may arise within a year demand considerable virement.

Mini budgets covering part of the year which have become a feature of public sector finance since the early 1980s are, in all but name, structured virement.

At operational level the freedom a manager has to vire is a measure of the real budgetary delegation obtaining within the organization. If every proposed virement has to be discussed up the line to strategic level, then there is, in reality, no budgetary delegation at all.

NOTES

1. The terminology varies throughout the sector. In the NHS it is current practice to refer to the immediate suborganizations as directorates, whereas in local government the more traditional terminology is departments (headed, confusingly, by directors), which are increasingly grouped together in directorates. What is meant here is the major suborganizational grouping where the head reports to the chief executive. The head will also participate in some sort of policy co-ordinating group possibly termed a board or a policy committee.
2. Again the terminology is not consistent throughout the sector. By 'operational' is meant the lowest level of budget holder who may be in charge of a section or subsection within a department or directorate. An organization may not be structured on hierarchical lines (although most are) and thus we need to be clear that the operational manager is, typically, given a budget which is relatively light in cash terms although it may be quite large in staff pay terms. Another way of looking at the discussion we have undertaken so far is to ask about the degree of freedom to effect/authorize significant change. The greatest freedom is at strategic level. The least freedom is at operational level. In between is in between!

BUDGETARY REPORTS

THE CONTEXT

A budgetary report (sometimes known as a 'budgetary statement' or a 'monthly tabulation' or even, familiarly, as a 'tab') is a document which is issued, normally at monthly intervals, by the finance department to managers which sums up the finance department's view of their expenditure (and in some cases income) over the defined period. It also, crucially, compares it with the finance department's view of what they should have spent (earned), i.e. their agreed budget.

For managers it should be a key piece of information to assist with the management of their resources. How big a help it is depends, as with all information, on its timeliness, its accuracy and its relevance. Additionally, managers will feel more committed to working within the confines of a budget if they have participated in its making and have a sense that it is realistic. Thus, if budgetary statements are to be taken seriously by the managers who receive them, there must be a process of managerial involvement in the construction of the original budgets.

The context therefore is one which combines managerial practice with financial reporting and is clearly linked to the quality of the relationships between the finance department and the service departments.

THE KEY CONCEPTS

There are three main groups of concepts covered in this article:

1. The actual *shape of the budgetary statement: its lines and its columns*, and in particular columns, which do not appear on the original budget, which detail *cumulative spending* (income), and *variances*
2. The *quality of the information*, in particular its *timeliness, relevancy* and *accuracy*
3. The *utility* of the statement to the manager and, reverting to the themes of involvement and links with the finance department, *budget manuals* and *budget liaison officers*

Shape of budgetary statement: lines and columns, cumulative spending, variances

Figure B2.1 shows an extract from a typical budgetary statement as it would arrive at regular intervals on a manager's desk. It looks very similar to the budget to which the manager is working and that similarity is genuine, although there are key differences—the chief being that the budget is an estimate or prediction for a period ahead while the budgetary statement is an (accurate)

Cost centre: Bunsbury Leisure Centre   Period: month 2 (May 1996)

Item	Annual budget £	Period budget £	Expenditure in period £	Variance £	Cumulative budget £	Expenditure to date £	Cumulative variance £
Salaried staff	360,000	30,000	32,000	(2,000)	60,000	64,000	(4,000)
Weekly staff	540,000	45,000	41,000	4,000	90,000	86,000	4,000
Supplies	120,000	10,000	8,000	2,000	20,000	21,000	(1,000)
Services	60,000	5,000	4,000	1,000	10,000	8,000	2,000

Figure B2.1   Extract from a typical budgetary statement

statement of what has actually happened. Other differences include additional columns for cumulative spending (income) and variances. These are dealt with below.

Lines and columns   If the budgetary statement is to be helpful then the lines (horizontal) must correspond to the lines of the original budget. If for any reason they do not, then the reason and its effect must be explained in some way. Reasons which might obtain include agreed variation of the budget with the initiative stemming from the centre (mini budget?) or the manager (virement?), or possibly the combination of lines in order to permit some flexibility. It is absolutely essential, however, that the manager who receives the statement has the same notion of the budget as the finance department which issued it!

The columns (vertical) may be different from the original budget. If that was profiled (see Article B1) then the effects of that profiling will appear: if not, then each month will be one-twelfth of the total year budget. The additional columns for cumulative and variance are dealt with below.

Cumulative spending   Suppose an annual (unprofiled) budget line is for £24,000. It is reasonable to suppose that this will be spent at a rate of £2,000 per month. If the reports for months 1, 2, and 3, respectively, have shown monthly spending of £1,800, £3,000 and £600, then we may examine the cumulative effect of this data:

- For month 1, spending was £1,800 against a budget of £2,000, an underspend of £200.
- For month 2, spending was £3,000 against a budget of £2,000, an overspend of £1,000.
- If, however, the figures for months 1 and 2 are cumulated (i.e. added together to make cumulative totals), then the spending over two months totalled £4,800 against a budget of £4,000, an overspend of £800.
- For month 3, spending was £600 against a budget of £2,000, an underspend of £1,400. If the totals are cumulated, then the spending for the first three months totalled £5,400 against a budget of £6,000, an underspend of £600.

The cumulative columns therefore are related to the budget, by adding together the individual monthly authorizations over the period in question, and to the spending, by adding together the individual monthly expenditure over the same period. The same argument would apply to income.

Cumulative figures are of much more significance to the manager than monthly totals. The manager's job is to keep annual spending on course, and the cumulatives are a better guide than any individual month. For the finance department, any cumulatives which represent significant overspending or underachievement of income may also represent a cash flow problem, even if it is known that the manager will bring things back into line by the year end. In such cases then a re-look at the profiling of the budget may be called for. A well-profiled budget should not show significant errors month by month.

Variances   The overspends and underspends referred to above (as well as any underachievement or overachievement on the income side) are known as variances. Typical budget statements include lines which total the pay budget/pay expenditure (cumulatively) and the non-pay budget/non-pay expenditure (cumulatively). Variances in individual lines may well be tolerated provided these key lines show reasonable comparison (i.e. small variance) between budget and expenditure. How to deal with variances forms the subject of Article B3.

Quality of information: timeliness, relevancy, accuracy

There is no doubt that one of the chief sources of disaffection for public sector managers is poor-quality financial information. The private sector, in general, cracked this problem many years ago. The public sector has improved greatly over recent years, but there are still many complaints and much room for improvement. The key concepts are *timeliness*, *relevancy* and *accuracy*.

Timeliness   To have maximum effectiveness a budgetary report should show minimum possible delay. In the private retail sector financial reports, covering the previous week up to Saturday evening, are frequently in place on the managers' desks by Monday lunchtime—a delay of less than 48 hours. In the public sector monthly reports are produced with a typical delay of a fortnight and worst-case delays of up to six weeks. The fortnight delay may be acceptable: the six-week delay is certainly not.

One important problem with delay is that it reduces scope for corrective action, particularly later in the year. A report for February (usually month 11) which does not arrive until April (month 1 of the next year) is useless. Underlying this problem, however, is a malaise which may be presented as one of commitment and motivation (managers do not see reports as important if the finance department cannot be bothered to get them out on time) or one of credibility (if it is impossible to take corrective action, then clearly no-one bothers about meeting budgets).

Poor timeliness, for which there is little if any excuse, is a major factor in budgetary overruns. If the sector is serious about controlling its spending (and income), then it must take its reporting seriously.

Relevancy   It should go without saying that managers receiving budgetary reports should perceive them as relevant to their management tasks. Unfortunately this is not always the case. There are two sorts of problems. The first is concerned with the scope of the budgetary report. The second is concerned with its detail.

1. The scope of the report should broadly accord with the scope of a manager's responsibilities. There is value in giving middle managers an idea of what is going on at strategic level and there is value in them having an idea of what is going on around them, but the thrust of the information which they receive should be concerned with what they can directly influence. This is, of course, another way of saying that the financial information system in use and the

cost centres/activity centres which it uses as focuses for its analysis should reflect the management structures actually in use within the organization.

2. The information should be at a level of detail which is comprehensible to the manager concerned, being neither overcluttered, which is confusing and unhelpful, nor overgeneral, which is often bland and equally unhelpful. These points are alternative ways of indicating that the managers concerned should be participants in the design of the information which they receive, interacting with the finance department so as to produce reports which are of maximum assistance to them in managing. If what comes out of the process is helpful to the managers but not so helpful to the finance department then another set of reports for internal, finance department use could be generated. These should be totally compatible with the reports generated for managers provided the same data set has been used. It may be that reports at different levels of detail should be generated for different levels of the organization, but it is often the case that the catering manager and the chief executive are looking at the same reports, which are too detailed for one and too general for the other: neither profits by the experience!

Accuracy The accuracy of the statements depends upon three factors. The first is the quality of the initial data. The second is the quality of the entry of the data into the system. The third is more subtle: it is to do with the purposes for which the information is intended and a possible conflict of purpose between finance department and service managers.

1. Typical data supplied by managers to finance (perhaps indirectly via personnel or some other route) includes sickness, overtime and casual staff utilization. It goes without saying that inaccuracies here will show up as inaccuracies on the reports. Such inaccuracies will almost certainly be picked up through payment procedures, and can be corrected, but this may take time. While this may not be significant early in the year it may have an effect later on.

2. There is always a possibility of error in transcribing manually generated data into electronic format via the computer keyboard. Again, such inaccuracies will usually be picked up at some stage either by manual checking procedures (e.g. a manager knowing that a figure is totally wrong or a cheque authorizer feeling that a figure is unlikely to be right) or through internal audit procedures or by failure to reconcile different parts of the generated accounts. The same significance as noted above applies.

3. More subtly, the service manager and the finance department have different interests. The manager wants to know 'How much have I got left?', i.e. 'What have I spent or promised to spend?' The finance department is ultimately interested in producing its overall report which is geared to the traditions and practices of financial accounting (longer term looking back) rather than management accounting (shorter term snapshots and extrapolations). Unless the problem is addressed then there is scope for confusion in interpretation of what the manager has been presented with. There should be no problem in re-presenting the same data set in different formats. The problem has been that managers in general have not known what they needed and the design of the systems has been driven by accountants. There is a general move throughout the sector towards commitment accounting, i.e. recording what has been committed rather than what has actually been spent, and this trend, provided it is understood by all parties, should remove some of the difficulties.

It is clear from what has been discussed that timeliness, relevancy and accuracy must be defined in terms that are acceptable both to the managers and to the finance department and that reporting practices are acceptable to all on the basis of this shared understanding.

Utility: budget manuals, budget liaison officers

Such a shared understanding is key to any discussion of the utility of budget reports. Two helpful institutions which have become relatively commonplace in the past decade or so have been the growth in the use of budget manuals and budget liaison officers. The common features are training, development and the building of understanding in the workplace.

Budget manuals   A budget manual is simply a set of explanations and procedures which accompany the budget itself and should be near to hand in the manager's workspace. These manuals typically contain an explanation of the main features of the budget for a particular year, a statement of the meaning of the lines and columns of the report itself, a copy of the financial instructions for the organization and a summary of any procedures which are of particular relevance to managers.

In principle, these should be really helpful documents of great relevance to managers. In practice, they can be overdetailed and cumbersome and therefore relegated to a cupboard rather than used on a desk. It is one of the key tasks of organizations to get their managers to that level of financial competency which they need to perform their work. Budget manuals are a useful tool in this developmental process, but the manuals themselves should be revised and developed over a period of time as feedback comes from managers to their authors and, indeed, as procedures themselves change in the light of circumstance.

The issuing of a budget manual, especially for the first time within an organization, can be a great opportunity for training and development; managers meeting with finance department representatives for the exchange of information and views.

Budget liaison officers   A second most helpful innovation practised in some organizations is the development of a set of budget liaison officers who are members of staff of the finance department and who have, as an important part of their workload, responsibility for assisting, either by telephone 'hot line' or by planned meetings, a set of managers in a service department.

Such an institution is truly developmental:

1. It is clearly of assistance to the managers who should get answers to their questions when and where they need them, thus reducing the scope for misunderstandings and consequent wrong actions/lack of actions. If the assistance is of good quality, then the managers will learn from it and ask elementary questions progressively less frequently. They will also reach a position where their questions become more searching and they may also be able to contribute ideas.
2. It is also developmental for the budget liaison officers. Provided that they are sympathetically chosen, having regard to their capacities for effective communication, they should be motivated by the work of encouraging others as well as profiting from any training that they themselves are given. When the service managers start asking the difficult questions and making suggestions and observations, they have an enhanced role in interpreting these and feeding them more generally into the finance department.
3. The organization itself develops because of the enhanced capabilities of its managers and their liaison officers. Equally importantly, the sorts of questions asked and the sort of suggestions made can show up weaknesses in information systems and information provision and therefore make for improvements in this area. Of great importance is the development of a learning culture which recognizes the potential for all members of the organization to support and assist each other in meeting both personal and organizational goals.

There is a theme which has bound together these last few paragraphs: it is the theme of constructive interaction between the finance department and the service departments. The financial reporting procedures, if properly supported, can make possible an enhanced relationship which is of benefit to the departments, their staff and the organization itself.

VARIANCES AND HOW TO DEAL WITH THEM

THE CONTEXT

A budgetary report, as discussed in Article B2, is a printout of the expenditure and/or income of a cost or activity centre as compared with its budget (as discussed in Article B1).

The concept of a variance was discussed in detail in Article B2: in brief it is a discrepancy between the budgetary forecast/authorization and the actual level of expenditure/income.

A manager required to keep expenditure within strict cash limits and maybe also required to meet income targets will pay attention to the variances as revealed on the regular budgetary reports. It is an important financial management skill to recognize when a variance is significant and a manager needs to have an armoury of techniques for dealing with significant variances.

This article deals with both aspects, first tackling the question of how one knows if a variance is likely to be significant and then looking at some key techniques.

THE KEY CONCEPTS

There are three main groups of concepts covered in this article. It deliberately concentrates upon adverse expenditure variances, leaving aside the question of under- or overachievement of income. The first is concerned with the significance of variances: it deals with the questions of *profiling* and *non-recurrent spending*. The second covers a group of techniques which can bring staff expenditure back into line. These techniques are related to *slippage, temporary staff*, and *bonuses and overtime*. The third covers non-staff variances, looking at *stock reduction* and *virement*.

Profiling

This concept has already been dealt with in some detail in Article B1. In essence it is the prediction across a year of how expenditure will occur on a month-by-month basis. For regular salaries the profiling is flat and regular. For some seasonal activities the profiling will reveal peaks and troughs. Any budget manager faced with a variance should first be satisfied that the variance is genuine and not the result of incorrect profiling or, indeed, no profiling at all. There are several categories of budgetary lines which should be profiled: any factor which is genuinely seasonal, for example energy costs or staffing when service demand is likely to fluctuate predictably, should be scrutinized in this light if it presents apparent variances.

Non-recurrent spending

A particular case in point is spending under various 'non-recurrent' heads, which may be counted as either capital or revenue in any given organization. One such head is 'furniture'. If an expenditure of £3,000 was budgeted for and the manager spent it all in month 1, it might well show up as an apparently serious adverse variance (one-twelfth of £3,000 is £250 less the £3,000 actually spent to make an adverse variance of £2,750). This is because no attempt was made either to profile the budget (as above) or to consult with the manager as to when the budgeted expenditure was likely to be incurred. If a manager knows that this sort of factor is at the root of the variance then there is no problem.

Slippage

The most serious source of variance is likely to be on staffing. Although basic wage and salary costs are almost entirely out of the control of line managers and in this situation variances tend to pile up as the months go by, there are occasions when opportunities for control occur. Such occasions arise when a member of staff leaves, and then it is quite common within the public sector to delay a refilling the vacancy for period of up to six months, thus saving up to half a salary.

The disadvantage of this is that it can put a serious strain on the colleagues of the person who is not immediately replaced. The advantage (apart from financial saving) is that it affords a breathing space to allow for consideration of whether the workloads can be redistributed in some way so as to provide a more effective use of staff time and talents. Vacancies can and should be seen as opportunities for restructuring and reappraisal and it should never be assumed that a straight replacement of the leaver is the most appropriate action. All such changes, of course, depend upon co-operative staff: financial management and person management are intimately related.

Temporary staff

When vacancies do occur they can be filled in the first instance by persons on temporary contracts. The hourly rates are frequently lower than the corresponding salary level. There are no future incremental costs to consider and there are often reductions in salary-related costs. Such use of casual staff, although increasingly frequent within the sector, should be regarded as nothing more than a temporary expedient.

More seriously, however, there is a longer term move within both public and private sectors towards the 'casualization' of staff. In essence this consists of creating a core of established/tenured staff, i.e. staff with 'permanent' employment, and a periphery of staff with various forms of temporary contract. This method of organization has clear advantages in terms of reduction of overall staffing cost—although it may increase expenditure on the personnel department! There are, of course, potential recruitment problems and maybe an increase in training costs. The morale of both permanent and temporary staff may also suffer.

There is no doubt that the employment of temporary staff when the opportunity arises can be an effective means of pulling back an adverse variance. Any long-term move towards casualization should, however, be seen as a matter for strategic management: there are clearly a number of major implications with regard to the quality of service delivery and labour relations as well as the dimensions already discussed.

Apart from the financial and flexibility advantages outlined above, one by-product of the employment of temporary staff which may appeal to the manager is the possibility of treating periods of temporary employment as some sort of probationary period. A person who proves effective in a role while employed temporarily may be employed with more confidence if a permanent position becomes vacant.

Bonuses and overtime

Weekly waged staff often see the possibility of earning bonuses or doing overtime as attractive features of a job. Both features present problems to managers. Bonuses have in some areas become so easy to earn that they have effectively become a part of the basic rate. Overtime, which should be an occasional feature, has in some areas become a regular feature, depended upon by employees as an expected part of the job.

Variances can, provided one is prepared to tackle working practices and patterns, be pulled back by reducing both bonuses and overtime. But the proviso is a very important one. Permission, possibly at the level of strategic management, will need to be sought in order to tread on the delicate ground of changing bonus patterns. Reduction of systematic overtime, however, will probably be encouraged by the management although resisted by the workforce.

It should be noted that reduction of bonuses is, in effect, a requirement for staff to work harder for their basic pay. The reduction of overtime is, in effect, a requirement for staff to do their work in less time. These requirements are not likely to be popular and considerable person management skills are needed to implement them. There can, however, be little doubt as to their effectiveness as potential tools for pulling back variances.

One further point needs to be made about overtime. Longer term, systematic overtime is very expensive. If the staff of a section are doing 40 hours' overtime per week between them, and being paid therefore for 50 hours or more (at time and a quarter or more), then the money so spent might be far better employed in hiring an additional member of staff, if only on a temporary contract. Money equivalent to a quarter or more of a weekly wage would be saved and there might be effectiveness gains from new blood and less tired workers.

Stock reduction

On the non-pay side the control of stock is in itself a serious matter. Overstocking uses valuable finance and incurs expenses for storage, deterioration, overrunning use-by dates and, unfortunately, pilferage. It can also encourage a certain degree of wastefulness if staff know that the cupboards are full. Overstocking is thus a practice to be avoided. Non-pay variances can sometimes be brought back by running stock levels down.

It should be remarked, however, that unless there is a serious and systematic overstocking situation, organizations are unlikely to make significant long-term savings by reduction of stocks. In the short term, however, it remains a useful tool for service managers.

Virement

It is possible that a budgetary statement shows a mixture of overspends and underspends. If this is the case then, once the manager is clear that the variances are not due to misprofiling or misrepresenting non-recurrent expenditure, the possibility of viring expenditure from one head to another can be considered.

Possible revenue virements are as follows:

- Within the pay heads, which may be allowed after consultation, but not if it implies any hidden restructuring or the possibility of creating a longer term problem for the organization
- Within the non-pay heads, which is frequently allowed with the minimum of fuss
- Between pay and non-pay heads which is rarely sanctioned at operational level, although as a strategic device it has considerable potential and is, of course, the basis of the move to replacing operatives by machines

Capital virements will rarely come the way of junior managers, but in some parts of the sector the possibility of viring from capital to revenue is a useful tool.

AUDIT: KEY CONCEPTS AND INTERNAL AUDIT

THE CONTEXT

Audit[1] in the public sector has three dimensions[2]:

1. Checking and validating the accuracy and integrity of the financial practices, records and reports of an organization
2. Ensuring that expenditure financed by public funds has been spent on those purposes, and only on those purposes, approved by Parliament when voting funds
3. Ensuring that, in addition to the financial probity aspects, organizations seek value for money in the form of economy, efficiency and effectiveness in pursuing agreed policy objectives

The first of these dimensions is shared in common with audit in private sector organizations. The second is special to the public sector (except in those cases where government has made a grant to a private sector or voluntary organization). The third is implicit throughout the sector but explicit only for local government and the NHS.

This article, together with Articles B5 and B6, explores the way in which public sector audit works. This article is concerned with some basic terminology and the work of an organization's internal audit department. Article B5 turns attention to the aspect of external audit and the work of the Audit Commission. Article B6 focuses on the important concept of value for money (VFM) and its components.

THE KEY CONCEPTS

Any organization will have a set of rules to which all its financial operations must conform. Such rules are typically known as *standard financial instructions (SFIs)*, but may have a different but similar title. These instructions are supported by a set of financial and organizational *systems* which provide the means for operationalizing the rules: i.e. ensuring that all financial transactions do in fact take place within the framework of the rules. For public sector organizations these systems will include some sort of reference to the purposes of the organization as expressed in the intentions of Parliament in setting up the organization.

These rules and systems are to do with the financial integrity of the organization. The audit of their working in practice is sometimes known as *probity audit* and is one of the two important dimensions of public sector audit. The other dimension is *value for money (VFM) audit* which will not be dealt with in this article as B5 and B6 will consider it in detail. There are other *functions of audit* and these will be considered.

Historically, *internal audit* has chiefly been concerned with probity audit and, although this is changing, with a growing emphasis on VFM audit, this article places more emphasis on the investigation of system security and the *implications for managers* should the systems be found to be insecure. A diagram which attempts to explain the relationship of various bodies which have to do with auditing in the public sector is given in Article B5, but could conveniently be glanced at while reading this article.

The *standing financial instructions* of an organization are its financial ground rules. They have been drawn up, probably by the treasurer/chief financial officer/director of finance, and approved by the policy making executive committee. They do not have the force of law and a breach, of itself, is neither a criminal nor a legal offence. They are, however, firmly embedded in a matrix of legal requirements and should be regarded as quasi-legal documents and thus treated with great respect. It should be noted that breach of such instructions will almost certainly be a disciplinary offence within any public sector organization.

The instructions should be widely available throughout an organization. They are often included in a manual (often loose leafed for easy updating) available to all employees. Managers, at whatever level, should certainly have easy access to them and be aware of their main thrusts, even if not of the detail. CIPFA[3] has published various model SFIs for different parts of the sector and thus there is a considerable overlap, if not identity, of such instructions.

Typically, there are three major sections. The first of these, which draws on relevant Acts of Parliament, defines the roles of the various parties in financial decision making. It also deals with financial planning and budgeting and matters of virement.

The second section deals with various matters of tendering and contracts. The emphasis in the past has been on external tendering and contracts with external parties. Clearly these are still of great importance, but the advent of the internal market has thrown an increasing emphasis on internal tenderers and service-level agreements as proxies for contracts.

The third section consists of regulations for such matters as accounting, audit, banking, insurances, inventories, payments, salaries and expenses. All managers should be aware of the general thrust of all these sections and the detail of any matters which directly affect them.

As indicated, these rules must be backed by a set of *systems* which ensure, if they are sufficiently robust, that the rules are kept. Organizations differ in detail, but the principal systems, common to all organizations in one form or another, cover the following matters:

1. A payroll system designed to ensure that the right people get paid the right amount of money, on time and consistently with other (external) systems such as for tax, national insurance superannuation and the banking system
2. An expenses system designed to ensure that employees who incur expenses in the course of their duties can be repaid promptly on receipt of appropriate authorization
3. A requisition system designed to ensure that goods and services are ordered by authorized people at competitive prices, such a system being linked to (internal) inventory and stock control/stores systems
4. A petty cash system designed to ensure that a limited amount of money is available for immediate purchase of small items required urgently without offering the potential for abuse or major theft
5. A budgetary control system designed to ensure that managers are clear as to the extent and limitations of their spending/authorization powers and that they have accurate and up-to-date information as to how close they are to their targets so that remedial action can be taken if necessary

All the above systems have, of course, an element of recording about them so that appropriate accounts can be produced. For the first four systems the accounts will be of a financial nature. For the last the information will mainly feed the management accounting system. Thus two more systems should be added to the list:

6. A financial accounting system designed to produce accounts of record mainly for external audiences
7. A management accounting system designed to produce figures of value to managers for control purposes

Functions of an audit

The functions of audit may be listed as follows

1. The routine and regular examination of the working of the various financial systems in operation throughout an organization and, in the light of this examination, the drawing of management attention to structural, departmental, sectional and personal weaknesses
2. In the light of overall confidence in these systems, the certification of the published accounts of the organization as representing accurately the summation of a host of authorized transactions
3. In the light of any lack of confidence in these systems, the recommendation of any changes in structure or practice needed to rectify the deficiencies
4. The recommendation of any changes in practice within existing structures and systems which can bring about positive improvements in value for money service delivery
5. The recommendation of changes to structures and systems which can bring about more fundamental improvements in value for money service delivery

These functions are shared between internal and external audit and the emphasis, particularly in local government and the NHS, has changed and is still changing in the light of the work of the Audit Commission and other government initiatives. Table B4.1 summarizes the situation with regard to internal and external audit in relation to the five functions listed above.

Probity audit

That part of audit which concentrates on the conformity of financial transactions to the rules and to the systems is known as probity audit and is chiefly the concern of the internal audit department. It consists of a regular review of the workings of all sections and departments usually on a rotating and planned basis with the foreknowledge of the managers concerned.

From time to time there will be spot checks, particularly if some irregularity is suspected, but in general the image the internal auditor wishes to cultivate is that of an internal consultant able to help sort out weaknesses, rather than a police officer or watchdog sniffing out individual malpractice.

Value for money audit

This is concerned with ensuring that the organization conducts all its financial affairs with economy, efficiency and effectiveness in mind. It is dealt with in much more detail in Articles B5 and B6, but an initial remark can be made to the effect that seeking economy, i.e. buying goods

Table B4.1   Changing responsibilities for the functions of audit

Function	Responsibility	Note
Examination of systems	Internal audit	Checked by external auditors
Certification of accounts	External audit	On the basis of confidence in the internal audit process
Identification of problems with systems	Internal audit	Can be backed by external audit if problems are serious
Identification of VFM improvements without major structural change	Internal audit	External auditors can produce general guidance on such matters
Identification of VFM improvements which need major structural change	External audit	Through management letters; internal auditors are gradually learning this role

and services at the cheapest possible rate consistent with adequate quality, has long been seen as a legitimate part of internal audit, simply because those parts of the SFIs which deal with purchasing, tendering and contracting usually require it. On the other hand, the search for efficiency, i.e. the conversion of non-cash resource into maximum output, has been seen until recently as the purview of middle management and not within the scope of internal audit. Similarly, the search for effectiveness, i.e. the consideration of the organization's goals and the best way of achieving them to the satisfaction of both quality and resource criteria, has been seen as the task of strategic management and not the role of audit in any sense.

Internal audit and implications for managers

When properly carried out an internal audit has implications for managers at all levels. At strategic level any major value for money recommendations should be considered and, if necessary, appropriate restructuring/reorganization put into place. At intermediate level less radical value for money recommendations can be considered and implemented without restructuring. At operational level systems can be tightened where necessary.

The great majority of internal audit findings and recommendations do not involve fraud. They are usually concerned with incidents where managers, for whatever reason, have circumvented the systems, possibly through ignorance. There is, in the public sector as in any other, always a certain level of petty fraud in the form of inflated expense claims, overstated car mileage or abuse of time sheet procedures, but the normal system failures are due to the following factors:

- Ignorance of the systems—employees do not know what they are supposed to do.
- Laziness—it is easier to take a short-cut than to follow the relevant procedures.
- Genuine belief that the systems waste money—for example a belief that 'High Street special offers' are cheaper than goods on the purchasing section's authorized list.

- Departmental/sectional interest—for example a belief that ignoring procedures could produce a desired outcome quickly, or indeed that following proper procedures would block a desired outcome.
- Absence of a system to follow—in situations of change people feel that they have to make up the rules as they go along.

The most obvious remedy for this sort of system abuse is through education and training and making the systems transparent. In some cases the systems will need changing, and that is a task where management and the finance department, in consultation with the auditors, should work together.

In those cases where something seriously amiss is found, there are certain procedures to be followed. The report should go beyond the audit department and the department concerned to the director of finance and/or the chief executive. If personal fraud or criminal malpractice is suspected then there is a duty to involve the police[4]. Internal disciplinary procedures can and should be invoked either to supplement police investigation and criminal charges or to replace them if the police decide to take no action. Suspicion of criminal activity usually involves summary suspension with appropriate warnings given in the presence of a witness. There are also precautions to be taken to ensure that the suspect does not have opportunity, through desk access say, to tamper with the evidence. It should be emphasized that such cases are not common, but managers who do not follow the procedures strictly to the letter are laying themselves open to criticism and possibly to serious charges of obstructing justice.

NOTES

1. The notion of 'audit' (a word derived from the Latin *audio*, 'I hear') grew up in the period when the owners of business were becoming separate from those people who actually ran them: their 'stewards' or as we would say, 'managers'. The owners needed an 'account' of what was going on, predominantly in financial terms, hence 'accountancy' and 'stewardship accountancy'. They also needed an independent confirmation that the accounts were accurate. The provision of such a confirmation was the responsibility of the auditor.
2. This initial account draws heavily on Professor John Perrin's book, *Resource Management in the NHS*, 1988, Chapman & Hall, London.
3. The Chartered Institute of Public Finance and Accountancy (CIPFA) has great influence and authority in the field of finance throughout the public sector and its research arm, the Public Finance Foundation, has contributed and continues to contribute much valuable material to our understanding of how public finance works.
4. This duty is explicit in the Criminal Law Act of 1967 and should be seen to override any desire expressed by senior managers to avoid publicity, protect personnel, use internal disciplinary procedures and so on.

EXTERNAL AUDIT AND THE AUDIT COMMISSION

THE CONTEXT

The work of internal auditors as described in Article B4 is supplemented in two ways by the work of public sector external auditors:

1. The external auditor acts as a check that the internal auditors have done their work properly and that therefore: (a) the accounts of the organization are reliable and likely to be correct; and (b) the activities of the organization have been in accordance with the requirements of Parliament.
2. The external auditor for local government and for the NHS is a special body, the Audit Commission[1] which is charged with ensuring value for money. This concept is discussed in detail in Article B6.

THE KEY ROLES AND INSTITUTIONS

The basic role of the external auditor, which is common throughout the public and private sectors, is to certify that the published accounts of the organization concerned are accurate. This certification is not done on the basis of scrutinizing every document: it is done on the basis of checking that the internal auditors have gone about their business correctly and have done their work well. Thus spot checks on the routine practices of internal audit sections and checks on the quality of their work will provide an assurance that the financial systems of an organization are in good shape and that therefore the accounts are to be trusted.

Public sector organizations have additional duties: to ensure that their expenditure is directed towards fulfilling their aims and objectives as laid down by Parliament when the organization was established; and to ensure that their expenditure in a given year conforms to the authorization voted to them by Parliament when the estimates were approved. To this end a rather complex set of bodies has emerged over the years. See Fig. B5.1.

Parliament is the supreme authority in matters of public finance, although in practice the government of the day, supported by the civil service, makes most of the decisions and is relatively rarely challenged. In order to support Parliament in its work of ensuring that the money it has voted is spent in accordance with its wishes, two committees have been set up.

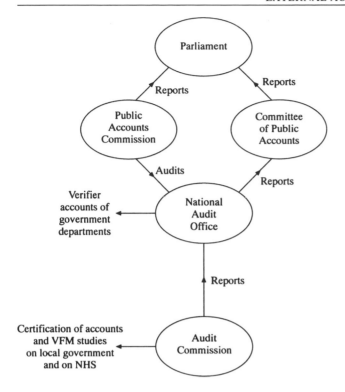

Figure B5.1 Organizations concerned with public sector audit

- The *Public Accounts Commission* is in effect the auditor of the National Audit Office. Its role is technical in the sense that its main duty is to ensure that the processes of the National Audit Office conform to its own rules.
- The *Committee of Public Accounts* is in effect the interpreter of the work of the National Audit Office to Parliament. It gives MPs the chance to understand what is being said by the National Audit Office and its dependant the Audit Commission.

These committees are supported by two public bodies.

- The *National Audit Office* is headed by the Comptroller and Auditor General. It is responsible for the verification of the accounts of the various government departments including all those which have to do directly or indirectly with local government and the NHS. Its work is carried out partly by civil servants working for agencies and partly by private firms which employ staff experienced in the field.
- The *Audit Commission* has two main tasks: the verification of the accounts of local authorities, health authorities and NHS trusts (this task is often subcontracted to firms of private accountants) and the encouragement of the search for value for money in local government and the NHS.

Thus depending on what part of the public sector is being considered, the certification aspect of external audit is carried out, either directly or indirectly, by either the National Audit Office (for government departments) or by the Audit Commission (for local government and the NHS).

These bodies report via the Committee of Public Accounts to Parliament, which is assured that the National Audit Office is doing its work properly by the Public Accounts Commission.

The Audit Commission

The VFM aspect of audit (see Article B6 for a fuller discussion) is pursued mainly by the Audit Commission in its dealings with local government and various health service bodies.

There are two main ways in which it proceeds:

1. By encouraging individual organizations to take steps to improve their VFM performance. This specific advice is conveyed to the organization concerned in the form of a 'management letter' which is aimed at the strategic managers and suggests ways in which economies and efficiency savings could be made and points to possible effectiveness improvements, some of which might require radical surgery.
2. The circulation throughout the relevant sector, local government or NHS, of reports which examine specific aspects of activity. NHS directed reports have included *The Virtue of Patients*, which was concerned with the activities of nurses, and *Lying in Wait*, which was concerned with effective bed use in acute hospitals. Local government directed reports have included *We can't go on meeting like this*, concerned with the effective use of valuable officer and member time, and *People, Pay and Performance*, concerned with aspects of effective personnel usage. Such documents point out ways in which performance has been enhanced within individual organizations and discuss key performance indicators.

Improving VFM may seem like a universally acceptable goal. The quest for VFM has, however, side-effects. It usually requires people to work harder/differently. It may imply a reduction in employment—a shake-out at both managerial and operational levels. It may involve an alleged loss in quality of service/professional integrity. It may involve organizational restructuring. It will certainly involve change. The strength of the Audit Commission lies in its ability to amass and circulate evidence that such changes can be undertaken, that they do work and that the effects are not disastrous.

NOTE

1. The full name of the Audit Commission is The Audit Commission for Local Government in England and Wales and the National Health Service. Scotland has its own commission. The Audit Commission was established by the Local Government and Housing Act of 1982. The NHS was added to its remit in 1990.

VALUE FOR MONEY: ECONOMY, EFFICIENCY AND EFFECTIVENESS

THE CONTEXT

Value for money (VFM) may be seen as one of the key terms of the 1980s and early 1990s. It has been referred to in Articles B4 (on audit) and B5 (on the Audit Commission). It is statutorily required (through the Acts defining the purpose and purview of the Audit Commission) that the two major deliverers of state services, the NHS and local government, shall seek VFM in all they do. The concept supersedes earlier terms, such as 'cost-effectiveness', by having a wider import embracing a dimension of quality.

The introduction of the concept as a major force in the public sector was politically motivated as part of the totality of successive Conservative governments' search for ways in which the public sector could be made to use its resources better. Although it was designed to enhance financial performance there have been by-products, in the form of performance indicators (to be discussed in Article C10) which have a bearing on reporting and accountability.

One way in which public sector VFM may be characterized is as 'a proxy for profit', i.e. as a goal which may be pursued by public sector managers who are not seeking profit and whose departmental income does not primarily depend on either the volume or the quality of their service. Although the internal market and its ramifications (see Articles B8–10) have reduced the size of this proportion of the sector, there are still substantial parts where no other proxy for profit or commercial parallel obtains, and VFM remains a relevant concept.

THE KEY CONCEPTS

The three well-known components of VFM are *economy*, *efficiency* and *effectiveness*, sometimes known as the 'three Es' which can be linked together in the *value for money chain*. In order to explain them and VFM properly, however, it is necessary to deal first with some more fundamental concepts: *inputs*, *outputs* and *outcomes*. The utility of the VFM concept as a reporting/accountability device leads to the consideration of various *performance indicators* having both financial and quality dimensions, and here some subconcepts, including *fitness for purpose/threshold standards*, *consistency/systems* and *customer satisfaction* should be discussed. Each of these latter concepts has a *political dimension*, and the discussion of this aspect along with the concept of *equity* will conclude the article.

Fundamental concepts: inputs, outputs and outcomes

The fundamental input of any non-voluntary delivering organization is financial. Without any doubt, cash/money may be seen as the primary input. In very few cases of service delivery, however, is cash of itself much use. To enable them to learn, students need teachers and books, not piles of cash. To enable them to recover, hospital patients need nurses, doctors, beds and drugs, not piles of cash. The cash must be converted into something more usable.

The secondary, usable input is thus what the cash buys. Clearly, this includes the staff resource—the people who directly or indirectly deliver the service. It also includes the capital resource—buildings, equipment, vehicles and so on—as well as the consumable resources—paper, drugs, polish, petrol used by the staff for delivering the service, maintaining the buildings or running the vehicles.

The main outputs are the services delivered and these may be expressed in different ways. A social worker may list the cases handled in the course of a year. The number of operations of various sorts performed by a surgeon may be logged. The output of a university may be measured in terms of its successful graduates, postgraduates and staff-authored research papers. Any part of the public sector which directly interfaces with the public will have some measure of output. Within an organization there will be outputs which are not perceived by the public. The payroll section of a local authority may issue 20,000 pay cheques (or their equivalent) per month. The cleaners of a university may service 1,000 offices daily. These are outputs for internal functions never seen by the public at all.

The concept of outcome is harder. It is a measure of what has been achieved. For example, in October 1994 a measles epidemic was widely forecast on the basis of good scientific evidence. A crash programme of vaccination with a high take-up rate was implemented and there was no epidemic, very few new cases of measles and no deaths either from measles or from the vaccine. Assuming that the forecast was well founded, then the desired outcome, i.e. preventing an epidemic, was achieved.

A further example occurred in the late 1980s and early 1990s, when the Government was concerned with a number of matters concerning the quality of school education. The introduction of a national curriculum and the concentration of effort on certain aspects of literacy and numeracy were required. The intended outcomes included improved performance in future years by the adults who were then children, which might enhance both their employability and the economic performance of the country as a whole.

These examples illustrate the difficulty of the concept. The first seems relatively simple, but it is, of course, possible that the forecast was misjudged and/or that some other factor averted the epidemic. The second is intrinsically harder both to quantify and to measure. Consider yet another example, which has difficulties in a number of dimensions. Over the years since 1948 the health of the nation has improved markedly. A number of key indicators such as steadily increasing life expectancy and the reduction in the incidence of key illnesses such as rickets or tuberculosis point to outcomes linked to the foundation and success of the NHS. It is, however, widely acknowledged, including from within the medical profession, that many of these outcomes stem from better housing, better sanitation, better education, shorter working weeks, longer holidays, the change to a service based rather than industrially based economy and so on. The measurement of the effect of any of these factors presents enormous difficulties. To determine which input produced what outcome is just not possible.

Whereas the primary input (cash) and the secondary inputs (e.g. staff, capital resource and consumables) are easy to measure and the outputs, e.g. the units of service produced, present little difficulty, the outcomes present both theoretical and practical difficulties and are, in addition, beset with problems of desirability, which can have political dimensions of great significance for the public sector.

Key concepts of VFM: economy, efficiency and effectiveness—the value for money chain

The 'three Es' can be defined in terms of input, output and outcome and present successively greater problems.

Economy   This is concerned with the conversion of the primary input—cash—into the usable secondary inputs—staff, consumables and capital items.

Very few people would quibble with the notion that items such as consumables should, provided they are fit for purpose, be bought at the lowest possible price. 'Shopping around' makes sense in personal terms: it makes sense in public terms.

Similarly, very few people would quibble with the notion that capital purchases should be undertaken with care. The purchase of a vehicle is just another case of shopping around, this time for something which will last a fair time. A project such as a new school or hospital should involve even more care in choosing location, drawing up the design, formulating the specifications, inviting tenders and, providing one has confidence that the tenderer can deliver appropriate quality on time and within tender price, awarding the tender to the lowest bidder.

There are more arguments concerned with staff! It clearly makes sense to purchase staff, provided there is competence, at the cheapest possible rate, bearing in mind the desirability of avoiding industrial dispute, securing loyalty and maintaining appropriate motivation. There are arguments regarding the desirability or otherwise of retaining a core of well-paid, multiskilled, loyal and well-motivated staff and supplementing these people as and when required by a periphery of casualized labour. Be that as it may, economy in personnel terms is about securing adequate staff at the minimum possible overall cost.

Efficiency   This is concerned with the conversion of the usable resource into outputs. It includes such matters as making best use of buildings and equipment so that they are utilized fully and are not standing idle. The goals of filling hospital beds or school classrooms are both directed at using capital efficiently.

The expectation that drugs will not be wasted by having stocks so large that a proportion pass their 'use by' date is an efficiency expectation. So too is the expectation that a tin of floor polish will cover so many square metres of floor.

On the staffing front, the growth of class sizes at all levels of education, the reduction in the standard time for procedures as diverse as sweeping a street, servicing a council house gas boiler or performing an appendix operation are all aimed at the efficient use of staff time.

There are also important interrelations between these aspects of efficiency. Capital expenditure can serve to save staffing costs. A street cleaner with a machine may be able to do the work of three street cleaners with brushes at only twice the total cost. This would be an efficiency gain made possible by investing in the capital cost of the machine and saving the staffing costs of two cleaners.

Effectiveness   This is about ensuring that the efficiently produced outputs are directed to achieving the desired outcomes. This implies, of course, that the desired outcomes have been formulated and that there are appropriate systems in place intended to monitor the outcomes. There are some difficulties with this!

In the first place, the outcomes cannot often be expressed simply in ways which are amenable to monitoring. We have already seen how the desirable outcomes of an educational system or a health service are not easily defined in any sensible way. To say that 'the desired outcome of an education system is that people should be better educated' is tautological, i.e. it tells us nothing new. To say that 'the desired outcome of a health service is that the nation's health will be better' is both tautological and, for reasons already discussed, likely to prove immensely difficult if not impossible to monitor.

It is, of course, possible to specify more precise desired outcomes. The avoidance of a measles epidemic was one such. So too would be the growth in numeracy as measured by a set of standard tests delivered at various ages. There would be arguments here, however, as to whether such testing would truly reflect a growth of numeracy of the sort which might underpin a genuine increase in the numerical capabilities of the workforce.

There are also problems of a political nature. It is argued by some that increased investment in nursery education, so that the great majority of children have extensive contact with nursery schools from the age of three, would not only make post-nursery school education more effective, but would also decrease disciplinary problems at school, reduce crime and improve the lives of mothers. Such claims, however well founded, would not be universally accepted. They would therefore have a political dimension: to put resources into nursery schools might imply reducing resources for secondary schools, for the police force and for those social workers who have to cope with the stress problems of mothers. To change the pattern of public spending is always a political matter: to change it on the basis of a contestable argument would be highly controversial.

There is also a dimension of quality associated with a consideration of outcomes. The question is often asked in a variety of contexts: 'We have decreased the inputs, we have increased the outputs, we are more economical and more efficient, but we have lost something—where is the quality of what we used to do?' We will return to the issue of quality shortly.

The value for money chain   Figure B6.1 shows a diagrammatic way of representing 'the three Es'.

● Converting primary resource (cash) to secondary resource (usable inputs) must be done economically.

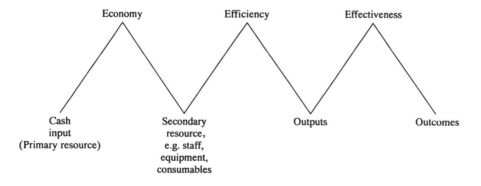

Figure B6.1   The value for money chain

- Converting usable inputs, whether of staff, consumables or capital, to measurable service outputs must be done efficiently.
- Comparing the achieved outcomes (related to outputs) with the desired outcomes (as specified in the original decision to provide a service) gives a measure of effectiveness.

One note should be added. The first two links in the chain, economy and efficiency, are relatively straightforward and may be combined to give output figures per unit of cash. Such a combination, often looking very much like a unit cost, is sometimes described as cost-effectiveness. This usage should be avoided: it lacks the evaluative dimension associated with the understanding of effectiveness as discussed above.

Performance indicators: some initial comments

Performance indicators will be dealt with in more depth in Article C10, but some initial comment may be made regarding the way in which the search for VFM has resulted in the production of various sorts of indicators. These may be divided into two sorts: those having relation to cost and those having relation to quality in some form.

Cost indicators   These have already been discussed. They are very closely related, if not identical, to unit costs, and the VFM emphasis which concentrates on outputs as related to money is clearly technical and relatively simple.

Quality indicators   These, on the other hand, are much more contentious. In general terms, the definition of quality may be approached in three ways which are conceptually distinct although in practice they impinge on one another: fitness for purpose/threshold standards, consistency/ quality systems and customer satisfaction

- *Fitness for purpose* is a term which queries whether something is suitable for the job it is intended to do. A small mass-production car is perfectly suited to town traffic. It would need modifications (e.g. larger fuel tank, oil cooler, underbody strengthening) to participate in a round the world rally. *Threshold standards* pose the question as to whether the specification has been met to an adequate standard. If the oil cooler has been bolted on loosely or the underbody strengthening is flimsy then, although the specification might be all right, the threshold standards have not been met.
- *Consistency* is about minimizing underperformance. It is about providing the same service on Friday afternoons as on Tuesday mornings, in summer and in winter, whoever is behind the desk or making the call. Ultimately the goal is 'zero defects': nothing goes wrong. *Quality systems* are those internal mechanisms which monitor performance and check that if there are variations leading to underperformance, inconsistency and defects, then something is done about both the immediate problem and the structural problems which may have caused it. The concept of 'total quality management' (TQM) is relevant here.
- *Customer satisfaction* is almost self-explanatory. The satisfaction of those people for whom the service is being provided and who, in one way or other are paying for the service, must be regarded as the prime goal of the organization. In the private sector 'the customer is king' is a well-known slogan. The problem with the public sector is that the customer is not always easily identifiable. In the NHS, for example, is it the government (which provides the vast majority of the funding) or the patient who pays little directly (although of course whose taxes

help fund the NHS) but is the direct recipient of the treatment? The various 'charters' are, in part, attempts to resolve this dilemma.

Put together, the search for all three dimensions of quality will probably produce 'value'. The combination of satisfactory 'value indicators' and satisfactory 'cost indicators' is the best approximation currently available for value for money.

The political dimensions

Each of these aspects of quality has a political dimension. It should be noted that the word 'political' is used in a wide sense: it does not here mean 'party political'.

- The aspect defined as *fitness for purpose/threshold standards* is obviously to do with the definition of the service to be provided in the first place. It is to do with the strategic understanding of what outcomes are desired and the best way in which these outcomes may be achieved.
- The aspect defined as *consistency/systems* has implications for working practices and labour relations. Whereas a call for increased throughput (productivity) may be challenged on traditional employee/employer grounds, the call for increased quality in terms of increased expectations of consistency and few (if not zero) defects, implies a co-operative and well-motivated workforce. It also implies a well-trained and flexible workforce and this in turn has implications in terms of equal opportunities and job security.
- The aspect of *customer satisfaction*, which has thrown emphasis onto the demands of non-professionals, is again political in the sense of requiring a reallocation of priorities and the devaluation of professional judgement as compared with the judgement and expectations of lay people.

One other political dimension should be discussed. It has been suggested that the 'three Es' should be expanded to embrace a 'fourth E': *equity*. This concept, related to equality, includes the notion that any service should be targeted to those who need it most, rather than being issued on an equal basis. Aristotle, an early Greek philosopher who provided a seminal discussion of the concept, wrote that 'it (was) as unjust to treat unequals equally as it was to treat equals unequally'. His argument was in terms of justice and the merits of recipients to fair treatment.

Today we might add the efficiency of targeting argument. If there are limited resources it is better to focus them on those who need them most. This too is political although in a dual and, to some, contradictory, way. In one sense it accepts the view of the right that there are limited resources. In another it is redistributive. The resources, however limited, come primarily from the better-off members of society. If they are then targeted, the recipients are likely to come primarily from the less well-off members of society. However we see the argument, it is at least tenable to say that good value includes not wasting resource on those who do not need it.

THE INTERNAL MARKET: COSTING, PRICING AND SERVICE-LEVEL AGREEMENTS

THE CONTEXT

The public sector has been under pressure since 1980 (or even beforehand on some reckonings) to reduce its overall expenditure and at the same time to increase both the quantity and the quality of the services it offers. Among the mechanisms which have been introduced are 'compulsory competitive tendering' (CCT) for local government, and its cousin 'market testing' for various branches of the civil service. Both of these devices require the public sector to tender, in competition with private sector and quasi-private sector[1] organizations, for the right to provide goods or, more importantly, services at a price.

A second mechanism used in this deliberate and sustained governmental pressure on the public sector has been the 'internal market'. This device has required organizations to operate a system whereby different branches of the organization sell their goods and services to other parts of the same organization at agreed and carefully calculated transfer prices. Such an internal market system operates both within local government and, in a different form, within the NHS. It is discussed below.

Both CCT and market testing are logically and conceptually different from internal market mechanisms, but there are practical links, the chief of which is the need to make accurate calculations of costs (and hence prices/transfer prices) of the various goods and services provided. This brings into the open the whole question of overheads.

THE KEY CONCEPTS

The main focus of this article is the *internal market* and that is discussed first, as tendering, whether for internal or for competitive purposes, is discussed in Article B9.

When an organization offers goods or services for sale it needs to know how much these goods or services *cost* so that, with an appropriate 'mark-up', it can determine a selling price. The cost, as will be explained more fully both below and in Article C5, is made up of various components. Important among these components are *overheads* of various types, and in a competitive situation it is important from several points of view that these overheads should be accurately known, reduced to their minimum level and attached in some acceptable way to the various goods and services produced by the organization. This article provides an initial discussion of costs and the allocation of overheads. Article C5 expands this discussion more rigorously.

If the internal market situation is in operation the supply of goods and/or services from one part of an organization to another demands a system of *transfer pricing* which is a specialized form of pricing. This will be dealt with in outline below and more fully in Article C6.

The public sector is mainly concerned with producing services rather than goods and so there is a need to define both the quantity and the quality of any service being provided within the sector. The mechanism for doing this is the *service-level agreement (SLA)* and that is discussed below.

The internal market

This is quite simply a device which enables one part of an organization to purchase clearly defined goods and services from another part of the organization at clearly defined prices. The fact that it is one part of an organization buying from another throws emphasis onto the 'internal'. The purchase of goods and/or services at a price throws emphasis onto the 'market'. The stressing of clarity in the definition of goods/services highlights the associated need for SLAs, and the stressing of clarity in the definition of price highlights the associated need for sensible and transparent costing systems.

The internal market is not solely a public sector concept. Indeed, it has its origins in the private sector. ICI in Britain, for example, has been divisionalized since its inception and has had an internal market for the supply and purchase of power, processes and services for over twenty-five years. More recently IBM, the US computer company, has divisionalized and introduced an internal market where its managers are free to purchase from outside the company if the internal division cannot produce the required goods and services to time, to quality and to price in line with external competition. The main aims of the divisionalization were to reduce costs and to streamline the bureaucracy of an enormous corporation. It ought to be added that among the British public sector antecedents of the internal market were the 'recharges' used within the NHS and local government for simple internal transfers.

Local government and the NHS practise different versions of the internal market although it could be argued that the versions are different in emphasis rather than concept. In local government when one department purchases from another the service provided is usually one which does not benefit external consumers, i.e. the general public directly. Thus when cleansing (as client) purchases financial or legal services from the treasury or the solicitor's department (as contractors), or education (as client) purchases building maintenance or grass cutting from works or recreation (as contractors), it is not the external consumer who benefits primarily. On the other hand, in the NHS, when the district health authority (as purchaser) contracts with a trust (as provider) for the supply of so many operations or a home-visiting chiropody service, the beneficiary is the general public.

The difference is, it can be argued, one of emphasis. The NHS has many examples of goods and services being supplied and purchased within the organization and local government is increasingly moving to a situation of having purchasing sections within departments where other sections of the same departments are responsible for providing, either internally or externally, services for clients. The concept of the 'enabling authority' has relevance here.

Costs and overheads

This section contains an initial discussion of the key terms and some simple examples to illustrate the concept and some of its inherent difficulties. The main technical treatment of overheads is in Article C5 on costing.

The purpose of costing is to work out as accurately as possible how much some operation, whether manufacturing or service provision, actually costs in money terms. Although a costing exercise looks quite complex, the principles are relatively straightforward. There is a snag in that the answers produced look straightforward, but this conceals an important truth regarding costing: except in the simplest cases it is not an exact science since it includes both estimates and judgements. There is room for discussion and that room can lead to quite serious arguments within organizations if different judgements or different estimates work to the advantage or otherwise of different departments!

If we consider a person who is in business making and selling garden sheds, all constructed to an identical design, there is no difficulty with costing. The cost of one shed is the total expenditure on materials, labour, rent, transport, advertising and so on during a period divided by the number of saleable sheds produced in that period. If the person makes 400 sheds in a year for a total expenditure of £40,000, then each shed has cost £100 to produce and must be sold at more than £100 if a profit is to be made.

That example could not be simpler. If, however, the business becomes complicated so that an A type shed and a B type shed are produced, the costing of each type becomes more complex. Some costs, e.g. the materials and the labour, are relatively easy to determine. The person knows how much material is used for each type and how long each one takes to produce. On the other hand some items, for example rent, transport and advertising, cannot so easily be divided up between each type of shed.

- The first sort of cost—the cost of labour and materials—is known as a *direct cost*.
- The second sort of cost—the cost of rent, transport, advertising and many other such items—is known as an *indirect cost* of which *overheads* are a particular type. For the purposes of this initial explanation indirect costs and overheads will be regarded as the same.

Typically in the public sector there are three layers of costs:

1. The direct cost of the operation being performed
2. The overheads of the section/department performing the operation
3. The overheads of the organization itself

For example, the cost of a foot operation, performed off-site by a community chiropodist employed by an NHS trust, will have three components corresponding to the above:

1. The direct cost of the operation in terms of the chiropodist's time, the materials used and, maybe, the travel costs
2. The overheads of the chiropody service—secretarial, administrative, management, in-service clinical training, etc.
3. The overheads of the trust itself—premises, administration, management, non-clinical education and training, marketing, etc.

It should be noted that even at this level there is room for discussion. The cost of the materials used and the travel are likely to be so small in relation to the cost of the chiropodist's time that they may be treated as sectional overheads. There may be no distinction drawn between clinical training and non-clinical education: it may all be 'staff development' and so on. For the moment, however, it is the principle which is important.

Among the overheads which must somehow be tied into the costs of any particular service or operation are:

- Salary and related costs of middle and senior management
- Salary and related costs of clerical, administrative and support staff
- Costs associated with the tenure, upkeep/maintenance and utilization of premises
- Costs associated with the ownership/leasing, maintenance/repair and utilization of vehicles, equipment and machinery
- Costs of education, training and staff development
- Running costs such as for heat, light and water
- Consumable costs such as stationery
- Other sundry items which, although taken one by one are usually smaller, may yet amount to a considerable sum in total

Supervisory management could be included as either a direct operational cost or an overhead. Many organizations would include small direct costs as overheads for reasons of simplicity. Figure B7.1 shows schematically how the total overhead costs of an organization can be allocated to an individual unit of service such as the chiropody operation discussed above. The question of how this is achieved is in theory resolved by breaking all overheads down in stages, although in practice some fairly crude approximations may be used.

Let us suppose that the chiropody service used in our example has three main thrusts to its work: clinic-based foot care, home-based foot care and foot care education. Let us suppose also that we are considering allocating the costs of the departmental secretarial service to the particular foot operation in question. If the secretarial service costs £20,000 per year, then some of that £20,000 must be tied in to each discrete activity undertaken by the section. The question is, how much?

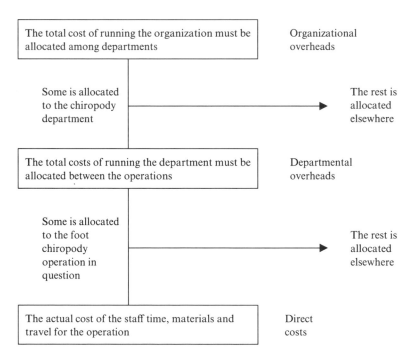

Figure B7.1   Allocation of costs: overheads and direct costs

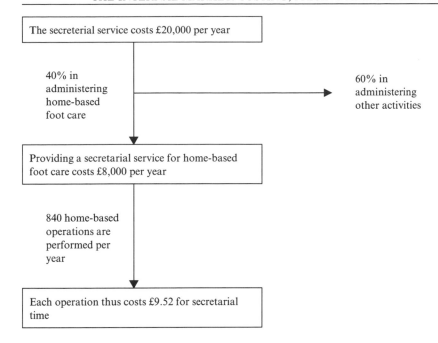

Figure B7.2   Example of allocation costs

The answer is to be found through a number of stages (Fig. B7.2):

1. An estimate of what proportion of the service is devoted to home-based foot care. The key to this may well be the proportion of clinician time spent on this enterprise. If the answer is '2 days a week (out of 5)' then 40 per cent is one estimate that could be used. In the absence of any other suggestions it is probably quite a good answer. The remaining 60 per cent might be spent as $2\frac{1}{2}$ days (50 per cent) on clinic-based services and $\frac{1}{2}$ day (10 per cent) on foot care education.
2. An estimate of how many home-based foot care operations the chiropody department actually performs in a year. If the answer is, say, 840 (a figure which should be available for previous years from the records and corresponds to 45 minutes per operation/travelling time on a 45-week year basis), then we can proceed to a calculation.
3. 40% of the total secretarial costs is devoted to home-based foot care, i.e. £8,000 (40 per cent of £20,000).
4. This £8,000 facilitates 840 home-based foot care operations, equivalent to £9.52 each.

Now it must be stressed that these figures are fictional. Even if, however, they were strictly accurate and a real-life example could be produced to match them, they could be subject to the following criticisms:

*   Is 'we spend 2 days a week on home-based foot care, and so we are allocating 40 per cent of secretarial time to this activity' the best way of doing it? Might it not be more accurate to observe the secretary in action and to see what proportion of secretarial time was actually spent on this thrust of the section's work? The answer to this lies in relative importance. For a relatively small overhead, the gain in accuracy from a detailed work study would almost

Overhead/activity	Managerial £000s	Secretarial £000s	Premises £000s	Running £000s	Total £000s
Home-based foot care	20	8	10	5	43
Clinic-based foot care	30	10	40	15	95
Foot care education	10	2	10	5	27
Total	60	20	60	25	165

Figure B7.3   Chiropody department: overhead allocation

certainly not be worth while. If the overhead were larger and serious questions of resource were being asked, then it might be.

- The assumption was that the secretarial time was equally divided between the clients of the various foot operations. Might it not be that Mrs Higgins was a reliable patient, always in and never changing an appointment, while Mr Starkey was frequently on the phone and frequently had some reason for making life difficult? In which case is it fair to cost the same secretarial time for Mrs Higgins as for Mr Starkey? The answer here is that fairness would only be an issue if Mrs Higgins and Mr Starkey were being charged 'full cost' for their treatment. If the object of the exercise is to allocate an overhead for internal market purposes, then an average where the rough is taken with the smooth is acceptable.

There is one further point, of great importance, to be made. In taking the various non-productive (indirect or overhead) costs of the section and allocating them somehow to the various productive activities of the section, we must ensure that all the overheads are included and that all are allocated somewhere. There must not be any loose ends.

In principle therefore, the total departmental overhead costs must be completely allocated to the various activities. In our example we have three activities. Let us suppose that we have four sorts of overhead cost: managerial, secretarial, premises and running costs. Then we can construct a matrix, as shown in Fig. B7.3.

There are three key points about this matrix:

1. The figure in the bottom right-hand corner—the grand total—must sum to the total overheads of the department.
2. The figure at the end of each row must be equal to the total overhead borne by each activity.
3. The figure at the bottom of each column must be equal to the total cost of each type of overhead.

The implication of this is significant. If, in the course of negotiations, one figure is argued down, for whatever reason, there must be an increase (or equivalent increases) elsewhere. It is essential that all parties concerned understand and agree the basis of overhead allocation, particularly if some degree of internal subsidization is being practised.

Transfer pricing

There are, in principle, three ways in which a price may be established:

1. By calculating the cost of a good, a service or an activity and then adding to that cost an amount, the 'mark up', which is usually expressed in percentage terms and represents the

profit on that good, service or activity. This is known as the *cost plus* method. It is by far the most common method in the private sector and is increasingly common in the public sector, although the percentage mark-up may be nominal.

2. By looking at the prices charged by one's competitors and then fixing one's prices in relation to theirs. This is known as the *competition awareness* method. It is possible to fix prices lower than the competition in order to gain customers and in so doing to fix prices lower than the corresponding costs, i.e. to make a loss. This is practised in both private and public sectors, but it has to be appreciated that there must be a corresponding source of additional profit to countervail the loss, otherwise there will be problems leading, in the private sector, to failure of the company, and in the public sector the need for some sort of rescue operation.

3. By considering the buying habits of potential customers and fixing the price in relation to this. This is known as taking into consideration *what the market will bear*. In the private sector this is practised in certain industries, for example fashion, where customers are willing to pay a premium for novelty. It has virtually no relevance in the public sector.

Service-level agreements

The service-level agreement (SLA) is a proxy for a contract. A contract in law is an agreement. It therefore follows that an SLA must be an agreement built on negotiation. It should not be imposed, either by one party on the other or by a third party, say a finance department, on two others.

The Local Government Management Board[2] offers the following contents checklist with respect to SLAs:

1. What is the service being provided?
2. What quantity will be provided? What is the unit of measurement?
3. What methods of charging will be used?
4. What is the rate of charge?
5. What is the acceptable range of variation of quantity (and quality)?
6. How will variations be dealt with? Will there be any penalties?
7. Who will act as arbiter in case of disagreement between the two parties?
8. What is the duration of the 'contract' (SLA)?
9. What period of notice is required to terminate the SLA?
10. How will parties know that the SLA is being fulfilled, i.e. what output measures are to be used?

NOTES

1. The term 'quasi-private sector' refers to those organizations which are formally separated from their parent organization and maintain separate records, premises and books. Their staffing, management and culture, however, maintain strong continuities with the organization from which they have been separated. Examples include companies formed to operate groups of former local authority old peoples' homes and some groups of bus companies. Apart from their origins in the public sector, the chief feature which distinguishes them from genuine private sector firms is the fact that many of them operate on a break-even 'not for profit' basis (or else on a requirement for nominal profit) while the private sector companies, of course, seek a commercial rate of return on capital.

2. From *Cost Centre Management: a guide for central support services*, Local Government Management Board, Luton, 1990. Similar lists are to be found in other publications from across the sector.

BUSINESS PLANNING

THE CONTEXT

The business plan is a concept which has gained considerable ground in the public sector over recent years. The idea originated in the private sector where its meaning was a document which set out the way in which a business hoped to develop either from a starting point (a new business) or from an established position where there was an intention to grow in some way. The originator of the business plan was the business itself, and the audience for whom the business plan was intended was a potential lender of money, say a bank, which would need to be assured that there was a probability that the business would succeed, and thus that the loan was reasonably secure. The plan would have sensible estimates of future sales and income, the expenditure necessary to support such sales and the anticipated cash flow.

Within the public sector the concept has taken on a meaning with two different emphases. In the first place, it is far less about money and far more about matching service provision to demand. In the second place, most of the audiences for business plans are internal to the sector or even to the organization. Within my own university, for example, each subject group produces a business plan which is read within the relevant school. Each school produces a business plan which is read within the university, and the university produces a plan which is used as a basis for resource negotiation with the university's chief funder, HEFCE.[1]

The overall context of the public sector business plan is thus one of resource allocation rather than of business funding and, usually, of maintaining the status quo ante with incremental change rather than with dimensions of start-up or significant expansion. It may be seen as a document which has a status and format intermediate between an overall strategy plan (which covers several years in general terms) and a budget (which usually covers one year in detail). The significance of business planning, in both private and public sectors, is that such plans focus attention on matters such as mission, marketing, employment and premises, and not solely on finance.

THE KEY CONCEPTS

This article considers the business plan under three main headings: the *scope* of the plan, i.e. the areas which should be considered within the typical public sector plan; the *implementation* of the plan, i.e. the way in which a business plan can and should be used; and the *dimension of change*, i.e. the way in which business planning is both a response to change and a way of maintaining change.

Scope

The scope of business planning may be illustrated with reference to a section or unit within an organization, say a local authority leisure centre, although, with some variation, the scope would apply to most public sector organizations. The business plan might deal with the following matters:

- A description of the leisure centre as it is with a statement of what it wishes to achieve in the short, medium and longer terms and an outline of how it wishes to effect the changes.
- The proportion of its overall income to be generated by various activities in the year to which the business plan refers.
- The ways of staffing the centre to cope with the various seasonal and daily peaks and troughs in demand.
- The ways of raising the profile of the centre in the public perception including general marketing and, perhaps, the possibility of achieving a real reputation in some field.
- A schedule of necessary maintenance and improvement of premises and capital expenditure on equipment and how it is proposed to fund such expenditure.

There are two key points to be noted in respect of this outline account:

1. Such an account must be credible. Forecasts must be based on reasonable interpretations of past performance in the light of current trends. If the utilization rates have been declining steadily for some years, for example, then a good and believable set of reasons must be given to support any plan which depends upon reversing this trend.
2. The whole notion of business planning assumes a culture in which managers have some control over the finances of the business they manage. In the example cited, managers would need to be able to vary prices in line with demand, to negotiate flexible working practices with their staff, to compete with other public and private centre leisure centres and to have some control over the interrelationship between capital and revenue budgets.

Implementation

Implementing business plans once written is an ongoing process. The Local Government Management Board[2] sees the process of implementation as having nine stages:

1. Identification of current activities
2. Identification of current clients/customers
3. Assessment of services currently offered
4. (Discussion of) services to be provided
5. (Determining) the best way of providing services including a (possibly radical) reappraisal of structures
6. Setting objectives
7. Monitoring progress
8. Marketing
9. (Taking) other considerations (into account)

This list is sensible and helpful within the current climate of the public sector, not just local government. It can be seen, however, that there are major omissions, the most important of which is that there is no mention of finance. This is in line with the LGMB's definition of business planning which is 'a methodology for identifying and matching supply and demand for services' or alternatively, 'a strategy to meet the needs and requirements of users'. This lack of reference to finance is clearly different from the tightly focused concept originating in the private sector!

The dimension of change

If business planning in the public sector is to develop in a really useful way then there are several aspects of the dimension of change which must be considered. The sector itself is changing in a direction which gives more power to managers and more delegated freedom to manage finance. This means that the concept of business planning within the sector must also change. It will always be different from the private sector notion, but it must approach it more nearly, particularly in regard to the more explicit inclusion of finance and financially related matters.

The key changes which must occur in the sector if business planning is to be a really useful tool are as follows:

1. Managers must not be constrained by centrally determined inflexible personnel policies. There must be freedom for managers to use contracts which match their needs and the needs of their clients and do not tie up money in staff who are surplus to requirements when demand is not high. Clearly, any organization, say a local authority or a NHS trust, both of which have legal responsibilities in regard to budgeting and budgetary control, will be wary of delegating too much power to their managers, but some must be delegated or services will remain over-costly.
2. Managers must not be constrained by centrally determined pricing policies, or at the very least their business plans should be explicit enough on the matter to serve as a basis for department-by-department negotiation or even as the stimulus for change in such policies across the organization.
3. Competition is real and that must be recognized. It is organizational ability to react to competition by varying price, by increasing quality or by increasing customer convenience which distinguishes the best private sector firms from their competition. Public sector organizations must be able to react in the same way that demands the freedoms outlined above.
4. Success is one of the factors which allows organizations to grow. If there is competition for a relatively stable market, the concomitant of one organization's growth is another organization's decline. If the success of the leisure centre we have used for an example is the decline of other leisure centres, be they publicly or privately owned, then this must be faced up to. Business planning which is constrained by protectionism is pointless. Business planning which exists in an environment of genuine competition is healthy.
5. Managers must be more free to manage finance. The skills needed to manage a tender won in accordance with a business plan in a culture of competition are different from the skills needed to manage a traditional revenue budget. This must be recognized and managers given freedom, within limits, to vire on their revenue accounts and to use capital investment to generate income and to make revenue savings. Articles B3 and C8 have relevance here.

It is recognized that some of these prescriptions are politically contentious. This dimension is usually more apparent in the public sector than in the private. But the real political issue is not a matter for dispute between parties, nor between employers and unions, nor between central government and its suborganizations such as the NHS or local government: it is to do with ensuring that in the move towards providing value for money in an environment of internal market, business planning and competition, the ultimate consumer and the ultimate provider of funds, the taxpayer, is not forgotten.

NOTES

1. HEFCE:The Higher Education Funding Council for England. For a fuller description of the way in which resource allocation in higher education is negotiated and funded, see the case study of Sheffield Hallam University by B.M. Jones and H.K. Scholes, in Darwin, J. and H.K. Scholes, *Public Sector Case Studies*, PAVIC, 1995.
2. This list is taken from *Cost Centre Management: a guide for central support services*, pp. 9–12, Local Government Management Board, Luton, 1990.

TENDERS AND TENDERING[1]

THE CONTEXT

The idea of tendering for contracts both within the public sector and between public sector organizations and the private sector is by no means new. The standing financial instructions of all public sector organizations have contained sections on such matters for many years. The compliance of organizations with their own tendering procedures has proved a rich field for auditors to mine! What is new is the emphasis, which has become stronger throughout the 1980s and early 1990s, on the compulsory nature of tendering for a much wider variety of goods and services, and the realities of cash limitation and competition: the idea that it matters to the organization that tenders should be right financially when the public sector is buying and the idea that they should be right in terms of quality and price when the public sector organization is tendering to sell.

One context of this article is therefore the growth of the requirement to tender accurately in a climate of increased customer expectation of value for money and delivered performance.

A second important dimension is the growth of managerialism. The days when tendering matters could be 'left to finance' have long since gone. In whatever part of the public sector we consider, managers are expected to deliver on financial targets, for both cost limitation and income generation, and on output targets, for both quantity and quality. This has meant that non-financial managers are directly involved in the tendering processes much more frequently than in the past. They are key stake-holders in the business of getting tenders right on all these dimensions. The second context of the article is therefore the increased importance of tendering to public sector managers.

THE KEY CONCEPTS

A *tender* is an offer to supply goods and/or services to a specified quantity and quality, over a specified time-span and at a specified price. The tender is usually made in response to an *invitation to tender* in which the specifications and timescale are laid down. The normal outcome of a successful tender in the private sector is a written *contract* and such a contract is a legally enforceable agreement, binding on both parties. The totality of the precontract activity is sometimes known as the *tendering process*.

The tendering process

There are several stages for different parties involved in the tendering process:

1. The intending purchaser's process of creating the tender specification
2. The intending provider's process of response to the invitation to tender (noting that in a competitive situation there will be more than one intending provider)
3. The intending purchaser's decision as to which tender to choose, or indeed whether to go ahead with the purchase
4. Drawing up the contract in the light of both the invitation to tender and the tender document together with any agreed precontract variations

Public sector managers on any one occasion may therefore be involved in the tendering process in one of two main ways. Of course, they are likely to be involved in both ways on different occasions, but never (at least in principle) both at the same time[2]:

- They may be intending purchasers/clients, in which case they are particularly interested in drawing up an accurate specification and making a sensible choice of contractor.
- They may be intending providers/contractors, in which case they are particularly interested in winning the contract by matching quantity/quality to the specification and price to their feel for the likely competition.

Once at the contract stage, managers with whatever hat they are wearing are interested in sorting out the way(s) of dealing with any variations.

Public sector managers may also be involved in two different modes:

- They may be operating within an internal market, in which case the outcome may be a service-level agreement[3] rather than a contract.
- They may be operating in a genuinely[4] competitive situation with internal and external competitors.

Whichever mode should make little if any difference. The specification should be the same whether the successful tenderer is internal or external to the organization. The tender itself should match the specification and the price should be calculated on the basis of at least covering full costs and should not, normally, be chosen with an eye to beating the competition with no regard to the actual costs.

In drawing up the *tender specification*, the key is consultation with all those parties concerned to ensure that the quality aspect of the specification is satisfactory. The quantity aspect will almost invariably have two dimensions: one based on history, the other on change. There is always a knowledge of what volume was handled in the last time period. This almost inevitably forms the starting point for the quantity specification. There will always be change factors, some due to changing patterns of demand, some due to changing availability of resource to purchase service, which will act to moderate the historically based starting point. It is in the interest of the potential purchaser to get both the quantity and quality aspects right.

In *making the choice between tenderers*, three key factors should be considered:

1. The price—other things being equal, the lowest tender should be accepted.
2. Confidence in the ability of the various tenderers to deliver what they promise in terms of both quantity and quality. This confidence can be quantified in terms of the costs to the purchaser of monitoring the operation.

   A belief that private sector organizations cut corners on quality has previously been part of the public sector culture, and has led to many tenders from private sector organizations being rejected. There is no evidence that private sector contractors are systematically worse than public sector contractors in fulfilling their obligations. There are, of course, horror stories about private contractors. Less well-known, although equally valid, are the horror stories about public sector contractors who cannot meet their obligations within their artificially low quoted prices.

Unless there is clear evidence to the contrary, private sector and public sector tenderers should be treated as equally competent.

3. The ability of the various tenderers to respond to changes in demand. Most tenderers can cope with change if there is sufficient notice. Some tenderers cannot cope with the fluctuations in demand, sometimes utterly unpredictable, which are made at short notice upon public sector organizations.

The way in which demand fluctuations are to be coped with should be an integral part of the tender specification and form an important part of post-tender, precontract negotiation. The terminology for dealing with demand fluctuations is 'variation'/'variation order'.

The tender document

This document is the potential contractor's response to the invitation to tender. It is a formal document and may be either a pro forma designed by the purchaser to reflect the various requirements as set out in the invitation, or it may be a document with a set of numbered paragraphs, again carefully matched to the required specification.

Either way, the key parts will show the following:

1. The potential contractor has understood the purchaser's requirements with regard to quantity (and possible quantity variations) and can meet them.
2. The potential contractor has understood the purchaser's requirements with regard to quality (and quality monitoring) and can satisfy them.
3. A clear statement of the price for various quantities of goods or service, together with any terms of payment, e.g. monthly in arrears, or any discounts for prompt payment/penalties for late payment.

It is in the interest of the potential contractor to make sure that the purchaser's requirements are understood and responded to. The days of a 'take it or leave it' attitude are going if not gone. The purchaser has the money or resource and is increasingly in a position of some power with respect to the potential provider.

It is in the interest of the potential contractor to calculate the costs accurately and to base the tender securely on the calculated costs. The price for the main volume of the contract should be based on a full absorption costing calculation (see Articles B7, C5 and C6), although relatively small volume increases may be priced on the basis of marginal costs (C5, C6). Larger anticipated volume changes may need special techniques of costing/pricing.

The contract

This is a legally binding document[5]. It is an agreement to provide something for a consideration. The 'agreement' is between the client and the contractor. The 'something' is the good or service under discussion. The 'consideration' is the price.

The stage between the acceptance of a tender in principle and the signing of the contract is important. It allows for last-minute variations of specification and consequent last-minute variations of price. It also allows for negotiation if the contractor's tender has not been exactly as anticipated by the client although near enough to make negotiation worth while.

For the client, the contract provides a reference point for quantity, quality and price. If monitoring shows that the quantity and quality are not being supplied, then there are grounds for demanding rectification or a renegotiation of price.

For the contractor, the contract specification provides the measure of what must be done. If the contractor, at the request of the client, does more then there is a basis for additional payment.

It is in the interest of both parties to ensure that the contract is accurately drawn up and that it is understood by both parties. The chief disputes are likely to centre upon quality and variations in quantity. Experience suggests that a good working relationship, likely to lead to smooth variations in the shorter term and renewal of the contract in the longer term, is built upon such mutual understanding. Although research suggests that such understanding is more important than the contract itself, this does not negate the importance of the contract should the understanding, for whatever reason, break down.

NOTES

1. I am grateful to my colleague Dr Peter Vincent-Jones of the School of Financial Studies and Law, Sheffield Hallam University, for a particularly thorough and rigorous critique of a first draft of this article. Most of his criticisms have been heeded and the article is the stronger for it. Any remaining weaknesses, errors and omissions and emphases of interpretation are, of course, my responsibility.
2. Within public sector organizations when an internal tendering process was taking place there was a tendency for senior managers to get involved in both aspects of the tendering process. This tendency was particularly marked in the early days of learning what the internal market was all about and it was exacerbated by a feeling that the whole affair was somehow to be circumvented and that therefore the internal tenderer had somehow to be advantaged.

    In local government for example, there was almost certainly a high degree of internal protectionism surrounding the first set of CCT which resulted in a high proportion of contracts won in-house. For the second round, some years later, where the rules had been learnt more thoroughly, even though internal tenders were more competitive, there has been a higher proportion of contracts awarded to outside organizations.

    Most organizations now separate formally the businesses of purchasing and provision within the internal market situation. Purchasers and providers have their own business plans and targets and at least at operational and middle management levels there is a genuine separation of purpose and personnel. At the strategic level of management, however, I suspect that there is still a fair degree of control over the freedom of the tendering and contracting processes.
3. A service-level agreement (SLA) is not a contract. Within local government an SLA serves as a quasi-contract within a situation where one section/department services another with, for example, personnel, payroll, IT services. In the NHS the term SLA is used in two senses. The first is as above, within a trust. The second use, perhaps improper, covers the detail of a contract between two organizations, often, but not necessarily so, in the same health authority, where the contract is general but the detail is contained in an annexe, the SLA. Thus a GP fundholder may contract with a community trust for a certain service, and the level of that service is commonly referred to as an SLA even though it is an appendix to a contract.
4. Vincent-Jones (see Note 1) stresses that many of the market situations within which the public sector is currently working are best regarded as 'quasi-markets'. I agree with him. Where we differ is in interpretation. He feels that the situation is becoming 'softer' and that there may be less emphasis on the 'market' and more on the 'quasi': I feel that the reverse is likely to be the case. This difference may be due to the location of our research. His is substantially within local government: my recent experience is within the NHS. Whatever the interpretation, we are agreed that this is a most interesting area although we differ about its potential to effect good practice within the respective sectors!
5. The SLA, see Article B7, serves within organizations as a proxy for a contract. It cannot be a legally binding document as the organization cannot contract with itself and the individual components of the organization, however separate they are in organizational terms, are not corporate entities capable of contracting. Thus one local government department or one directorate of an NHS trust cannot contract with another. The correct term for contract-like arrangements in these circumstances is service-level agreement. Such agreements, although not legally binding, are very important and should be taken seriously.

NUMERICAL TECHNIQUES WITH EXAMPLES

WHAT THIS SECTION IS ABOUT

The context

The public sector is currently expected to behave increasingly more like a set of business enterprises. Consequently, concepts and techniques which for many years have been routinely used in the private sector are increasingly part of the vocabulary and armoury of the public sector manager.

This section deals with a select number of such concepts and techniques. The selection has been based on three main criteria:

- Concepts and techniques examined by the major professional bodies
- Concepts and techniques which I have observed being used (or occasionally misused!) in public sector organizations
- Concepts and techniques which are taught as part of the financial management courses within the public sector routes on the undergraduate programme of Sheffield Business School

In addition, practising public sector managers, some of whom I teach on MBA courses, have been consulted in an effort to ensure relevance.

The key concepts

There are two underlying themes to the concepts and techniques discussed in this section:

1. Articles C2 C4 are relevant to the theme of *investment appraisal*, i.e. the evaluation of the utility of spending capital in order to provide a service, make savings or achieve surpluses which can be used to ease pressures on the revenue budget. The topics dealt with include payback, discounted cash flow and break-even analysis.
2. Articles C5–C7 are relevant to the theme of *budgeting and controlling budgets*, i.e. making the financial plans and ensuring that any departures from them are monitored and appropriate action taken in both the shorter and longer terms. The topics dealt with include costing, pricing and variance analysis.

Concepts and techniques in Articles C1 and C8–C9 are applicable to both these themes. The topics dealt with include cash budgeting, cost of capital, forecasting and performance indicators. The order of presentation does not map exactly onto the themes for reasons of logic and clarity, for example the topic of cash budgeting, although primarily a budgetary matter, is dealt with before payback and discounted cash flow because it makes sense in teaching terms.

HOW TO USE THIS SECTION

This section consists of discussions of ten topics which are relevant to the manager in the public sector. Each one is treated in the following manner:

- A discussion of the context in which the concept/technique is used. Readers can use this discussion to check out whether the material is what they need.
- A discussion of the key concepts which underpin the topic. Readers can use this discussion to check out their existing knowledge and to familiarize themselves with the concepts prior to embarking on the quantitative material.

- An explanation of the technique in simple terms and using very limited examples to establish the key principle(s).
- One or two fully worked examples of a standard appropriate to cover the examination syllabuses of academic and professional bodies.

Two exercises in the form of unworked mini case studies of a similar standard which focus upon the material of the topic under consideration are included for each Section C topic in Section D. The reader is advised to work these before consulting the answers contained later in the book. Tutors are advised that worked solutions to these mini case studies can be obtained on application to the publishers.

The section can be used in one of three main ways:

- For students, it can be used as an introductory study, in which case it is advisable to work through it steadily, perhaps taking a week's study time over each section. It might be advisable to work just one of the mini case studies in Section D, leaving the other for a revision aid.
- For practising managers, it can be used to dip into in order to learn or refresh some technique needed to satisfy a work-related demand. It may be necessary to underpin such understanding by looking at one or more of the previous themes, but this should be readily apparent. The practising manager will not need to work the mini case studies (unless it is felt necessary as an aid to confidence) but should be able to test out understanding by applying the technique to the real-life problem in hand.
- Anybody can, of course, use the section as an aid to revision or clarification of existing ideas. In this case a mixture of dipping into and systematic working through will probably prove helpful.

The mini case studies are focused on the particular technique. Real life is often not so tidy and the reader is advised that Section D also includes some less highly structured and less focused case studies. These should be considered/discussed in the light of material from each of the preceding sections.

CASH BUDGETS

THE CONTEXT

The need for cash budgeting and cash flow management exists at two distinct levels within any public sector organization:

1. At the level of the treasurer/chief financial officer it is important that the global expenditure of the organization is matched in quantity and phasing to the global receipts of the organization. In particular it is important, especially at any time of relatively high interest rates, to minimize any deficit which would have to be met by short-term borrowing, as for example by utilization of bank overdraft facilities.
2. At the level of any section or project manager who is working with both income and expenditure it is important to ensure both that in the shorter term the chief financial officer is assisted in this task by prudent management, and that in the longer term care has been taken in drawing up the financial aspect of the business plan to indicate the planned cash flows over the life of the project.

While the first level is of great importance and, indeed the global management of cash flow and the techniques for investing any short-term surpluses to the advantage of the organization are sometimes referred to as 'financial management', this section concentrates on the lower level of section or project management.

THE KEY CONCEPTS

Four basic concepts are used in setting out a cash budget:

1. It is first necessary to have a very good idea of the *pattern of expenditure*, not just in terms of cash but, very importantly, in terms of when the cash is to be spent.
2. It is equally necessary to have a very good idea of the expected *pattern of income*, again not just in terms of cash but also when the cash is likely to arrive.
3. Once these patterns are established they can be entered on a *schedule* which indicates the phasing of income and expenditure.
4. From this schedule can be derived a *cash budget forecast*.

The planning of how much is likely to be spent/received and when this expenditure/income is due is an important part of any business planning in the private sector. It has in the past been seen as less important in the public sector, but this is changing and is definitely a factor of which public sector managers should be aware.

Table C1.1 Schedule outline

Form 1						Month							
Schedule	1	2	3	4	5	6	7	8	9	10	11	12	Total
Income items													
Total income													
Expenditure items													
Total expenditure													

The construction of the schedule is relatively straightforward and leads to a cash budget forecast. It may also lead to the construction of a project cash flow or payback period table as discussed in the next section.

The schedule

This is normally set out in the form of a table. An outline is shown in Table C1.1.

It is important that all expenditure and income is entered as accurately as possible. From the point of view of any operation it is invariably better if income can be front loaded and any expenditure deferred, i.e. cash should ideally be received as early as possible and bills should be paid as late as possible (subject to avoiding any penalties). In constructing the schedule with an eye to reality it is better to be pessimistic on these scores. If in doubt, expenditure should be entered earlier and income later. If, on the other hand, the intention is to present one's position in a flattering light then expenditure should be presented as likely to be later and income as likely to be earlier! My view is that, on this topic, pessimism is to be preferred.

Deriving a cash budget (sectional cash management over a time period) from the schedule

This is normally set out in the form of a table similar to Table C1.2.

Table C1.2 Cash budget

Form 2						Month						
Cash budget	*1*	*2*	*3*	*4*	*5*	*6*	*7*	*8*	*9*	*10*	*11*	*12*
Start	[1]											
In	[2]											
Total	[3]											
Out	[4]											
Leaves	[5]											

N.B. If bank in *credit* plain, e.g. £400, if bank *overdrawn* in parentheses, e.g. (£125).

Into the table are entered against each month:

- The starting position [1], i.e. the likely opening cash balance.
- The gross income from all sources [2].
- The total [3] of (1) and (2).
- The gross expenditure on all items [4].
- The difference [5] between [3] and [4] noting that if [4] is greater than [3], i.e. a cash overspend/ bank overdraft is indicated, it is conventional to place the overspend/overdraft in brackets, e.g. (£4,350). The figure [5] thus derived becomes the figure [1] for the next month.

From this table, the cash budget, it can be seen clearly what arrangements must be made in advance to cover any shortfalls or, if there are surpluses, to plan for their effective utilization.

EXAMPLE OF A CASH BUDGET FORECAST: MATILDA HIGGINS

A student, Matilda Higgins, has the following financial circumstances:

1. She starts the year on 1 October with a credit balance of £400 which she has earned during the summer vacation.
2. Her grant comes in three instalments: £350 (October), £350 (January) and £300 (May).
3. She takes out a student loan for £1,000 in two instalments, £500 in November and £500 in February.
4. Her parents make a regular contribution of £125 per month for 9 months (October to June) and allow her to live free at home from July to September.
5. She takes a job averaging £100 per month from 1 December to 30 April.
6. Her flat deposit of £250 is paid on 1 October and is reclaimable on 30 June.
7. Her initial expenses amount to £500 and are paid for equally in October and November.
8. She will have extra travelling expenses of £50 for going home over Christmas (December), Easter (April), and summer (June).
9. Her normal living expenses are £125 per month (October to June).
10. Entertainment during term costs her £75 per month (October to June) but only £50 per month in vacation (July to September).

11. Her rent comes to £250 per month (October to June) and she may put down a retainer in July of £250 if she likes her flat.
12. She intends to buy presents as follows for her family: December £170 (Christmas and birthday), £20 each in March, June and September.

Required

1. Draw up a cash flow statement for Matilda Higgins.
2. Discuss the necessity or otherwise of taking out the student loan.
3. How much must she earn over the next summer vacation to give her a starting point of £600 for next year?
4. Advise MH on her financial affairs.

Solution to Matilda Higgins

Begin by using the information in items 2–12 of the question to complete a schedule as in Table C1.1. It is always as well to be pessimistic, i.e. reckon on things going against you. Thus enter the £250 retainer which Matilda might put down in July (item 11). You should find that your schedule looks like Table C1.3.

Table C1.3 Schedule for Matilda Higgins

Form 1

Schedule	Oct	Nov	Dec	Jan	Feb	Mar	Apr	May	Jun	Jul	Aug	Sep	Total
Income items													
Grant (2)	350			350			300						1000
Loan (3)	0	500			500								1000
Parents (4)	125	125	125	125	125	125	125	125	125				1125
Job (5)	0		100	100	100	100	100						500
Flat reclaim (6)									250				250
Total income	475	625	225	575	725	225	525	125	375				3875
Expenditure items													
Flat deposit (6)	250												250
Initial exp. (7)	250	250											500
Extra trans. (8)			50				50		50				150
Living (9)	125	125	125	125	125	125	125	125	125				1125
Entertainment (10)	75	75	75	75	75	75	75	75	75	50	50	50	825
Rent and retainer (11)	250	250	250	250	250	250	250	250	250	250			2500
Presents (12)			170			20			20			20	230
Total expenditure	950	700	670	450	450	470	500	450	520	300	50	70	5580

Table C1.4 Cash budget for Matilda Higgins

Form 2

Cash flow	Oct	Nov	Dec	Jan	Feb	Mar	Apr	May	Jun	Jul	Aug	Sep
Start	400	(75)	(150)	(595)	(470)	(195)	(440)	(715)	(740)	(885)	(1185)	(1235)
In	475	625	225	575	725	225	225	425	375			
Total	875	550	75	(20)	255	30	(215)	(290)	(365)	(885)	(1185)	(1235)
Out	950	700	670	450	450	470	500	450	520	300	50	70
Leaves	(75)	(150)	(595)	(470)	(195)	(440)	(715)	(740)	(885)	(1185)	(1235)	(1305)

N.B. If bank in *credit* plain, e.g. £400, if bank *overdrawn* in parentheses, e.g. (£125).

Once you have done that you are in a position to enter the figures on to the cash budget form, remembering to start with the opening balance of £400 (item 1). When you have done this your cash forecast should look like Table C1.4.

Once you have done this you will have satisfied Requirement 1. You will see that she is always overdrawn and that she finishes the year £1,305 overdrawn. Since she started with £400, that represents an overspend of £1,705 and that checks with the difference between her income (£3875) and her expenditure (£5580).

Requirement 2 invites you to discuss whether she should take out the student loan. Not mentioned here is that the student loan is interest free while her overdraft will almost certainly cost her considerably in bank charges. She is therefore advised to take out as big a loan as possible as early in the year as possible so as to minimize these charges. You could argue that this might make her spend more, and that is a possibility you might wish to explore under Requirement 4.

Requirement 3 invites you to calculate the summer vacation earnings necessary for her to start next year with £600. This is clearly made up of two components, the £1,305 necessary to reduce her overdraft to zero and the £600 to give her a good start, totalling £1,905. This is straightforward calculation with no subjective element at all. You could add that this averages to about £150 a week, or more if she takes any holiday!

Requirement 4 asks you to advise Matilda on her financial affairs. This is subjective. Some might consider the entertainment figure, averaging nearly £16 per week over the year, was high. Others would have been meaner with the presents while yet others would criticize the rent as being about double what she might pay in a provincial city. The best advice is not to say 'you are doing this wrong' (we don't know all her circumstances), but to ask her to consider every line of her expenditure for herself and make any changes in the light of her own reflection on her own experience.

EXAMPLE OF A CASH BUDGET FORECAST: XY LTD

The following information relates to XY Ltd.

Month	Wages incurred (£000s)	Materials purchased (£000s)	Overheads (£000s)	Sales (£000s)
February	6	20	10	30
March	8	30	12	40
April	10	25	16	60
May	9	35	14	50
June	12	30	18	70
July	10	25	16	60
August	9	25	14	50
September	9	30	14	50

1. It is expected that the cash balance on 31 May will be £22,000.
2. The wages may be assumed to be paid within the month they are incurred.
3. It is the company policy to pay creditors for materials three months after receipt.
4. Debtors are expected to pay two months after delivery.
5. There is a one-month delay in paying the overhead expenses.
6. 10 per cent of the monthly sales are for cash and 90 per cent are sold on credit.
7. Agents receive 5 per cent commission on all credit sales in the month after the sale is made.
8. It is intended to repay a loan of £25,000 on 30 June.
9. Delivery is expected in July of a new machine costing £45,000 which will be paid for in three equal instalments in July, August and September.

Required

1. Prepare a cash budget for each of the three months June, July and August. (You may assume that overdraft facilities are readily available.)
2 Comment on the practices indicated in items 3, 4 and 5.

Solution to XY Ltd

As before, the first stage is to draw up a schedule on the Form 1. The process this time is complicated by the information in items 3, 4 and 5 regarding the phasing of payments and receipts and items 6 and 7 regarding the commission on credit sales and when it is paid.

The schedule when complete should look like Table C1.5. You should study the following explanations for the relevant lines very carefully:

1. The separation of the sales into cash and credit elements follows the 10 per cent cash, 90 per cent credit guideline given in item 6. The phasing puts the cash element into the relevant sales month but delays the credit element by two clear months (item 4). Thus February's £30K sales divides into £3K cash (in February) and £27K credit which is not received until April, two months later.
2. On the expenditure side, the entry of wages is straightforward (item 2), but there is a three-month delay in entering the materials purchase (item 3) and a one-month delay in entering the

Table C1.5 Schedule for XY Ltd (all figures in £000s)

Form 1	Feb	Mar	Apr	May	Jun	Jul	Aug	Sep	Total
Income items									
Cash sales	3	4	6	5	7	6	5	5	41
Credit sales			27	36	54	45	63	54	279
Total income	3	4	33	41	61	51	68	59	320
Expenditure items									
Wages (2)	6	8	10	9	12	10	9	9	73
Materials (3)				20	30	25	35	30	140
Overheads (5)		10	12	16	14	18	16	14	100
Commissions (6), (7)		1.35	1.8	2.7	2.25	3.15	2.7	2.25	16.2
Loan (8)					25				25
Machine (9)						15	15	15	45
Total expenditure	6	19.35	23.8	47.7	83.25	71.15	77.7	70.25	399.2

overheads (item 5). The commission on the credit sales is 5 per cent of the credit element and is entered a month behind the sale (item 7).
3. The entries for the loan repayment and the machinery purchase are straightforward.

Once the schedule is complete the cash budget can then be drawn up for the required months using the £22K starting point indicated in item 1. You should arrive at the figures shown in Table C1.6. You should note that only the relevant months, June, July and August are included. This meets the first requirement.

The second requirement invites you to comment on the practice of paying three months in arrears (item 3), paying overheads one month in arrears (item 5) and asking for payment only two months in arrears (item 4). Cash flow is aided by paying late and getting income early. In that way any interest paid on an overdraft is minimized and any to be gained by running a credit balance is maximized.

Table C1.6 Cash budget for XY Ltd (all figures in £s)

Form 2			
Cash flow	Jun	Jul	Aug
Start	22,000	(250)	(20,400)
In	61,000	51,000	68,000
Total	83,000	50,750	47,600
Out	83,250	71,150	77,700
Leaves	(250)	(20,400)	(30,100)

N.B. If bank in *credit* plain, e.g. £400, if *overdrawn* in parentheses, e.g. (£125).

PROJECT CASH FLOWS OR PAYBACK PERIODS

THE CONTEXT

The idea of the cash budget/cash flow explored in Article C1 can easily be extended to a use as a helpful tool for project appraisal. Instead of drawing up the figures as in Article C1, they are drawn up so as to throw into emphasis the cumulative effects of both income and expenditure flows. At some point the planned income may match or exceed the planned expenditure, and at this point 'payback' has occurred. The technique can also be used if 'savings' rather than income are planned.

THE KEY CONCEPTS

Three of the concepts are identical to those involved in cash budgeting:

1. It is necessary to map the pattern of *investment* and *expenditure* over the project's life span.
2. It is necessary to map the pattern of *income* or *savings* over the project's life span.
3. It is necessary to draw up a *schedule* of these patterns of investment/expenditure and savings/income.

There are two more concepts:

4. *Cumulative net expenditure/income*, i.e. the total effect of what has happened up to any given point in the project's life span.
5. This may be positive (a net surplus), negative (a net deficit) or at some point exactly neutral—this point is the *payback period*.

Deriving a cash flow forecast (project management over a time-span) from the schedule

This is normally set out in tabular form as shown in Table C2.1. Three conventions should be used in drawing up the table.

Table C2.1   Cash flow forecast outline

Year	Expenditure	Income	Surplus or (deficit)	Cumulative surplus or (deficit)
0				
1				
2				

1. Year 0 is now, the starting position, while year 1 is the first year of operation, etc.
2. Expenditure is shown as a negative, i.e. with a minus sign, – , while income is shown as positive, i.e. with a plus sign, + .
3. Any cumulative surplus is shown without parentheses, while any cumulative deficit is shown in parentheses, ( ).

Into the table are entered against each time period:

- Any carry forward from a previous project [1], entered in year 0
- The anticipated expenditure in any year(s), including any substantial initial expenditure in year 0 [2], i.e. any investment
- The anticipated income/savings in any year(s) [3], typically this starts in year 1
- The difference [4] between [2] and [3], using the convention described above.
- The cumulative surplus or deficit [5], taking into account any initial cash position.

The payback period in years is the point at which the anticipated cumulative deficit changes to an anticipated cumulative surplus.

EXAMPLE OF PAYBACK FORECAST: SIDWELL SPORTS CENTRE

A small sports centre is estimated to cost £500,000 to build and equip which will be paid for up front. The running expenses are estimated at £50,000 annually from year 1 and the income at £50,000 in year 1 and £100,000 annually from year 2.

Using a tabular method demonstrate when the sports centre is anticipated to move into a position of cumulative surplus.

Solution

See Table C2.2. All the conventions are illustrated here in this artificially easy example!

Table C2.2 Solution for Sidwell Sports Centre

Year	Expenditure	Income	Surplus or (deficit)	Cumulative surplus or (deficit)
0	– 500,000		(500,000)	(500,000)
1	– 50,000	+ 50,000	0	(500,000)
2	– 50,000	+ 100,000	50,000	(450,000)
3	– 50,000	+ 100,000	50,000	(400,000)
4	– 50,000	+ 100,000	50,000	(350,000)
5	– 50,000	+ 100,000	50,000	(300,000)
6	– 50,000	+ 100,000	50,000	(250,000)
7	– 50,000	+ 100,000	50,000	(200,000)
8	– 50,000	+ 100,000	50,000	(150,000)
9	– 50,000	+ 100,000	50,000	(100,000)
10	– 50,000	+ 100,000	50,000	(50,000)
11	– 50,000	+ 100,000	50,000	0
12	– 50,000	+ 100,000	50,000	50,000

- There is a large initial expenditure shown in year 0 by a negative sign in the expenditure column and in parentheses in the surplus/(deficit) and cumulative columns.
- The first year income matches the first year expenditure, thus showing a zero in the surplus/deficit column and no change to the cumulative column.
- From year 2 onwards there is a regular excess of income over expenditure, i.e. a surplus which has the effect of reducing the cumulative deficit at a regular rate.
- In year 11 the cumulative deficit is reduced to zero. This is the payback period.
- The next line is, strictly speaking, not necessary, but it is given to show the effect on the final figure as the operation moves into a cumulative surplus.

EXAMPLE OF PAYBACK FORECAST: GAS V. OIL

A small hospital is considering two tenders for the supply of a new boiler:
- A gas-fired system will cost an initial £50,000 and it is estimated that it will save £7,500 annually (as compared with the current system) over a 10-year working life.
- An oil-fired system will cost an initial £60,000 and it is estimated that it will save £7,000 annually (as compared with the current system) over a 15-year working life.

Draw up a table showing the cash situation for each boiler for the whole of its anticipated working life and comment on the outcomes.

Because we are told the annual savings rather than the income/expenditure we can simplify the working somewhat and combine both boilers in Table C2.3.

Table C2.3 Payback forecast for gas v. oil

Year	Gas Expenditure	Gas Saving	Gas Cumulative	Oil Expenditure	Oil Saving	Oil Cumulative
0	− 50,000		(50,000)	− 60,000		(60,000)
1		7,500	(42,500)		7,000	(53,000)
2		7,500	(35,000)		7,000	(46,000)
3		7,500	(27,500)		7,000	(39,000)
4		7,500	(20,000)		7,000	(32,000)
5		7,500	(12,500)		7,000	(25,000)
6		7,500	(5,000)		7,000	(18,000)
7		7,500	2,500		7,000	(11,000)
8		7,500	10,000		7,000	(4,000)
9		7,500	17,500		7,000	3,000
10		7,500	25,000		7,000	10,000
11					7,000	17,000
12					7,000	24,000
13					7,000	31,000
14					7,000	38,000
15					7,000	45,000

The gas-fired boiler is initially cheaper and shows a net saving during year 7. Its projected life span is 10 years and over this period the anticipated savings net of initial expenditure amount to £25,000.

The oil-fired boiler is initially dearer and shows a net saving during year 9. Its projected life span is, however, at 15 years considerably longer and over this period the anticipated savings net of initial expenditure amount to £45,000.

The choice seems to be a balance between the availability of money now, the strength of desire for an earlier rather than a later payback date and the strength of the desire for greater rather than smaller net savings over the whole life period.

DISCOUNTED CASH FLOW

THE CONTEXT

The technique of 'discounting' the cash worth of future transactions (whether for cash expenditure, receipts, losses or savings) is used mainly in the general areas of option or investment appraisal.

Like many techniques, it was first developed in the private sector where interest payments are of fundamental significance, but it is now increasingly applied within the public sector for evaluating, in particular, the future utility of present capital investment. In some cases it is required by statute or regulation and in these cases a discount rate (the test discount rate, see below) is specified.

THE KEY CONCEPTS

The most important concept to grasp is that, because of the interest paid on borrowings or received on investments, transactions which are planned to take place in the future are of less worth in cash terms than apparently identical transactions taking place at the present time.

Four key concepts are involved in performing the relevant calculations:

1. The *cash value* or *raw value* of the future transaction, i.e. the actual money which changes hands or is an anticipated 'loss' or is an anticipated 'saving'.
2. The *distance ahead in years* at which the transaction(s) is(are) predicted to take place. There may be a series of transactions at yearly intervals, each one successively further from the present time.
3. The *interest rate* at which money is borrowed or loaned. In the commercial sector actual current rates or estimates of future rates will be used. In the public sector a *test discount rate* specified by the government or an agency of government is normally employed.
4. The *net present value (NPV)* of the future transaction/loss/saving as calculated by operating on the cash value in the light of its distance ahead in time and the appropriate discount rate.

It must be noted that all these are to do with interest rates. They have nothing to do with inflation.

How and why it works

Consider a person who has £1,000 and invests it at an interest rate of 10 per cent. The growth in cash worth of this sum over three years is as in Table C3.1.

Table C3.1

Year (year 0 is now)	Cash value £
0	1,000
1	1,100
2	1,210
3	1,331

A person who needed £1,331 in three years' time would only need £1,000 today. Conversely, a person expecting to receive £1,331 in three years' time could, on the strength of that expectation, borrow £1,000 today if the interest rate for borrowing was reckoned at 10 per cent.

Another way of putting this is that the *net present value* of £1,331, three years hence at a discounting rate of 10 per cent, is £1,000.

The table can be redrawn slightly differently, putting the emphasis on a final value of £1,000 rather than on an initial value (Table C3.2). The interest rate is still reckoned at 10 per cent.

What this implies is that a future transaction worth £1,000 taking place at the end of year 3, i.e. three years hence, could be substituted by a transaction worth £751 today, i.e. the NPV of £1,000 three years hence at an interest rate of 10 per cent is £751.

Three things need to be stressed:

1. The figures have been rounded for simplicity.
2. In Table C3.1 the figures were obtained by multiplying onwards successively from £1,000 by a factor of 1.1 (i.e. 1 + 10 per cent). In Table C3.2 the figures were obtained by dividing backwards successively from £1,000 by that factor of 1.1.
3. You will find that the tables, allowing for marginal rounding errors, are identical as far as the ratios are concerned. In each case the cash worth in Table C3.2 is approximately 0.751 multiplied by the corresponding cash value in Table C3.1.

Table C3.2

Year (year 0 is now)	Cash worth £
0	751
1	826
2	909
3	1,000

How it works in practice

The conventional way of tackling the question is to use published tables of discounted cash flow factors. These set out the factor to be used for any interest rate from 1 per cent upwards at time distances ranging from 1 year to 25 years or more. The basic calculations have been performed. All the user must do is look up the factor to be used in discounting a future transaction by choosing the right column for interest/discount rate and the right row for distance in time. This will give a factor, say 0.624. If the cash worth of the future transaction is say £2,000, then its NPV is 0.624 × £2,000 = £1,248. Table C3.3 shows discounted cash flow (DCF) factors.

The required calculations are, of course, ideally suited for computer application, and any finance department should have the appropriate application software. It is, nevertheless, helpful to understand the principles involved and to be able to work the calculations out manually, partly because it is required by the syllabi of many academic and professional bodies but, more importantly, because it is in many cases quicker! For this reason a set of graded examples are included.

EXAMPLE: THE GREENHOUSE

An advertisement appears in a gardening magazine. 'Greenhouse £170: nothing to pay until 12 months time!' followed (in small print) by 'or you can pay £150 now'. A reader who knows that the current interest rate for borrowing is 10 per cent is working out which is the better bargain.

Solution

- Payment next year: Price £170   Time 1 year   Discounting factor 0.909   NPV £154
- Payment now: Price £150   Time 0 years   Discounting factor 1.000   NPV £150

It looks as if payment now is the better bargain, as indeed it is in this example. It is worth examining the various figures:

- For 'payment next year' the discounting factor is looked up in Table C3.3. Where the 10 per cent column crosses the year 1 row the figure is 0.909. This is multiplied by the cash value of the future transaction (£170) to give £154.53 which is rounded to £154.
- For 'payment now' the discounting factor does not need to be looked up. For current/present/ 'now' transactions it is always exactly 1.000, whatever the interest rate. The NPV of a current transaction is thus always the same as the monetary value, in this case £150.

EXAMPLE: THE LORRY FLEET

Rothcaster MDC's cleansing department needs five lorries. It has been quoted a price of £20,000 for purchase. The treasurer has advised that loan charges at the rate of £120 for each £1,000 borrowed are payable for 10 years.

The dealer has also quoted a leasing arrangement which would cost £3,300 per year per lorry with an option to purchase at the end of the 7-year lease period for £1,000 per vehicle.

In both cases the first payment is made immediately and subsequent payments on the anniversary of purchase/lease.

The transport manager has stated that he would expect such a lorry to last for at least 10 years before the cost of maintenance and repair became uneconomical.

Table C3.3 DCF factors

Year	5%	6%	7%	8%	9%	10%	11%	12%	13%	14%	15%	20%	25%	30%	40%	50%	Year
1	0.952	0.913	0.935	0.926	0.917	0.909	0.901	0.893	0.885	0.877	0.870	0.833	0.800	0.769	0.714	0.667	1
2	0.907	0.890	0.873	0.857	0.842	0.826	0.312	0.797	0.783	0.769	0.756	0.694	0.640	0.592	0.510	0.444	2
3	0.864	0.840	0.816	0.794	0.772	0.751	0.731	0.712	0.693	0.675	0.658	0.579	0.512	0.455	0.364	0.296	3
4	0.823	0.792	0.763	0.735	0.708	0.683	0.559	0.636	0.613	0.592	0.572	0.482	0.410	0.350	0.260	0.198	4
5	0.784	0.747	0.713	0.689	0.650	0.621	0.593	0.567	0.543	0.519	0.497	0.402	0.328	0.269	0.186	0.132	5
6	0.746	0.705	0.666	0.630	0.596	0.564	0.535	0.507	0.480	0.456	0.432	0.335	0.262	0.207	0.133	0.088	6
7	0.711	0.665	0.623	0.583	0.547	0.513	0.482	0.452	0.425	0.400	0.376	0.279	0.210	0.159	0.095	0.059	7
8	0.677	0.627	0.582	0.540	0.502	0.467	0.434	0.404	0.376	0.351	0.327	0.233	0.168	0.123	0.068	0.039	8
9	0.645	0.592	0.544	0.500	0.460	0.424	0.391	0.361	0.333	0.308	0.284	0.194	0.134	0.094	0.048	0.026	9
10	0.614	0.558	0.508	0.463	0.422	0.386	0.352	0.322	0.295	0.270	0.247	0.162	0.107	0.073	0.035	0.017	10
11	0.585	0.527	0.475	0.421	0.388	0.350	0.317	0.287	0.261	0.237	0.215	0.135	0.086	0.056	0.025	0.012	11
12	0.557	0.500	0.444	0.397	0.356	0.319	0.286	0.257	0.231	0.208	0.187	0.112	0.069	0.043	0.018	0.008	12
13	0.530	0.469	0.415	0.368	0.326	0.290	0.258	0.229	0.204	0.182	0.163	0.093	0.055	0.033	0.013	0.005	13
14	0.505	0.442	0.388	0.340	0.299	0.263	0.232	0.205	0.181	0.160	0.141	0.078	0.044	0.025	0.009	0.003	14
15	0.481	0.417	0.362	0.315	0.275	0.239	0.209	0.183	0.160	0.140	0.123	0.065	0.035	0.020	0.006	0.002	15
16	0.458	0.394	0.339	0.292	0.252	0.218	0.188	0.163	0.142	0.123	0.107	0.054	0.028	0.015	0.005	0.002	16
17	0.436	0.371	0.317	0.270	0.231	0.198	0.170	0.146	0.125	0.108	0.093	0.045	0.023	0.012	0.003	0.001	17
18	0.416	0.350	0.296	0.250	0.212	0.180	0.153	0.130	0.111	0.095	0.081	0.038	0.018	0.009	0.002	0.001	18
19	0.396	0.331	0.277	0.232	0.194	0.164	0.138	0.116	0.098	0.083	0.070	0.031	0.014	0.007	0.002	0.001	19
20	0.377	0.312	0.258	0.215	0.178	0.149	0.124	0.104	0.087	0.073	0.061	0.026	0.012	0.005	0.001	0.001	20
21	0.359	0.294	0.242	0.199	0.164	0.135	0.112	0.093	0.077	0.064	0.053	0.022	0.009	0.004	0.001	0.001	21
22	0.342	0.278	0.226	0.184	0.150	0.123	0.101	0.083	0.068	0.056	0.046	0.018	0.007	0.003	0.001	0.000	22
23	0.326	0.262	0.211	0.170	0.138	0.112	0.091	0.074	0.060	0.049	0.040	0.015	0.006	0.002	0.001	0.000	23
24	0.310	0.247	0.197	0.158	0.126	0.102	0.082	0.066	0.053	0.043	0.035	0.013	0.005	0.002	0.000	0.000	24
25	0.295	0.233	0.184	0.146	0.116	0.092	0.074	0.059	0.047	0.038	0.030	0.010	0.004	0.001	0.000	0.000	25

Table C3.4   Lorry purchase solution

Year	DCF factor	Lease (raw) £	Lease NPV £	Buy (raw) £	Buy NPV £
0	1.000	16,500	16,500	12,000	12,000
1	0.926	16,500	15,279	12,000	11,112
2	0.857	16,500	14,140	12,000	10,284
3	0.794	16,500	13,101	12,000	9,528
4	0.735	16,500	12,127	12,000	8,820
5	0.689	16,500	11,369	12,000	8,268
6	0.630	16,500	10,395	12,000	7,560
7	0.583	5,000	2,915	12,000	6,996
8	0.540	nil	nil	12,000	6,480
9	0.500	nil	nil	12,000	6,000
Totals		120,500	95,826	120,000	87,048

Neglecting any regulations which might apply, would you advise buying or leasing? Use a discount rate (interest rate) of 8 per cent.

Solution

The solution is set out in Table C3.4. You will see from this that the raw figures for leasing and buying are very similar, only £500 different in fact. After discounting, however, it is quite clear that it is more advantageous to buy than to lease. The buying method is well over £8,000 cheaper in terms of NPV.

Discounted cash flow techniques can also be applied to payback forecasts as discussed in Article C2. In order to demonstrate this the example about the hospital boilers can be reworked using a discount rate.

EXAMPLE OF PAYBACK WITH DISCOUNTING: GAS V. OIL

A small hospital is considering two tenders for the supply of a new boiler:

- A gas-fired system will cost an initial £50,000 and it is estimated that it will save £7,500 annually (as compared with the current system) over a 10-year working life.
- An oil-fired system will cost an initial £60,000 and it is estimated that it will save £7,000 annually (as compared with the current system) over a 15-year working life.

Using a discounted cash flow technique draw up a table showing the cash situation for each boiler for the whole of its anticipated working life and comment on the outcomes. Use a discount rate of 10 per cent.

Table C3.5

Year	10% DCF factor	Gas-fired Raw £	NPV £	NPV cumulative £	Oil-fired Raw £	NPV £	NPV cumulative £
0	1.000	− 50,000	− 50,000	− 50,000	− 60,000	− 60,000	− 60,000
1	0.909	+ 7,500	+ 6,817	− 43,183	+ 7,000	+ 6,363	− 53,637
2	0.826	+ 7,500	+ 6,195	− 36,988	+ 7,000	+ 5,782	− 47,855
3	0.751	+ 7,500	+ 5,632	− 31,356	+ 7,000	+ 5,257	− 42,598
4	0.683	+ 7,500	+ 5,112	− 26,244	+ 7,000	+ 4,781	− 37,817
5	0.621	+ 7,500	+ 4,657	− 21,587	+ 7,000	+ 4,347	− 33,470
6	0.564	+ 7,500	+ 4,230	− 17,357	+ 7,000	+ 3,948	− 29,522
7	0.513	+ 7,500	+ 3,847	− 13,510	+ 7,000	+ 3,591	− 25,931
8	0.467	+ 7,500	+ 3,502	− 10,008	+ 7,000	+ 3,269	− 22,662
9	0.424	+ 7,500	+ 3,180	− 6,828	+ 7,000	+ 2,968	− 19,694
10	0.386	+ 7,500	+ 2,895	− 3,933	+ 7,000	+ 2,702	− 16,992
11	0.350				+ 7,000	+ 2,450	− 14,542
12	0.319				+ 7,000	+ 2,233	− 12,309
13	0.290				+ 7,000	+ 2,030	− 10,279
14	0.263				+ 7,000	+ 1,841	− 8,438
15	0.239				+ 7,000	+ 1,673	− 6,765

Solution

The solution is worked out in Table C3.5. From this we can see that the gas-fired system is cheaper because, after discounting, it loses less than the oil-fired system. This is at variance with the figures which were obtained in when the calculation was worked without using discounting.

BREAK-EVENS

THE CONTEXT

Break-even calculations are performed when it is desired to know what quantity of a product must be produced and sold in order to recoup any initial investment. As a modification to this it is possible to perform such calculations to determine the minimum volume of production/sales activity necessary within a fixed time period, say a year, in order to recover not only the initial costs but also irreducible 'overheads' associated with the operation.

Although the technique was developed in manufacturing industry within the private sector as an aid to investment appraisal, it is valid to apply it (with some provisos and modifications) to service provision within the public sector.

THE KEY CONCEPTS

Three essential concepts underpin all break-even calculations:

- The investment which has to be recouped
- The cost of producing any particular item
- The charge which can be made for that item, i.e. the price at which it can be sold

These concepts apply to the simplest 'investment recovery' case. They are supplemented and modified when applied to more complex cases.

The basic formula

If the initial investment is £I, which is spent, say, on a special machine for producing widgets, and the cost of labour, energy and materials per widget produced is £V, and the widget can be sold at price £P, then each widget sold contributes £P − £V towards recovering the investment. This can be written £$(P - V)$.

If the number of widgets to be sold, the break-even quantity, is N, and since the investment was £I, then

$$N \times £(P - V) \text{ must equal } £I$$

or

$$N = I/(P - V)$$

Once that quantity of widgets (N) has been sold, the surplus $£(P - V)$ becomes a 'contribution' to profit. N is thus the minimum sales quantity for profitability.

The term 'contribution' is an important element in solving break-even problems.

The basic formula used to solve a simple example Suppose that a machine for producing widgets costs £2,000. Suppose also that the labour, materials and energy needed to produce each widget total £2. Suppose also that each widget can be sold for £3.

- The contribution of each widget to recovering the fixed cost is £3 − £2 = £1.
- It is thus clear that the number of widgets to be sold to break even is £2,000/£1 = 2,000.

Once 2,000 have been sold the fixed cost has been recovered and the operation has moved into profit.

The formula modified to meet real-life conditions

In reality, break-even calculations are only rarely as simple as this! The most basic complications are threefold:

1. The investment on plant or machinery becomes a capital cost.
2. In addition to the capital cost there are other costs associated with the operation which are independent of the volume of production.
3. The calculation can be performed within the context of a period, usually a year.

The modified formula can then be derived as follows:

Let $£F$ be the total annual fixed cost comprised of capital charges and other organizational fixed costs.

Let $£V$ be the variable cost (e.g. labour, materials, energy) associated with the production of one widget.

Let $£P$ be the charge which can be made for any one widget, i.e. the price.

Let N be the number of widgets to be produced and sold in order to break even.

Then contribution (C) per widget is $£(P - V)$ and so for N widgets the contribution is

$$N \times £(P - V)$$

To break even this must equal the fixed cost, $£F$, and hence:

$$N \times £(P - V) = £F$$

and thus

$$N = F/(P - V)$$

Once N widgets per year have been produced/sold the sale of widgets begins to contribute to the organization's annual profit.

The modified formula used to solve a simple example A widget-making machine is leased by a firm at an inclusive rate of £48,000 per year. It is located in a small factory where the total overheads amount to £52,000 per year. It is worked by operatives paid on a piece work basis of £1 per widget produced and the charge for materials, energy and so on comes to a further £3 per widget. Widgets command a ready sale at £6.50 each.

1. How many widgets must be produced annually for the widget factory to break even?
2. How many widgets must be produced and sold to make a profit of £40,000?
3. If the selling price of widgets falls to £6 owing to competition what effect does this have on break-even and profit figures?

Solution

1. The annual fixed cost is £48,000 + £52,000 = £100,000 (F).
   The variable cost per widget is £1 + £3 = £4 (V).
   The selling price is £6.50 (P).
   The contribution per widget is thus £6.50 − £4 = £2.50 ($P − V$).
   The break-even volume is $F/(P − V)$ and is thus £100,000/£2.50 = 40,000.
2. In order to make a profit of £40,000 a further £40,000/£2.50 widgets must be produced, i.e. 16,000 additional widgets.
3. If the selling price reduces to £6, then the contribution per widget reduces to £2 and thus £100,000/£2, i.e. 50,000 widgets must be produced to break even. For a profit of £40,000, an additional £40,000/£2 widgets must be produced, i.e. 20,000 additional widgets.

Points to note

1. Once the contribution is determined the calculation is straightforward—just divide the fixed costs by the contribution.
2. If a profit is sought (as it is in all commercial operations and may be in a public sector context) then the profit is provided by the contributions of all widgets sold once the break-even point has been achieved.
3. If the selling price of widgets falls the contribution per widget is reduced and thus the number of widgets to achieve break-even and the number of widgets required to achieve a stated profit both increase.

Graphical representations

It is often possible and helpful to represent the calculations in some form of diagram. The two most common of these diagrams are known as the *break-even diagram* and the *profit volume diagram*. They are not quite the same although they are closely related. The way they work will be illustrated in the next two examples. There is also a concept, the *margin of safety*, which will also be covered in both examples.

EXAMPLE OF A BREAK-EVEN CALCULATION INVOLVING A BREAK-EVEN DIAGRAM: NOSHERS

Noshers is a restaurant which has planned sales of 75,000 meals in a year with total receipts of £525,000 from these sales. The average variable cost per meal has been calculated at £4. The total annual fixed costs of the operation are £189,000.

Required

1. Calculate the break-even figure for the restaurant in terms of both number of meals sold and cash sales revenue derived from that number.
2. Calculate the margin of safety built into the plans in terms of number of meals.
3. Illustrate the calculation with a break-even diagram.

Solution

The average price per meal (P) = £525,000/75,000 = £7.
The variable cost per meal (V) has been given as £4.
The contribution per meal (C) is given by the formula $C = P - V$, so C = £7 − £4 = £3.
The break-even number of meals (N) is given by the formula $N = F/C$.
The fixed cost (F) has been given as £189,000, so N = £189,000/£3 = 63,000.
When 63,000 meals have been sold, the total sales income will be 63,000 × £7 = £441,000.

We now need to calculate the margin of safety, which is very simple:

Margin of safety = planned number of meals − break-even number of meals

In this case:

Margin of safety = 75,000 − 63,000 = 12,000 meals

The break-even diagram is shown in Fig. C4.1. Apart from the overall 'shape' of the diagram, which must be understood and memorized, the key fact to recall from your school mathematics is that straight lines are defined by two points. Thus if you know two points on a straight line, you can draw the line.

The break-even diagram consists of five straight lines. The first two lines are known as the *axes*:

1. The *horizontal axis*, which represents 'number', in this case *number sold*.
2. The *vertical axis*, which represents 'money', either *income* or *expenditure*.

The other three lines represent various factors in the calculation:

3. A *horizontal* line, which represents the *fixed cost*.
4. A line which represents the *variable cost* for different quantities of sales. It *slopes upwards* starting from where the fixed cost line crosses the vertical axis.
5. The last is a line which represents the *total income* from different quantities of sales. It *slopes upwards* starting from where the two axes cross (often known as the origin).

The stages in drawing Fig. C4.1 are as follows:

1. Draw the horizontal axis (1) near the bottom of the graph paper and choose a scale which allows for the full range of possible sales from zero to some number larger than break-even. In this case 75,000 is a convenient number as it is the hoped-for sales.
2. Draw the vertical axis (2) up the left-hand side of the graph paper and choose a scale which allows for the full range of possible incomes from zero to some amount larger than the break-even. In this case £525,000 is a convenient number as it is the hoped-for income at the planned sales level.
3. Draw a horizontal straight line (3) from the point on the vertical axis which corresponds to the fixed cost.

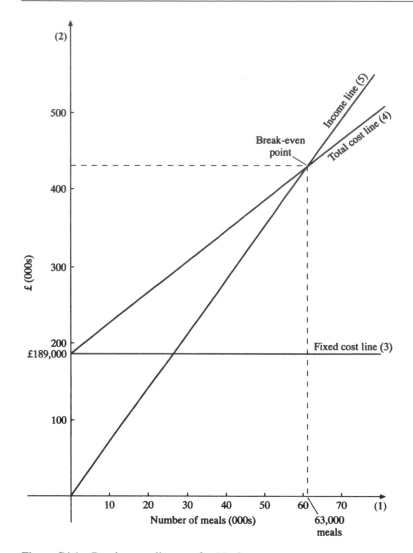

Figure C4.1 Break-even diagram for Noshers

4. Draw an upwardly sloping straight line (4) from the point on the vertical axis which corresponds to the fixed cost through to the total cost (fixed + variable) of producing a certain numbers of items. In this case the total cost of producing 75,000 meals is convenient as it is £189,000 (fixed) + £300,000 (74,000 × £4) = £489,000.

5. Draw an upwardly sloping straight line (5) from the origin (the point where the axes cross) through to the total income produced by selling a certain quantity of items. In this case the total revenue from selling 75,000 meals is hoped to be £525,000, and this is a convenient figure to use.

6. The point where line 5 crosses line 4 is the break-even point and corresponds on the horizontal axis to the number of meals sold (63,000) and on the vertical axis to the income generated by these sales (£441,000).

EXAMPLE OF A BREAK-EVEN CALCULATION INVOLVING A PROFIT VOLUME DIAGRAM: THE PHOTOCOPIER

A public library is considering installing a photocopier for the use of its clients. It has been quoted an annual rental of £1,400 together with a charge for toner, paper and service of 3p per copy. It is proposed to charge clients 10p per sheet for photocopying.

Required

1. Calculate the annual sales of photocopies which must be achieved in order to break even.
2. Illustrate this calculation by means of a profit volume diagram.
3. Use this diagram to show the profit which will be made if annual sales of 30,000 photocopies are achieved.

Solution

The price per copy (P) is 10p (given).
The variable cost per copy (V) is 3p (given).
The contribution (C) is given by the formula $C = P - V$. In this case $C = 10p - 3p = 7p$.
The annual fixed cost (F) is £1,400 (given).
The break-even figure (N) is given by the formula $N = F/C$.

In this case therefore:

$$N = £1,400/7p = 20,000$$

Thus 20,000 photocopies annually must be sold, each of which contributes 7p to recovering the fixed costs of rental.

The profit volume diagram is shown in Fig. C4.2. This is somewhat simpler than the previous diagram in that it has only three straight lines:

1. The vertical axis: this must be put in near the left-hand side of the paper and a zero point inserted about half-way up. Below the zero point represents financial loss. Above the zero point represents financial profit.
2. The horizontal axis: this must be put in through the zero point. It represents quantity sold.
3. The third line slopes upwards from the fixed cost (below the zero point) through the break-even number on the horizontal axis. Once it has passed the break-even point it is above the horizontal axis and represents profit.

The construction of Fig. C4.2 is as follows:

1. The vertical axis is drawn up the left-hand side of the paper and a zero point is marked approximately half-way up this line. The top end is labelled '£ profit' and the bottom end '£ loss'. A scale is chosen to allow for the fixed cost (in this case £1,400) to be marked on the loss part of the line near the lower end.
2. The horizontal axis is then drawn through the zero point and a scale chosen to allow for both the break-even figure (20,000) and the required figure (30,000) to be marked conveniently.
3. A straight line is then drawn sloping upwards from the fixed cost (a loss of £1,400) through the break-even quantity (20,000) and continued. This is the profit volume line.

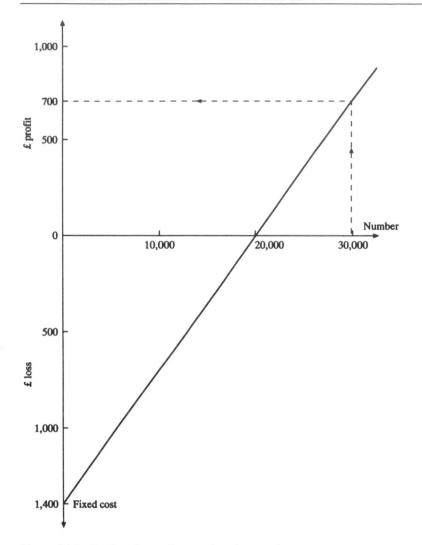

Figure C4.2   Profit volume diagram for photocopier

The question requires us to estimate the profit from sales of 30,000 photocopies. This is done by drawing a dotted line up from 30,000 copies to meet the profit volume line and then drawing a second dotted line horizontally towards the vertical axis which is crossed at £700. This is the annual profit for sales of 30,000.

The explanation of why this works is as follows:

- At zero sales, there is no income and considerable expenditure on the fixed costs. These represent a dead loss.
- At break-even sales, the fixed costs have been exactly balanced by the totality of contributions (total sales less total variable costs).
- These two points are absolutely key and a straight line can be drawn between them and continued.
- Once the fixed costs have been recovered any further sales result in a profit.

COSTING

THE CONTEXT

Costing has already been introduced (in Article B7) as the necessary prerequisite to pricing for an internal market and as a useful discipline in establishing how the total costs of goods or services are made up so that it can be more easily seen where economy or efficiency savings might be made.

It is foolish to expect one article in a more general book to explain all about costing—whole books are written on detailed aspects of the subject and there is a professional qualification, CIMA, which is primarily concerned with costing and its ramifications. Nevertheless, it is the ambition of this article to introduce the key concepts and provide enough material for the reader to be able to understand what the management accountant means when discussing costing matters.

One partial omission is justified on the grounds of length. There is no sustained treatment here of activity-based costing (ABC), a contemporary approach to the subject which focuses on activities rather than goods or units of service. Most modern costing texts contain at least one chapter on the subject and there are, of course, specialist books devoted to the topic.

THE KEY CONCEPTS

There are a number of important distinctions and definitions in the field of costing and they are presented here in the form of a non-alphabetical glossary with examples where appropriate. The glossary is arranged in an order intended to help the reader through various stages in the costing process.

Absorption costing, full costs and marginal costs

Absorption costing This is a technique of attributing the total costs of an organization to the various units of goods and service which it produces by a succession of calculations based on records, estimates and judgements. It is absorption costing which forms the focus of this article.

The full cost For any good or service the full cost may be established within reasonable bounds of accuracy using absorption costing techniques. Thus a car manufacturer can work out the cost of producing one example of a particular model, a civil engineering firm can cost a bridge, a social services department can cost some aspect of service provision for the elderly, or an NHS trust can cost a hip joint operation. Except in the very simplest of cases, for example an organization which produces only one type of good or service which is identically delivered to consumers, no costing is perfect, since there are assumptions, estimates and judgements built into the various processes.

The marginal cost   In contrast to the full cost, this omits the overheads and a number of indirect costs from the calculation. It is thus substantially lower than the full cost of an activity, process or product. It is useful as an aid to pricing once the planned volume of sales/service has been reached. See Article C6.

Direct and indirect costs

A direct cost   Any cost which has directly and clearly to do with the production of any good or service. The chief direct costs are the cost of labour and the cost of materials. The emphasis on each of these will be different for any organization. The public sector is composed of organizations most of which are labour intensive.

An indirect cost   Any cost borne by the organization which has to be attributed in some way (either by allocation or by apportionment) before the full cost of a good or service can be established. Thus the total cost of putting a teacher in a classroom in an LEA school for an hour is not just the £15 which the teacher might get paid for that hour. It includes such indirect costs as:

- The costs of providing and maintaining the teaching premises
- Some of the costs of all those members of staff, e.g. headteacher, secretary, whose job is primarily support rather than service delivery
- Some of the costs of providing an education office to deal with matters affecting all the LEA schools
- Some of the costs of providing the infrastructure of the local authority in which the LEA and thus the school is located

These are only a few of the indirect costs: you can probably think of some more. Some indirect costs are known as overheads.

Cost centres: production and service departments

Cost centre   Any organizational unit, process, activity, good or service to which it is felt useful to ascribe costs. Costs might be organized departmentally, with each department being a cost centre, or on the basis of some project. For the purposes of this article the department will be seen as the main type of cost centre with a distinction being drawn between those departments which are directly providing a service or producing a product (production departments) and those departments which are necessary for the running of the organization but which do not directly produce any saleable good or service (internal service departments).

Production department   Any unit of the organization which directly contributes to the production of goods or services which are bought by or delivered to an external customer/consumer. Thus in private sector manufacturing industry any manufacturing process (including assembly) counts as production. In the public sector any part of the organization which interfaces with the public to provide a service counts as a production department. Examples include teams of social workers in local government or a specialty, say orthopaedics, in an NHS trust.

(Internal) service department Any unit of the organization which contributes to supporting the work of production departments by providing a service within the organization. Thus, whether private or public sector, personnel, marketing, finance or maintenance departments, and many others, count as (internal) service departments. There is a possible confusion in that the public sector is mostly geared to providing services (rather than goods) to the public, but the word 'service' has traditionally been used in this field to refer to service departments (such as personnel) as referred to above. The 'service department' of, say, a washing machine manufacturer, i.e. the department which services and repairs customers' washing machines, is, confusingly, a 'production department' on this account! The acid test is whether the end user of the department is inside or outside of the organization. If inside, then the department is a service department: if outside then the department is a production department.

Key terms in cost attribution: allocation, apportionment and reapportionment

Allocation The process of looking at an indirect cost of some sort and placing it in an appropriate cost centre using some obvious criterion. For example, the cost of servicing a machine is allocated to the department which houses the machine, even though it cannot be directly tied to a particular job.

Apportionment The process of taking an overhead cost of some sort and dividing it up between a number of cost centres on the basis of some rational criterion. For example, the rent of the organization's premises might be apportioned between the various departments on the basis of the floor area which they occupy.

Reapportionment The process of taking the total of indirect costs or overheads which have previously been allocated or apportioned to non-production cost centres and dividing this total between production cost centres on the basis of some rational criterion. For example, the total costs of the personnel department might be reapportioned between the production departments on the basis of the number of employees in each production department.

The process of absorption costing

There are four main stages involved, the first two of which are closely related and often regarded as one stage:

1. (a) The *allocation* of *direct costs* to departments
   (b) The *allocation* of *indirect costs* to departments
2. The *apportionment* of *overhead costs* to departments
3. The *reapportionment* of the *total costs* of service departments to the production departments

The allocation of direct and indirect costs may be performed together, and in examples the substages are often treated as one.

Between these main stages there are some totalling activities. The key to doing absorption costing well is to lay out the material clearly, and this normally means in the form of a table. Before we reach this stage, however, it will prove helpful to illustrate each of the stages in a public sector context, using the example of a science department in a school and the calculation of an average hourly rate for teaching science.

Allocation of direct costs   The salaries of the teachers and laboratory technicians, together with any superannuation and national insurance payments, should be added to the cost of all materials and disposable equipment.

Allocation of indirect costs   Examples of indirect costs which could be easily allocated include any staff development activities, for example in-service courses especially geared to science, and any special equipment bought for science teaching purposes which will last longer than a year. The cost of this equipment has to be 'annualized' in some way, for example by applying a notional rate of interest on its capital value or by estimating that it will last, say, ten years. See Article C8 for a discussion of annualization.

Apportionment of indirect costs   The cost of the school's headteacher and secretary might be apportioned between the various teaching departments on the basis of the number of teaching staff employed. If the school had 100 teaching staff and the science department staff numbered 10, then $10/100 = 10$ per cent of the costs of the headteacher and secretary might be apportioned to the science department. Alternatively, if the school had 120 teaching and non-teaching staff and the science department had 15 staff (including technical support) then the science department might be apportioned $15/120 = 12.5$ per cent of these costs. There is a clear lesson that the apportionment criteria are often negotiable.

Reapportionment of indirect costs   One of the departments of the school which might be regarded as a service department rather than a teaching department is the library. It clearly has costs, direct and indirect, which can be totalled. Suppose they total £30,000 per year. One way of reapportioning the costs to the teaching departments might be to use the criterion of how many students take the various subjects. If 8 per cent of the school's teaching is devoted to science, then it is not unreasonable to reapportion the library's costs at 8 per cent of $£30,000 = £2,400$ to science. Another possible criterion might be on the basis of book stock. If 15 per cent of the library's stock were science books, then it would be equally plausible to argue that 15 per cent of £30,000, i.e. £4,500 should be reapportioned to science.

   It is absolutely necessary from a calculation point of view that the same criteria should be used for each department! It is absolutely necessary from the point of view of actually operating an organization that there should be agreement between the various departments as to how the costs should be apportioned and reapportioned.

Activity-based costing   This modern approach to cost analysis throws the emphasis on to a relatively small number of activities undertaken by an organization and costs each one. British Gas, for example, concentrates on six activities of which meter reading is one. All expenses can be attributed to one of these six activities using the techniques described above.

EXAMPLE OF COSTING PROCEDURES: ANYTOWN COMMUNITY TRUST[1]

Anytown Community Trust has a total budget of £20m. It is organized on a directorate basis, having three directorates (Personnel & Training (PT), Finance & Information (FI) and Maintenance (M)) providing services within the trust and three directorates (On-site Residential (OR), Adult Clinical (AC) and Child Clinical (CC)) providing services to the local community. The chief executive and her immediate support staff cost £120,000 and are accounted for separately, within the budget, and seen as an equal cost for each directorate. The costs of utilities (energy, water, etc.) and premises (capital charges, rates, etc.) are charged to the chief executive, but are divided between the directorates according to criteria set out in the notes below.

The budgeted expenditure is as follows (all budgeted figures in £000):

Chief executive	staff (5 persons)	120	
	non staff	3,000	3,120
Personnel & Training	staff (80 persons)	980	
	non-staff	180	1,160
Finance and Information	staff (100 persons)	1,380	
	non-staff	220	1,600
Maintenance	staff (60 persons)	680	
	non-staff	820	1,500
On-site Residential	staff (240 persons)	2,880	
	non-staff	1,000	3,880
Adult Clinical	staff (300 persons)	2,980	
	non-staff	2,000	4,980
Child Clinical	staff (215 persons)	1,980	
	non-staff	1,780	3,760
			20,000

Notes:

1. Chief executive non-staff costs are to be allocated in the following way: 10 per cent each to PT and FI, 20 per cent each to M, OR, AC and CC.
2. Total PT costs are to be apportioned according to the staffing levels of each directorate.
3. Total FI costs are to be apportioned according to the total costs of each directorate.
4. Total M costs are to be apportioned according to the non-staff costs of each directorate.
5. Any reapportionment is to be calculated according to similar criteria.

Required

1. A table showing the costs listed above allocated and apportioned between directorates according to the criteria indicated and reapportioned from PT, FI and M to those directorates (OR, AC and CC) having direct contact with the local community.
2. The total costs, after allocation, apportionment and reapportionment, of the three community contact directorates.

Solution to Anytown Community Trust

All figures in £000, all calculated figures rounded to nearest £000.

Item	PT	FI	M	OR	AC	CC	Total	Note
Staff	980	1,380	680	2,880	2,980	1,980	10,880	
Add CE staff	20	20	20	20	20	20	120	1
Non-staff	180	220	820	1,000	2,000	1,780	6,000	
Add CE n/s	300	300	600	600	600	600	3,000	2
Total	1,480	1,920	2,120	4,500*	5,600*	4,380*	20,000	3
App PT	119	149	89	357	446	320	1,480	4
App FI	142	184	204	432	538	420	1,920	5
App M	114	122	334	377	612	561	2,119	6
Sub-total	375	455	627	1,166*	1,596*	1,301*	5,519	7
Reapp PT				119	149	107	375	8
Reapp FI				141	176	138	455	9
Reapp M				152	248	227	627	10
Subtotal				412*	573*	472*	1,457	11
Total				6,078	7,769	6,153	20,000	12

Explanation and notes   The first stage is allocation. This is straightforward, except for notes 1 and 2:

1. 120 divided equally by 6 makes 20 in each column.
2. 3000 divided in proportion 10, 10, 20, 20, 20, 20 inserted in each column.
3. A cross-checked total after allocation.

The next stage is apportionment of the costs of the non-contact directorates to all directorates including themselves on the basis of the given criteria. Notes 4, 5 and 6 apply:

4. PT 1,480/995 multiplied by x, where x is staffing numbers for each directorate in turn. Note that the CE and staff have 'got lost' but it does not matter!
5. FI 1,920/20,000 multiplied by y, where y is total costs for each directorate in turn.
6. M 2,120/9,000 multiplied by z, where z is non-staff costs for each directorate in turn.
7. This is a cross-check total after the apportionment of PT, FI and M. Note that there is a small rounding error: 5,519 should be 5,520, but it is of no significance.

   The next stage is reapportionment of the non-contact directorates to the community contact directorates on the basis of similar criteria. Notes 8, 9 and 10 apply:

8. PT 375/755 multiplied by a, where a is staffing numbers for each directorate in turn. Note 755 is the total staffing figure for the community contact directorates.
9. FI 455/14,480 multiplied by b, where b is total costs for each directorate in turn. Note 14,480 is the total costs of the community contact directorates.
10. M 627/6,580 multiplied by c, where c is the non-staff costs of each directorate in turn. Note 6,580 is the total non-staff costs of the community contact directorates.

11. This is a cross-check total after the reapportionment of PT, FI and M. Note that there is a small rounding error: 1,457 should be 1,456, but it is of no significance.

Finally, the totals for each of the community contact directorates may be obtained. Note 12 applies:

12. This gives the total costs for each of the three community contact directorates after initial allocation of costs, subsequent apportionment of non-contact directorate costs and final reapportionment of non-contact directorate costs. The cross-check of the starred subtotals gives confirmation of the accuracy of the calculation.

The solution to the following example is left as an exercise for the reader.

EXAMPLE OF COSTING PROCEDURES: EASTHAMPTON MDC[2]

Easthampton Metropolitan District Council has set up a trading organization, run on commercial lines, within its works department for the purpose of making double glazed units for itself and other local authorities. The windows pass through three production processes, frame forming (F), glass forming (G) and assembly (A). In addition, the organization has two service sections, personnel (P) and maintenance (M).

An enquiry has been received to fulfill an urgent order for 500 special bay windows and the appropriate costing and pricing is being undertaken on the basis of the figures in Table C5.1, obtained from the current year's business plan.

Additional data is as supplied in Table C5.2.

Required

Prepare a statement showing the total costs of operating the three production departments after the costs of the service departments have been reapportioned.

(*Note*: the machine hours and direct labour hours figures given in the last two lines of Table C5.2 will not be needed until a development of this example is considered in Article C6.)

Table C5.1

	Dept F £	Dept G £	Dept A £	Dept P £	Dept M £	Total £
Direct materials	28,000	8,000	7,000	–	–	43,000
Direct labour	10,000	11,000	12,000	–	–	33,000
Indirect materials	2,717	4,221	363	–	3,980	11,281
Indirect labour	7,000	2,000	1,920	–	1,200	12,120
Power (machinery)						16,000
Rates						15,000
Machine insurance						11,000
Canteen expenses						9,000

Table C5.2

	Dept F	Dept G	Dept A	Dept P	Dept M	Total
Machine horsepower	25,000	15,000	7,000	–	3,000	50,000
Floor area, m²	23,000	16,000	12,000	3,000	6,000	60,000
Machinery book value, £	5,000	3,000	2,000	–	1,000	11,000
Employees	6	10	4	1	4	25
Maintenance hours	500	300	200	–	–	1,000
Machine hours	1,800	1,200	600	–	–	3,600
Direct labour hours	800	2,800	800	–	–	4,400

Solution to Easthampton MDC

All figures in £. All calculated figures rounded to the nearest £.

	Production			Service			
Item	F	G	A	P	M	Total	Note
Direct mat.							
Direct lab.							
Subtotal							1
Indirect mat.							2
Indirect lab.							3
Power							4
Rates							5
Machine ins.							6
Canteen							7
Subtotal							8
Reappt P							9
Reappt M							10
Subtotal							11
Total							12

Explanation and notes

1. Subtotal gives total direct costs for the production departments. There can be no direct production costs for non-production (service) departments.
2. Indirect materials costs have already been allocated.
3. Indirect labour costs have already been allocated.
4. Apportion power on the basis of machine horsepower (proportion of 50,000 h.p.).
5. Apportion rates on the basis of area (proportion of 60,000 m²).
6. Apportion machine insurance on the basis of book value (proportion of £11,000).
7. Apportion canteen on the basis of employees (proportion of 25).

8. Note cross-check total of £74,400. This line gives the subtotals of indirect costs after allocation and apportionment but before reapportionment.

9. Personnel is reapportioned on the basis of number of employees in production departments (6/20, 10/20, 4/20).

10. Maintenance is reapportioned on the basis of maintenance hours for production departments (500/1,000, 300/1,000, 200/1,000).

11. This gives the subtotal costs for the re-apportionment. A cross-check is possible: 1,110 + 10,080 = 11,190; 5,373 + 3,579 + 2,238 = 11,190.

12. This, by adding the starred subtotals, gives the total costs of the production departments and a cross-check total of 150,400.

NOTES

1. This trust and its method of organization are completely fictitious. Anyone who actually organized a trust in this grossly oversimplified manner would be making life very difficult for themselves. Nevertheless, the principles of costing can be illustrated through the simple model.

2. This example, set by the author, was included in the Local Government Financial Management paper of the Institute of Chartered Secretaries and Administrators (ICSA) in June 1995. It is included by permission.

PRICING

THE CONTEXT

In the private sector virtually all income is received from the sale of goods or services. It is therefore essential that the price of these goods or services is fixed at a level so as to maximize income, bearing in mind the costs of production of the goods or delivery of the service and an estimate of the willingness of potential purchasers to buy at any given price.

In the public sector a very high proportion of income derives ultimately from taxation and a much lower proportion of income derives from the sale of goods or, more usually, services. Furthermore, these goods and services are directed at different sectors of the community and the price charged for them varies on a spectrum from completely free to a full commercial price. For example:

- Free: primary school education, NHS prescriptions for pensioners
- Nominal charge: NHS dental inspection, use of music library
- Subsidized charge: NHS prescription lenses, many local authority leisure activities
- Full price: rents for council dwellings, NHS charges to private sector for services

There are, of course, many other examples in each category.

In addition to charges levied on clients/customers external to the organization, there is also the important question of the prices to be levied within an internal market situation, and the complicating factor of prices to be levied internally when there is, possibly as a result of legislation, external competition to provide the same good or service.

One dimension of the context of pricing is therefore the nature of the public sector as a service provider funded predominantly from taxation, while another is the dimension of providing value for money (the reasoning behind the internal market) while yet another is potential competition. Finally, the context of all pricing is rooted in costing. Without accurate knowledge of the costs of a good or service, it is not possible to know either the degree of subsidy or the 'correct' commercial price. Costing has been dealt with in outline in Article B7 and more fully in Article C5.

THE KEY CONCEPTS

The main private sector models of pricing for external purchasers are: *full cost plus*, *marginal cost plus*, *competition* and *what the market will bear*. Any individual pricing decision will be based on one of these models or a combination of two or more. The public sector also uses these models, but the decision as to how to use them depends upon political factors, statute and the nature of the client as well as upon commercial considerations.

The two sectors also have to decide prices for internal markets. Here the main models are *full cost*, *full cost minus*, *competition* and *distorted full cost*. Again, any of these models may be used singly or in combination.

Full cost This is just what it says. A proper calculation of cost, probably based on absorption methods as discussed in Article C5, is carried out for any good or service. It is likely that this calculation has been done very accurately in the private sector and that the public sector is learning rapidly both the importance of the calculation and the ways of doing it.

It must be stressed that there is (except in very simple cases) no such thing as a perfect cost calculation—there are always estimates of proportions, choices of criteria and judgements as to weightings which must be made—and therefore that any costing exercise could lead to a range of 'correct' solutions. In labour intensive organizations, such as most parts of the public sector, this range is not likely to be enormous provided all labour costs are attributed in some way to each activity and that the total indirect cost/overheads of the organization are also included in some rational manner.

Full cost plus This is simply full cost with a percentage 'mark-up'. The mark-up is what leads to profit in the private sector and indeed in some parts of the public sector, for example local authority direct labour organizations which are required by statute to make a 5 per cent return on capital. The most likely method of calculating full cost is some form of absorption costing, although activity-based costing (ABC) methods might have more bearing in the next decade.

Full cost minus This is simply full cost with a percentage mark-down. The retail branch of the private sector regularly uses this method as a means of inducing customers to purchase. 'Loss leaders' are items, e.g. sugar, which may be well advertised and sold cheaply in order to get customers into a store where they will, it is hoped, buy other profit-making items. This specialized usage has no deliberate application in the public sector (although it may occur if the full cost calculations are not done anything like correctly!), but it is used in both public and private sectors as an internal transfer rate. This can both motivate potential competition to bring down its prices and make it not worth while for internal purchasers to go outside the system.

Distorted full cost This is based on a deliberate miscalculation of full cost. The most obvious way that this can be done is to misallocate central establishment charges away from front line departments which have to compete in an external environment. This has the effect of making their services appear cheaper while the services of other departments, in consequence, appear dearer. It must be remembered that any costing system has to locate the total costs of the organization somewhere and therefore that if some aspect of costs is not allocated in one place it must be allocated somewhere else. There is some evidence that local authorities in the early to mid-1980s protected their direct labour organizations in this way, and that in the late 1980s and early 1990s those aspects of service required by legislation to compete for work were likewise protected. It is, of course, impossible to protect the whole organization in this manner! Sooner or later the full cost calculation must be done properly and the overhead costs attributed in line with financial rather than political criteria.

Marginal cost plus   This can be used when the organization has achieved or nearly achieved its targets for sales and is based on the direct costs of any operation rather than its full costs. Personal experience tells us that the full cost of running a car (which includes capital costs, garage cost, tax and insurance) may be, say, 40p per mile whereas the marginal cost for an extra mile is not far different from the cost of the fuel, say 8p per mile. If we reckon on covering a certain annual mileage, say 8,000 miles per year, then once that figure is reached we may legitimately cost any extra miles at the marginal rate. The same is true in any organization: once it has reached its planned sales output and therefore the customers have paid the organization's overheads, it is legitimate to relax the pricing regime and, maybe, reduce the price for additional items to favoured customers.

Competition   This is an important guide to pricing. If the customer can get goods or services of equivalent quality more cheaply and conveniently elsewhere, then sooner or later most customers will do so! Thus in any situation of genuine competition it is imperative that the organization keeps its eyes fixed on what competitors are charging. This is a serious matter for all organizations, both public and private sector.

What the market will bear   This is a pricing technique used for certain goods and services which has little if anything to do with costs and a great deal to do with accurately estimating what customers are prepared to pay for what are essentially overpriced items of goods or services! The private sector worlds of fashion and entertainment provide many examples. The justifications for high prices include risk, exclusivity and the value added by the skill of performers. The public sector has little if anything to compare, but an inversion of the technique might be applied if the notion of subsidy is considered. If the potential customers are poor, then a service can be priced down in order to make it available to them.

HOW THESE PRICING TECHNIQUES MAY BE APPLIED IN THE PUBLIC SECTOR

It is worth first reiterating the distinction between pricing in competitive and non-competitive situations. The public sector is increasingly in competitive situations with regard to tendering, but whereas the private sector must in general make a profit on the sale of its goods and services, the public sector is required only to break even or to make a notional profit. It should therefore be in a position of advantage with respect to tendering. On the other hand, it is frequently alleged that public sector costs are higher than need be, by which is often meant that the direct costs of service provision are more than they need be and/or that the overhead costs of departmental and organizational administration are unduly high. There is an added complication in that, until comparatively recently, the public sector's capital accounting was poor and the costs of capital were not necessarily included accurately in calculating prices: in some cases they were not included at all.

The starting point must be an accurate costing exercise. The organization must know what its various activities cost on a fair and reasonable basis of cost attribution, including a reasonable estimate of capital costs. It must also have a realistic understanding of the volume of service activity which is demanded by potential clients and the pressures of increasing value for money. Once it has these figures it is in a position to decide on what basis to price.

If the basis is not to be 'full cost' or 'full cost plus', where the 'plus' is a stipulated notional rate of return, then the justification for departure must be made explicit and the implications for other parts of the organization must be appreciated. The possibilities as discussed above are:

- 'Distorted full cost', in which case other parts of the organization absorb more of the overheads than they should and thus their costs are inflated. This will make it harder for them to sell in a competitive situation.
- 'Marginal cost plus', which should be used only when the department has reached its planned level of activity, which should not be set artificially low. One use of marginal costing is where an NHS trust sells its services for a certain volume priced at full cost and then specifies that any additional service in the same area may be charged for at a price derived from the marginal cost.
- What the market will bear, which, as has been indicated, applies in an inverse way in the public sector as a question of subsidies. If this is to be the case, it must be quite clear where the subsidy is coming from. It may be from central government, it may be from other users of the service or it may be from other departments. In the case of local government it may be from locally raised taxes. All these possibilities raise different questions of principle and pose different practical implementational problems.

The fixing of an internal transfer rate raises a set of very interesting problems. In one sense it must be competitive—or else the internal purchasers will wish to purchase from outside the organization. In another sense it does not matter what it is as long as it is well understood and is the same throughout the organization.

The nub of the problem lies in the distinction between what are often colloquially referred to as 'real money' and 'funny money':

- If an organization buys a service from outside then it pays with real money—a cheque is written—and that money is no longer available to fund any service within the organization.
- If a department within an organization buys a service from another department within the same organization, then the transaction is a paper transaction: no real money has changed hands and the resources of the organization are not diminished. What has happened is that the basic distribution of (human) resources within the organization has been legitimized with each transaction. The purchaser department recognizes the right of the provider department to its share of the total organizational resources in terms of level of resource and level of activity.

If an organization has got its resourcing about right and the level of activity of each department is recognized as comparable in terms of value for money, then there will be no problems with regard to internal transfers of 'funny money'. If any of these factors are wrong, then sooner or later a purchaser department will wish to spend real money in the outside world on purchasing something which could be obtained, maybe not very well and maybe (apparently) rather expensively, from within the organization.

When this occurs strategic management should recognize the problem and look for ways of alleviating it. One such way is to fix the transfer price low enough to remove the temptation to spend outside the organization while retaining some credible link with full cost. This is only a stopgap. The real solution is to get the balance of organizational resource and service delivery right. The transfer price then becomes almost irrelevant.

EXAMPLE OF PRICING: ANYTOWN COMMUNITY TRUST (continued)

Using the cost figures established in Article C5 for this NHS trust, calculate full cost figures for prices to be charged to external consumers (purchasers) for:

1. An average hour of the time of a clinician in the Adult Clinical directorate; and
2. One resident-day in the On-site Residential directorate.

Comment on any particular features of the calculations or their outcomes.
    Use the following notes for guidance:

1. The Adult Clinical directorate has 250 clinicians (all grades and types) who are each scheduled to work for 225 days at 7.5 hours per day.
2. The On-site Residential directorate has 1,000 beds, with an occupancy rate of 90 per cent.
3. A mark-up of 5 per cent is considered appropriate.

Solution to Anytown Community Trust (continued)

1. Total cost for Adult Clinical directorate = £7,769,000 (previously calculated).
    Total clinician working hours = $250 \times 225 \times 7.5 = 421,875$ hrs.
    So average cost per hour = £7,769,000/421,875 = £18.42 per hr.
    Thus, including 5 per cent mark-up, price to purchaser would be £19.36 per hr.
2. Total cost for On-site Residential directorate = £6,078,000 (previously calculated).
    Number of resident-days = $1,000 \times 365 \times 90\% = 328,500$ resident-days.
    So average cost per resident day = £6,078,000/328,500 = £18.50 per resident-day.
    Thus, including 5 per cent mark-up, price to purchaser would be £19.43 per resident-day.

The salaries of clinicians vary enormously and it might be better to break clinicians down into categories, for example medical staff, paramedical staff and nurses. If this were done some form of apportionment of overheads would have to be performed within the directorate.
    The justification for the 5 per cent mark-up is to allow for unexpected variation in costs (upwards) or throughput (downwards) and to make a 'safety margin' to allow for marginal costing/pricing for additional work.

EXAMPLE OF PRICING: EASTHAMPTON MDC (continued)

Using the cost figures established in Article C5 for this works department double glazing organization, and the information contained in the last two lines of Table C5.2, calculate:

1. Appropriate overhead apportionment rates (OARs) for the three production departments, Frame forming, Glass forming and Assembly
2. A price to be charged for a special order for 500 bay windows

Use the information in the following notes to support the calculation:

1. The estimate from the production departments as to the costs per window are as follows:
    Per window   Direct materials   £400
                   Direct labour   8 hours at £7.50 per hour
                   Frame forming   3 machine hours
                   Glass forming   2 machine hours
                   Assembly   4 direct labour hours
2. A mark-up of 20 per cent of cost price is to be applied.

Solution to Easthampton MDC (continued)

1. The appropriate OAR for Frame forming (Ff) is based on machine hours and is equal to total Ff overheads divided by estimated Ff annual machine hours:

(£30,627 + £5,373)/1,800 machine hrs = £36,000/1,800 machine hrs = £20 per machine hr

The appropriate OAR for Glass forming (Gf) is similarly based on machine hours:

(£21,621 + £3,579)/1,200 machine hrs = £25,200/1,200 machine hrs = £21 per machine hr

The appropriate OAR for Assembly is based on direct labour hours and is equal to total Assembly overheads divided by estimated Assembly direct labour (dl) hours:

(£10,962 + £2,238)/800 dl hrs = £13,200/800 dl hrs = £16.50 per dl hr

2. The cost for window is thus (all in £s):

Direct materials		400
Direct labour	8 × £7.50	60
Frame forming overhead	3 × £20	60
Glass forming overhead	2 × £21	42
Assembly overhead	4 × £16.50	66
Total cost		628
Add mark up 20 per cent		125.60
Price per window		753.60

So for 500 windows the full price would be £376.800.

VARIANCE ANALYSIS

THE CONTEXT

There are two dimensions/emphases to the context of the analysis of variances.

The first, which has its origins in the private sector, is an emphasis on changes in the direct costs of the production of manufactured goods owing to a number of factors of which those to do with the costs of labour and materials are the most important. In forecasting the costs of production certain assumptions, termed 'standard costs', are made. If these assumptions prove incorrect in practice, then there are consequential 'variances' which can be analysed according to relatively simple techniques.

The second, which has its origins in the public sector, is an emphasis on differences between the actual costs of running an operation and the budgeted costs. Variances are the differences between forecast and actual figures appearing on budgetary control statements and have been discussed in Articles B2 and B3.

The two can be linked if, in addition to the public sector emphasis on how much a service costs to provide, we add a dimension of quantified output. If it is expected that a service costing £30,000 will yield 1,500 outputs at a cost of £20 each, then if there are overspends on costs, say to £33,000 and underachievements on output, say to 1,320, then the cost per output rises to £25. The private sector technique of analysing variances can be applied to the public sector case to see how much of the £5 per output increase in cost is due to overspend and how much is due to underachievement.

Of course there are parts of the public sector, say works or buildings departments, where the private sector technique is directly applicable with little modification.

It must be added that the analysis of variance presented here is very basic and concentrates on two sets of factors only: those to do with labour and those to do with materials. A fuller treatment, to be found in any standard costing text, would include several other factors.

THE KEY CONCEPTS

It must be stressed that this is a very much simplified treatment of the subject covering only a limited range of causes of variance. The *variance* (V) we are looking for is the difference between the *actual cost* (AC) of producing an item (be it a manufactured item or a unit of service) and the *standard cost* (SC) (the cost predicted on the basis of forecasts of labour and materials costs):

$$\text{Variance} = \text{standard cost} - \text{actual cost}$$

or:

$$V = SC - AC \qquad (C7.1)$$

Note: convention dictates that a negative variance is adverse, i.e. against us, while a positive sign is favourable, i.e. benefits us.

The standard cost is made up of two elements, *standard labour cost* and *standard material cost*:

$$\text{Standard cost} = \text{standard labour cost} + \text{standard material cost}$$

The standard labour cost is made up by multiplying two elements, the *standard hours* (SH), i.e. the predicted time for the job, and the *standard rate* (SR), i.e. the predicted hourly pay rate:

$$\text{Standard labour cost} = \text{standard hours} \times \text{standard rate}$$
$$= \text{SH} \times \text{SR}$$

The standard material cost is made up by multiplying two elements, the *standard quantity* (SQ), i.e. the predicted amount of material needed for the job, and the *standard price* (SP), i.e. the predicted unit price of the material:

$$\text{Standard material cost} = \text{standard quantity} \times \text{standard price}$$
$$= \text{SQ} \times \text{SP}$$

Therefore:

$$SC = (SH \times SR) + (SQ \times SP) \qquad (C7.2)$$

Note: in working out the value of standard cost given by this formula it is essential to do the multiplying operations before the addition operation.

If we substitute the letter A (for actual) for the letter S (for standard) we can obtain a formula which corresponds to the above in all respects except that it is dealing with outcomes/actuals rather than predictions/forecasts:

$$AC = (AH \times AR) + AQ \times AP \qquad (C7.3)$$

An example to illustrate the use of the formulae

A householder plans to have a brick wall built, and estimates that it will use 800 bricks costing 22p each, and that it will take a bricklayer 5 hours at a rate of £10 per hour. In the event the wall uses 1,000 bricks costing 19p each and the bricklayer takes 6 hours at a rate of £9 per hour. Calculate the standard and the actual costs and hence the variance.

From (C7.2):

$$SC = (5 \times 10) + (800 \times 0.22) = £50 + £176 = £226$$

From (C7.3):

$$AC = (6 \times 9) + (1000 \times 0.19) = £54 + £190 = £244$$

And hence from (C7.1):

$$\text{Variance} = SC - AC = £226 - £244 = -£18 \text{ (negative, and therefore adverse)}$$

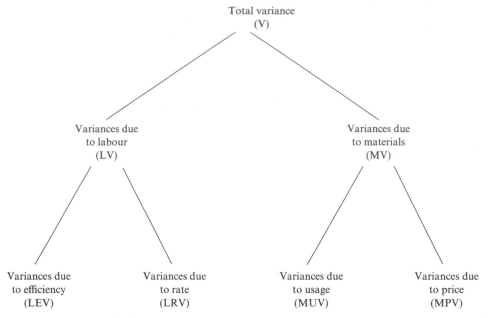

Figure C7.1 Analysis of variance

At this stage it may well be objected that all this is a matter of common sense and that we do not need formulae to work out what is essentially a very simple problem. That is absolutely true, but we do need the formulae to go on to the next stages of the argument, which enables us first to split the total variance into variance due to labour factors and variance due to materials factors, and then to split each of these into pairs of subvariances due to the four differences between standards (forecasts) and actuals (outcomes).

The first stage is the separation of total variance into variance due to incorrect labour forecasts and variance due to incorrect materials forecasts (Fig. C7.1). We can obtain three formulae:

$$\text{Variance, V} = \text{LV} + \text{MV} \qquad (C7.4)$$

$$\text{Labour variance, LV} = (\text{SH} \times \text{SR}) - (\text{AH} \times \text{AR}) \qquad (C7.5)$$

$$\text{Materials variance, MV} = (\text{SQ} \times \text{SP}) - (\text{AQ} \times \text{AP}) \qquad (C7.6)$$

We can test out the validity of these formulae using the figures from the example.

From (C7.5):

$$\text{LV} = (5 \times 10) - (6 \times 9) = £50 - £54 = -£4$$

From (C7.6)

$$\text{MV} = (800 \times 0.022) - (1000 \times 0.19) = £176 - £190 = -£14$$

And hence from (C7.4).

$$V = LV + MV = -£4 + -£14 = -£18 \text{ (negative/adverse)}$$

The second stage is to split the variances into four components each due to incorrect forecasts of the four factors which go into making up the original estimate. We can obtain two sets of formulae, each having three equations.

Set 1 (to do with labour)

Labour variance = labour efficiency variance + labour rate variance

$$LV = LEV + LRV \tag{C7.7}$$

Labour efficiency variance = standard rate (standard hours − actual hours)

$$LEV = SR(SH - AH) \tag{C7.8}$$

Labour rate variance = actual hours (standard rate − actual rate)

$$LRV = AH(SR - AR) \tag{C7.9}$$

Set 2 (to do with materials)

Materials variance = materials usage variance + materials price variance

$$MV = MUV + MPV \tag{C7.10}$$

Materials usage variance = standard price (standard quantity − actual quantity)

$$MUV = SP(SQ - AQ) \tag{C7.11}$$

Materials price variance = actual quantity (standard price − actual price)

$$MPV = AQ(SP - AP) \tag{C7.12}$$

These formulae have not just come 'out of the blue': they are logically derived from the successive splitting up of the total variance. (A 'proof' that they are valid for anyone who is interested in following the argument is provided at the end of this article[1]. It is not essential to follow this proof provided that the formulae are either learnt or easily to hand.)

EXAMPLE OF VARIANCE ANALYSIS: COOKESVILLE CATERERS

Cookesville Caterers provide refectory meals for the students of Cookesville University. It is anticipated that a week's catering can be provided at a total cost of £48,000 for food (48,000 units at £1.00 each) and £24,000 for labour (6,000 hours at £4.00 per hour on average). In fact the first week of operation costs £59,400 for food (54,000 units at £1.10 each) with labour costs being only £22,400 (6,400 hours at £3.50 per hour on average).

Perform a variance analysis using these figures and suggest reasons for any variances which you detect.

Solution to Cookesville Caterers

Stage 1 Identify the key terms for one week.

Standard quantity, SQ = 48,000 units   Actual quantity, AQ = 54,000 units

Standard price, SP = £1.00 per unit   Actual price, AP = £1.10 per unit

Standard hours, SH = 6,000 hours   Actual hours, 6,400 hours

Standard rate, SR = £4 per hour   Actual Rate, AR = £3.50 per hour

Stage 2 Working out total variance and labour/materials variances without using formulae.

Labour variance = £24,000 − £22,400 = £1,600 (positive, i.e. favourable)

Materials variance = £48,000 − £59,400 = −£11,400 (negative, i.e. adverse)

Total variance = labour variance + materials variance

$$= £1,600 + −£11,400 = −£9,800 \text{ (negative, i.e. adverse)}$$

Stage 3 Application of formulae.

Labour efficiency variance, LEV = SR(SH − AH) = £4(6,000 − 6,400)

$$= £4 × −400 = −£1,600 \quad \text{i.e. £1,600 adverse}$$

Labour rate variance, LRV = AH(SR − AR)

$$= 6,400(£4 − £3.50)$$

$$= 6,400 × 50p$$

$$= +£3,200 \quad \text{i.e. £3,200 favourable}$$

Materials usage variance, MUV = SP(SQ − AQ) = £1(48,000 − 54,000)

$$= £1 × −6,000$$

$$= −£6,000 \quad \text{i.e. £6,000 adverse}$$

Materials price variance, MPV = AQ(SP − AP) = 54,000(£1 − £1.10)

$$= 54,000 × −10p$$

$$= −£5,400 \quad \text{i.e. £5,400 adverse}$$

We may check these variances against our previous calculations:

Labour variance = £1,600 adverse + £3,200 favourable = £1,600 favourable as before

Materials variance = £6,000 adverse + £5,400 adverse = £11,400 adverse as before

Total variance = £1,600 favourable + £11,400 adverse = £9,800 adverse as before

Comment on variances

- *Labour*   It is often the case that cheaper labour takes longer for any task, but in this case we do not know whether the production was higher thus leading to a reduction in average labour price as managerial time decreases in proportion to operative time. A higher throughput could also explain the increase in labour time.
- *Materials*   We do not know how many meals were actually produced and so cannot comment on whether the higher materials usage was due to wastage or additional production. We do know that the price per unit was higher than anticipated.
- *Overall*   We cannot make an informed comment as we would need to know the total volume of meals produced and sold. It might well be that the apparently serious adverse variance was offset in part or in whole by increased sales revenue.

EXAMPLE OF VARIANCE ANALYSIS: SEAHAM SECRETARIAL

Seaham Secretarial is the in-house contracting service which provides the central word-processing facility for Seaham District Council. Its business plan for 1994–95 included the following estimates:

Documents to be generated	18,000 A4 pages
Material to be used (paper, binders, etc.)	18,000 units at 5p per unit = £900
Staff time	6,400 hours
Total staff pay	£38,400

As a result of its first year's activities the following outcomes were noted:

Documents generated	20,000 A4 pages
Material used (paper, binders, etc.)	30,000 units at 4p per unit = £1,200
Staff time	8,000 hours
Total staff pay	£40,000

Perform a variance analysis using these figures and suggest reasons for any variances which you detect. Comment on any management action which might follow from your analysis.

Solution to Seaham Secretarial

Preliminary stage   Reduction of actual figures to basis of forecast output.

The planned spending was £39,300. The actual spending was £41,200. The variance therefore was apparently £39,300 − £41,200 = −£1,900, i.e. £1,900 adverse. However, in addition to the causes of variance so far discussed, some of this total variance was due to producing more documents than expected.

As a preliminary calculation, it is necessary to reduce the outcome figures for material quantity used and staff time to the base of 18,000 forecast produced rather than the 20,000 which were actually produced. The factor is 18,000/20,000, i.e. 0.9 or 90 per cent, and the outcome figures for quantity and hours must be reduced by this factor. The cost for each unit of materials and each hour of time is unchanged.

Stage 1 Identify key terms for year's activity.

Standard quantity, SQ = 18,000 units   Actual quantity, AQ = 27,000 units
                                        (0.9 × 30,000)

Standard price, SP = 5p per unit   Actual price, AP = 4p per unit

Standard hours, SH = 6,400   Actual hours, AH = 7,200   (0.9 × 8,000)

Standard rate, SR = £6 per hour   Actual rate, AR = £5 per hour

Stage 2 Working out total variance and labour/ materials variances without using formulae.

Labour variance = £38,400 − £36,000 = £2,400 (positive, i.e. favourable)

Materials variance = £900 − £1,080 = −£180 (negative, i.e. adverse)

Total variance = labour variance + materials variance

$$= £2,400 + −£180 = £2,220 \text{ (positive, i.e. favourable)}$$

Stage 3 Application of formulae.

Labour efficiency variance, LEV = SR(SH − AH)

$$= £6(6,400 − 7,200)$$
$$= £6 × −800$$
$$= −£4,800 \quad \text{i.e. } £4,800 \text{ adverse}$$

Labour rate variance, LRV = AH(SR − AR)

$$= 7,200(£6 − £5)$$
$$= 7,200 × £1$$
$$= £7,200 \quad \text{i.e. } £7,200 \text{ favourable}$$

Materials usage variance, MUV = SP(SQ − AQ)

$$= 5p(18,000 − 27,000)$$
$$= 5p × −9,000$$
$$= −£450 \quad \text{i.e. } £450 \text{ adverse}$$

Materials price variance, MPV = AQ(SP − AP)

$$= 27,000(5p − 4p)$$
$$= 27,000 × 1p$$
$$= £270 \quad \text{i.e. } £270 \text{ favourable}$$

We may check these variances against our previous calculations:

Labour variance = £4,800 adverse + £7,200 favourable = £2,400 favourable as before

Materials variance = £450 adverse + £270 favourable = £180 adverse as before

Comment on variances

- *Labour* The adverse labour efficiency variance may have been due to using cheaper and less efficient staff. It is also possible that the initial estimate of how much work the staff could do may have been optimistic.

The positive labour rate variance was undoubtedly due to this factor and outweighed the apparent inefficiency of the staff.

- *Materials* There was a considerable (50 per cent) overusage of materials, an apparent wastage, and this may have been due to the inefficiency of cheaper staff. It could also have been due to an initial underestimate in wastage rate. Either way, this underlies the materials usage variance.

   The overusage was partially offset by the reduction in material price which underlies the materials price variance.

- *Management action* At first sight there is no need for any management action. The adverse variance was relatively small on the materials front which is not very significant in regard to the cost of labour. The labour variance was favourable and the output of the service was more than expected.

   This apparently satisfactory situation conceals, however, the need for an increase in productivity (thus improving the labour efficiency variance) and a considerable reduction in wastage (thus improving the materials usage variance). At the same time efforts should be made to maintain the supply of the cheaper materials and to keep down the average hourly cost of labour.

NOTE

1. Total variance = labour variance + materials variance

$$= \text{LEV} + \text{LRV} + \text{MUV} + \text{MPV} \qquad \text{(from C7.7 and C7.10)}$$

$$= \text{SR(SH} - \text{AH)} + \text{AH(SR} - \text{AR)} + \text{SP(SQ} - \text{AQ)} + \text{AQ(SP} - \text{AP)}$$
(from C7.8, C7.9, C7.11, C7.12)

These terms are then muliplied out:

Total variance = $\text{SR} \times \text{SH} \underline{- \text{SR} \times \text{AH} + \text{AH} \times \text{SR}} - \text{AH} \times \text{AR}$

$+ \text{SP} \times \text{SQ} \underline{- \text{SP} \times \text{AQ} + \text{AQ} \times \text{SP}} - \text{AQ} \times \text{AP}$

The underlined terms then cancel, leaving:

Total variance = $\text{SR} \times \text{SH} - \text{AH} \times \text{AR} + \text{SP} \times \text{SQ} - \text{AQ} \times \text{AP}$

$$= \text{LV} + \text{MV} \qquad \text{(from C7.5 and C7.6)}$$

We have thus worked back from the complex formulae to the simple formula. This is not a proof as such, but it is a demonstration that there is consistency in the formulae and that the four subequations (C7.8, C7.9, C7.11, C7.12) can be derived from the basic formulae which in turn are merely symbols added to common sense!

COST OF CAPITAL

THE CONTEXT

Any contemporary discussion of capital in the public sector must have at least two contexts in which it should be located:

1. The fact that within local government and the NHS, the distinction between capital and revenue (both as income and as expenditure) is clear, based on statute and reasonably well understood at all levels of the respective service. Central government did not draw the distinction, for its own purposes, until recently, but now the capital and revenue expenditure of all government departments is itemized separately.
2. The understanding, which is at the root of all commercial undertakings, that the investment of capital is a means of generating profits and that, within an organization, capital investment is justified in terms of expansion or effecting labour savings (both of which increase the capacity for making profits) or improving quality of output, thus enhancing the value of the product and increasing the organization's credibility in the market place.

Chapter 2 included an extended discussion, in non-numerical terms, of the distinction between capital and revenue, the connections between capital and revenue and the place of capital controls. This article attempts to build a more technical understanding of these matters in financial management terms.

THE KEY CONCEPTS

There are four senses in which public capital expenditure may be said to have a cost:

1. If the expenditure is financed directly from revenue (as is perfectly permissible within limits in both local government and the NHS and was standard practice within central government until recently) there is an *opportunity cost*, i.e. the money cannot be spent on something else which might be valued.
2. If the expenditure is financed (as is usually the case with local government and is increasingly the case with the NHS) from borrowing there are the *costs of borrowing*, i.e. the interest charges and loan repayment/debt redemption.
3. Once the expenditure has been undertaken and a capital asset purchased, there are inescapable *costs associated with ownership and utilization*.
4. Any asset once bought depreciates, i.e. loses its resale value over a period of years, and this *depreciation* represents a cost to the organization.

Each of these types of cost should be understood. The first is not usually a financial cost and will be treated briefly: the others undoubtedly are financial costs and will be treated at more length.

Opportunity cost[1]   This may be defined loosely as the costs of not doing something. In the commercial world this involves mapping the anticipated cash flows (both expenditure and income) of a series of possible actions over a number of years and considering what action, if any, to take in the light of such mapping. In the public sector the notion of investment bringing income is not so well understood, and thus the comparisons are usually in terms of non-numerical benefits associated with different potential capital expenditure.

The costs of borrowing   Referred to in local government as 'debt/loan charges', these comprise two elements, *interest charges* and *capital repayment charges*, which are analogous to the charges experienced by any private person who borrows money, for example through a mortgage for the purpose of house purchase. Just as a private person meets mortgage repayments from his or her regular income, these charges are ultimately met from the revenue income of public authorities and count as revenue expenditure.

There is a technical distinction between a loan (which must be repaid on a certain date) and a debt (which must be redeemed over a certain period). A debt is often financed by a series of loans, for example local authority buildings may be financed over sixty years. Few lenders are willing to have their money tied up over this period and so a series of loans, each for say three to five years, is arranged and the repayment of each loan is financed by the next loan. Interest is charged on the various loans, in sequence, at a rate of interest which is determined by conditions which prevail when the loan is taken out. This accounts for the interest aspect of the debt charge.

During the period of the debt, money must, in theory, be set aside on a regular basis so that when the term of the debt expires (concurrently with the term of the final loan) there is sufficient money available in what is termed a 'sinking fund' to repay the final loan and in so doing to redeem the debt. This sum of money set aside accounts for the capital repayment aspect of the debt charge.

If the permitted period of borrowing is for a shorter period, say five years for a vehicle, the debt and the loan will probably become the same: debt redemption and loan repayment are therefore not just concurrent, they are actually the same.

In practice, all these matters are looked after within a section of the treasurer's department which almost certainly operates a 'consolidated loans pool'. Such a pool aggregates debts, loans, interest charges and sinking funds into one large fund, covering all the borrowing of the organization, from which individual items of borrowing cannot readily be extracted.

This does not invalidate the principle of having two aspects to the charges. Interest on a variety of loans has to be met. Redemption of debt has to be fulfilled on due date within, for local government, a statutory limit depending on the nature of the original expenditure, e.g. five years for vehicles, sixty years for buildings.

The ordinary 'non-financial' manager needs to know how much any past borrowing cost or any intended borrowing will cost. To this end, organizations usually produce guides to the cost of borrowing based on the current average of the consolidated loans pool. It is impossible to be precise, but with the current (1996) relatively low rates of interest charges a figure of between £100 and £120 annually for each £1,000 borrowed would not be far out.

The costs of ownership and utilization   These include the maintenance necessary to ensure that the asset remains fit for its purpose and the labour and other costs associated with its utilization in service delivery. A van, for example, needs regular maintenance and maybe special renovation/ repair from time to time to keep it fit for any duty. It also needs a driver and fuel to perform its expected duties. A school or home for elderly people needs regular painting, decorating and cleaning. It also needs teachers or care workers to make use of it in providing a service for school students or residents.

The NHS has a phrase, revenue consequences of capital schemes (RCCS), which draws attention to these costs. In any part of the sector where capital expenditure is being considered, the ongoing revenue costs must be taken into account. So too, incidentally, should any savings that may be made. If a new item of laundry equipment can be worked effectively by four people rather than six, then the saving of two people's wages can be legitimately offset against the costs of operating the equipment.

In this connection, some capital expenditure may be incurred with income generation in mind. A leisure centre which installs floodlights, for example, presumably anticipates income from the outdoor sports groups and individuals who will use the facilities during the extended day. This does not invalidate the need to consider carefully the maintenance and running costs needed, for example replacement bulbs and the cost of electricity.

Depreciation   As an item considered routinely as a cost of capital, depreciation is not well established in those parts of the public sector which remain after the privatization programme of the 1980s and early 1990s, although it was practised extensively in the nationalized industries. It is well established in the private sector because, among other reasons, it essentially represents an expenditure which has the effect of reducing profits and thus reduces the liability to taxation.

Depreciation is the taking into account of the loss in resale value of an asset. Depreciation normally:

- takes place over a number of years, often five in the case of vehicles or plant and longer for buildings;
- starts from the value of the asset as purchased, normally its price; and
- works down to a nominal sum, often zero.

Thus a vehicle bought for £11,000 might be depreciated to the nominal value of £1,000 over 5 years at a rate of £2,000 per year, so that after 2 years it would be recorded as worth £7,000 and after 4 years it would be recorded as worth £3,000. Depreciation does not have to be 'linear' in this way, but equal annual depreciation is by far the most common method of depreciating the value of assets.

EXAMPLE TO ILLUSTRATE COST OF CAPITAL: THE ROTHCASTER CRECHE

A group of employees who are also parents is considering installing a self-managed crèche facility in the grounds of Rothcaster hospital using land which will be available free of all charges. The group is considering the annual capital costs of purchasing, installing and maintaining a second-hand portable building. The initial costs would be financed by a bank loan to be repaid over 5 years at a rate of £26 per month for each £1,000 borrowed.

The following information is available:

1. Cost of a suitable building delivered to site and erected on prebuilt pillars: £5,000.
2. Cost of initial connection of mains services together with decoration and making good: £6,000.

3. Annual cost of maintenance: £500.
4. Estimated usable life of building 5 years, after which the resale value would be £1,000.

Required

Advise the group as to the capital costs and how they should be built into the annual budget.

Solution to Rothcaster crèche

- Total initial capital costs are £5,000 + £6,000 = £11,000, and so monthly repayment to bank is 11 × £26 = £286, which is equivalent to £3,432 per year.
- Annual maintenance charge is £500 per year.
- The group starts with nothing, but finishes with a building worth an estimated £1,000, i.e. it will have gained the equivalent of £200 per year.

These statements are all true and derived from the information given. There is, however, an element of discretion in the advice to be given to the employee/parent group. The advice may be given as follows:

- The cost of the bank loan is £3,432 per year. This is undoubtedly a capital charge to be repaid out of the revenue account and, presumably, recovered from fees (or other income source) for using the crèche.
- The cost of maintenance is £500 per year. This is a revenue item, but is so closely associated with the capital item that it might as well be shown with it and recovered in the same way.
- The notional £200 per year capital gain, from a zero position (the group owns nothing to start with) to a putative £1,000 over five years, could be offset on revenue. It would, however, be far more advisable to forget it (as far as budgeting is concerned) and use it, if in fact it materializes, to offset any capital borrowing in the future.

The best advice, therefore, is to allow £3,932 per year (£3,432 + £500) as the annual revenue cost of owning and maintaining the building. This could sensibly be rounded to £4,000 per annum, which must be recovered from fees or any other source(s) of income.

NOTE

1. The technical meaning of 'opportunity cost' is sometimes defined (see Coombs and Jenkins (1991)) in relation to the discounting techniques applied to capital investment and discussed in article C3. I believe that this usage is sufficiently different from common practice as to be unhelpful. Discounting techniques are, of course, very useful and should be practised more widely in the public sector. It is, however, probably of more value in appraising capital investment decisions to consider opportunity costs more figuratively as applying to the intangible loss of benefits through not taking certain actions.

FORECASTING

THE CONTEXT

The likely volume of demand for a service or a provision is absolutely key to planning the level of provision to be made, the resource to be invested in making this provision and the charges, if any, to be made for people who make use of the service.

In the business world, a realistic estimate of the likely demand for a good or service is a key factor in persuading investors or lenders to finance a new business or potential expansion of an existing concern. In the public sector, likewise, forecasts of volume of demand must form an important part of the business planning process and the estimation of future viability of service provision.

The contemporary context is thus business planning (see Article B8), but the ideas are much older and all branches of the public sector were concerned with such estimates long before the advent of the new managerial culture. The relevant discipline is market research, a branch of the field of marketing, and textbooks of market research will provide a much fuller picture than can be drawn here.

There are essentially three main ways of making forecasts:

1. Forecasting on the basis of history, i.e. what people have done in the past. Provided the environment is not changing too rapidly and the history is reasonably recent, this is a cheap and relatively reliable method.
2. Forecasting on the basis of surveys and questionnaires, i.e. what people say they will do when asked. This is likely to yield an up-to-date picture which takes account of any, perhaps subtle, environmental changes. On the other hand, a reliable survey is expensive and people do not always do what they say!
3. Forecasting on the basis of behaviour, i.e. what people do elsewhere. Finding such information can be very easy or it can, particularly if any competitive interests are at stake, be very difficult. It is worth the effort, however, as it provides a very reliable source of information provided there are considerable similarities between the researched population and the population being planned for.

This article concentrates on the first method, looking at the question of how data in the form of a time series can be used to predict future behaviour.

THE KEY CONCEPTS

A *time series* is a set of figures representing past performance which can be used as a guide in predicting or estimating future performance. There are several techniques ranging from the simple to the complex. They all suffer from the limitation, mentioned above, that the past is not necessarily the best guide to the future. Additionally, each technique has its own limitations. We shall consider three techniques: *graphical, moving averages* and *exponential smoothing*.

Graphical techniques

In principle, a graphical technique just means drawing a graph of past performance and estimating how it can be extrapolated into future periods. It is exemplified below.

Example: Rainbow Bus Company   The number of miles worked annually by the Rainbow Bus Company over twelve years is as follows:

Year	1982	1983	1984	1985	1986	1987	1988	1989	1990	1991	1992	1993
Miles (000s)	92	104	170	184	208	255	276	312	340	350	360	365

Draw a graph representing these figures and discuss the implications for 1994.

The drawing of the graph is simple (Fig. C9.1). The horizontal axis is marked out evenly in years. The vertical axis is marked out evenly in thousands of route miles. The individual lines are plotted and joined by straight lines to form a 'curve'.

The overall impression is one of growth at one rate until 1990 and then at another, much more gentle rate, from 1990. Unless there are any known environmental factors to the contrary, it

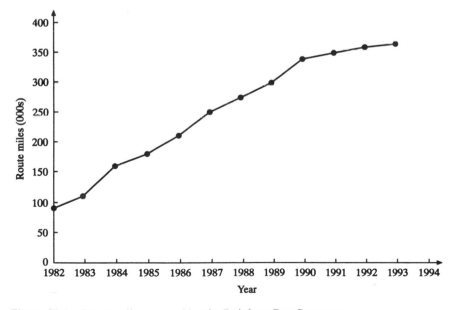

Figure C9.1   Route miles covered by the Rainbow Bus Company

seems reasonable to suppose that growth will continue at the slower rate for 1993–94 and thus that about 5,000 route miles will be added to the total worked.

The managers of the bus company are presumably concerned as to whether to obtain additional vehicles or to set on additional staff. Since 5,000 route miles represents less than 1.4 per cent of their current workings, it is likely that it could be absorbed by more effective use of their existing vehicles and staff.

On the other hand, if management were planning to open up a new route or there had been serious problems in making vehicles available to meet existing commitments, then a different conclusion might be drawn.

The lesson to be learned from this simple example is that numbers are only one factor to be taken into account when making decisions.

Moving averages

The curve for the Rainbow Bus Company was relatively smooth. Sometimes these curves are very erratic showing ups and downs. It may be felt desirable to smooth these out in some way in which case the moving average technique may be used. Any results may be presented graphically as in the previous example.

Moving average example: sales Consider Table C9.1 which gives sales data on a monthly basis for the past year and the January of a new year (in the first two columns) and then three different

Table C9.1 Moving average illustration

Past sales		Forecasts produced by		
Month	Actual sales (units)	3-monthly moving average	6-monthly moving average	12-monthly moving average
Jan	450			
Feb	440			
Mar	460			
Apr	410	450		
May	380	437		
Jun	400	417		
Jul	370	397	423	
Aug	360	383	410	
Sep	410	377	397	
Oct	450	380	388	
Nov	470	407	395	
Dec	490	443	410	
Jan	460	470	425	424

forecasts based on moving averages for successive 3-month, 6-month and 12-month periods, respectively.

The forecasts in each case are obtained by averaging the actual figures for the previous 3, 6 or 12 months, e.g. the 3-monthly forecast for April is found by adding the actual figures for January, February and March and dividing by 3. Thus on the basis of 3 months the April forecast is (450 + 440 + 460)/3 = 1,350/3 = 450.

If we consider the second January there are three different forecasts: the first is based on 3 months, October–December, and is 470; the second on 6 months, July–December, and is 425 and the third on 12 months, January–December and is 424. It should be noted that none of these corresponds to the actual figure for that month which is, in fact, quite similar to the actual for the previous January.

The 3-monthly and 6-monthly averages are plotted graphically in Fig. C9.2 along with the basic data.

It should be noted that:

- The various moving averages give successively greater smoothing for lengthening periods.
- This greater smoothing is advantageous if there is reason to believe that there is an underlying longer term trend.
- If there is reason to believe that shorter term trends are important then a shorter smoothing period should be used.

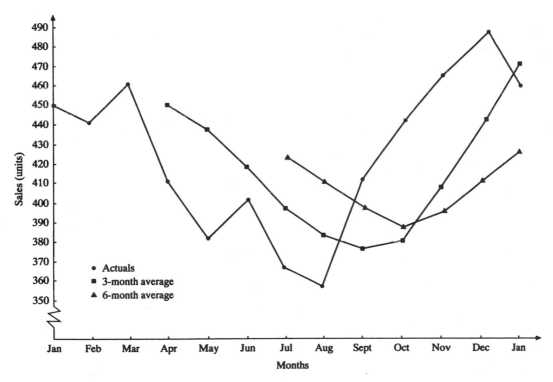

Figure C9.2 Actuals and 3-month and 6-month averages (figures from Table C9.1)

Table C9.2 Rainbow Bus Company moving average figures

Year	Actual	3-year moving average	5-year moving average
1982	92		
1983	104		
1984	170		
1985	184	122	
1986	208	153	
1987	255	187	152
1988	276	216	184
1989	312	246	219
1990	340	281	247
1991	350	309	278
1992	360	334	307
1993	365	350	328
1994		358	345

There are a couple of problems inherent in moving averages:

- There is a often a feeling that more recent actuals should be seen as more significant than older figures.
- There is often a feeling that seasonal sales variations, such as occur at Christmas or summer holidays, may be significant and therefore should not be smoothed out.

There is a serious problem with moving averages if a long-term trend exists. This can be illustrated by using the previous example of the Rainbow Bus Company's figures, working out 3- and 5-year moving averages and plotting them on a graph. The figures are given in Table C9.2. The graph is shown in Fig. C9.3.

It can be seen that the curves for the 3-year and 5-year moving averages are much smoother than the curve for the actuals, thus demonstrating clearly the way in which the moving average technique removes the troughs and peaks of normal progress. However, both smoothed curves underestimate the growth, the 5-year curve more so than the 3-year one.

This problem shows up only when there is growth or decline over the period in question. When the original figures are more random there is no such consistent trend in the averages. Two points can be made about this:

1. If a clear trend is obvious from the actuals line, then it may not be necessary to do the smoothing anyway. Intelligent guesswork may produce as reliable a figure as mathematical techniques!
2. The feeling that more recent figures should carry more weight reasserts itself as the reason for the consistent underestimates in a period of growth (or overestimates in a period of decline) is because in the moving average technique older figures carry as much weight as newer figures.

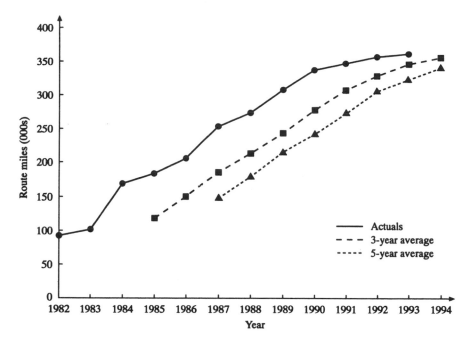

Figure C9.3   Rainbow Bus Company moving averages

Exponential smoothing

The under/overestimation problem can be solved to some extent by the use of a more complex technique known as exponential smoothing. This technique also allows more weight to be given to more recent history, but there is a trade-off between these two advantages, i.e. it is necessary to judge how much of each advantage is required in any given case. A smoothing factor, usually denoted as α (the Greek letter 'alpha') is chosen and used in a formula. The working can be done in tabular form, or, of course, using a computer program.

α is a figure between 0 and 1, and according to how it is chosen the formula will emphasize either smoothing or recency. If α is say between 0 and 0.5 then there is more smoothing; if α is say between 0.5 and 1 then the forecasts are more sensitive to recent figures.

The formula is:

$$F = \alpha \times A + (1 - \alpha) \times F$$

where A is the actual for a year and F is the forecast for the next year based on a series of preceding actuals and forecasts. The first F (which applies to the second time period) is the actual for the first time period.

The method of using the formula is much simpler than the formula might suggest:

1. Take a particular period's actual figure and multiply it by α.
2. Take the forecast for the period in question and multiply it by $1 - \alpha$.
3. Add these figures to give the forecast for the next period, noting that the forecast to be used for period 2 is actual for period 1, simply because there is no better figure available.

Table C9.3 Exponential smoothing calculation: sales ($\alpha = 0.3$)

Month	Actual (A)	$\alpha \times A$	$(1 - \alpha) \times F$	Forecast (F)
Jan	450			
Feb	440	132 ——— + ———	915	450 (period 1 actual)
Mar	460	138	313	447
Apr	410	123	316	451
May	380	114	307	439
Jun	400	120	295	421
Jul	370	111	290	415
Aug	360	108	281	401
Sep	410	123	272	389
Oct	450	135	276	395
Nov	470	141	288	411
Dec	490	147	300	429
Jan	460	138	313	447

Exponential smoothing example: sales The monthly sales over a period of a year are as shown in the previous example.

1. Plot the actual figures from January to December on a graph.
2. Compute the exponentially smoothed figures using an α value of 0.3 and hence make a prediction for the second January. (Calculations are given in Table C9.3).
3. Compute the exponentially smoothed figures using an α value of 0.7 and hence make a prediction for the second January. (Calculations are given in Table C9.4).
4. Add the predictions for 2 and 3 to the original graph (1). This is presented in Fig. C9.4.

Table C9.4 Exponential smooting calculation: sales ($\alpha = 0.7$)

Month	Actual (A)	$\alpha \times A$	$(1 - \alpha) \times F$	Forecast (F)
Jan	450			
Feb	440	308	135	450 (period 1 actual)
Mar	460	322	133	443
Apr	410	287	136	455
May	380	266	127	423
Jun	400	280	118	393
Jul	370	259	119	398
Aug	360	252	114	378
Sep	410	287	110	366
Oct	450	315	119	397
Nov	470	329	130	434
Dec	490	343	138	459
Jan	460	322	144	481
Feb				466

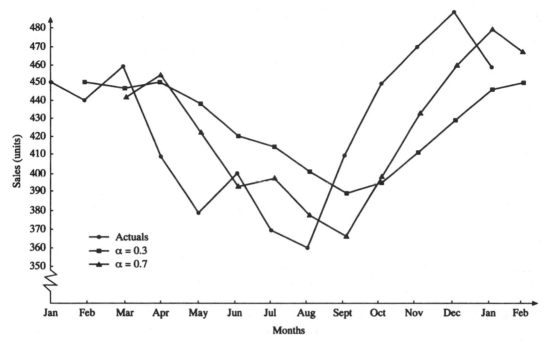

Figure C9.4   Sales, actuals and smoothed ($\alpha = 0.3$, $\alpha = 0.7$)

EXAMPLE OF GENERAL FORECASTING: PUDDLETOWN-ON-SEA PUTTING GREEN

The gross takings for the Puddletown-on-Sea District Council's putting green during the high season for the past ten years are shown in Table C9.5. (An inflation correction has been applied.)

1. Plot the actual figures on a graph and hence make a forecast for 1996.
2. Calculate a 2-year moving average and hence make a prediction for 1996.

Table C9.5   Puddletown-on-Sea putting green income figures

Year	Income, £
1986	21,000
1987	22,500
1988	20,750
1989	24,250
1990	22,500
1991	26,250
1992	25,000
1993	26,000
1994	24,750
1995	26,250

3. Calculate the exponentially smoothed figures using an α value of 0.7 and hence make a prediction for 1996.
4. Discuss the utility of the various predictions.

Solution to Puddletown-on-Sea putting green

1. The graph (Fig. C9.5) is erratic but appears to zig-zag in a generally upwards direction with a levelling out from about 1992. A prediction of about £25,000, i.e. approximately the 1994 figure, would seem sensible.
2. The figures for the 2-year moving average are shown in Table C9.6.

   Using a 2-year average period on figures which regularly zig-zag over a 2-year cycle has the effect of taking out the erratic nature of the growth. The average of the figures for 1994 and 1995, i.e. £25,500 can be used as a prediction for 1996.
3. The calculation of the exponentially smoothed figures ($\alpha = 0.7$) is shown in Table C9.7. On the basis of this calculation, based on the relatively high smoothing factor ($\alpha = 0.7$) which reflects the more recent figures, a forecast of £25,887 is made for 1996.
4. There are thus three different forecasts:
   - (a) £25,000 (made by inspection of the graph)
   - (b) £25,500 (made by using a 2-year moving average)
   - (c) £25,887 (made by using an exponential technique with $\alpha = 0.7$)

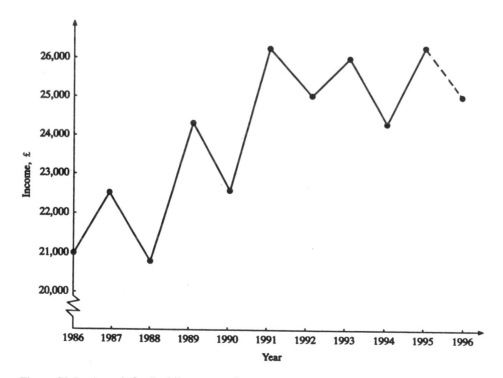

Figure C9.5   Actuals for Puddletown-on-Sea

Table C9.6   Two-year moving average calculation

Year	Income, £	Average of past two years, £
1986	21,000	
1987	22,500	21,750
1988	20,750	21,625
1989	24,250	22,500
1990	22,500	23,375
1991	26,250	24,375
1992	25,000	25,625
1993	26,000	25,500
1994	24,750	25,375
1995	26,250	25,500

Table C9.7   Exponentially smoothed calculation

Year	Actual (A)	$\alpha \times A$	$(1 - \alpha) \times F$	Forecast (F)
1986	21,000	–	–	–
1987	22,500	15,750	6,300	21,000[a]
1988	20,750	14,525	6,615	21,050
1989	24,250	16,975	6,342	21,140
1990	22,500	15,750	6,995	23,317
1991	26,250	18,375	6,823	22,745
1992	25,000	17,500	7,560	25,198
1993	26,000	18,200	7,518	25,060
1994	24,750	17,325	7,715	25,718
1995	26,250	18,375	7,512	25,040
1996	–			25,887

[a]The forecast for the second period (1987) is taken as the actual for the first period (1986) since no other figure is available.

The utility depends to some extent on what they are being used for! They are all 'down' on 1995 and thus, unless any serious change in opening hours or pricing structure is proposed, no additional staff or service is justified.

On the other hand, all the predictions lie well within the range which has come to be expected over the past few years and are all substantially higher than the earlier figures. Any figure in the £25,000–26,000 range could be taken as a reasonable forecast for budgeting purposes.

PERFORMANCE INDICATORS

THE CONTEXT

Performance indicators (PIs) are by-products of the pressure for value for money. Whether within central government, within local government or within the NHS, organizations are now required to produce and publish key indicators on a variety of fronts, and there is no doubt that these indicators influence the allocation of resources and the expectation for development in both quality and quantity of future performance.

PIs are also intimately related to the management of change. Intelligible indicators that can be accepted by the managers to whom they have relevance are potent levers for motivating and changing the behaviour of staff. Where organizational indicators are seriously adrift from national norms, managers at strategic levels may more easily make structural changes to their organization in the interests of both cost-effectiveness and personal/professional pride.

THE KEY CONCEPTS

This article first provides a *definition* of what a PI is and goes on to *classify the types of indicator*, discuss the *comparative nature* of PIs and raise problems regarding their *specificity*. A discussion of PIs based on the criteria of *internal and external usage* and *utility to different levels of an organization* is then attempted. Finally, the use of PIs as *levers for change* is raised.

Definition of performance indicator

A performance indicator is a numerical figure which can be used in comparison with other figures to indicate the relative status of some aspect of the performance of the organization in question.[1]
    It is essential to stress the three components of the definition:

1. A PI must be numerical. It may or may not, however, be financially related.
2. A PI must be used in a valid comparison situation, otherwise it is valueless.
3. A PI must be specific enough to enable the appropriate level of management to do something to improve it if necessary.

The performance of the organization, or any part of it, may be viewed in economy, efficiency or effectiveness terms, and hence PIs may be linked with any part or parts of the value for money chain discussed in Article B6. Some PIs look very much like costs and are linked to economy/ efficiency. Others relate to customer satisfaction or the matching of outputs to planned goals and are thus more to do with effectiveness.

Table C10.1 Types of performance indicators

	Internal audience	External audience
Effectiveness	Indicators with high level of generality such as 'overall completion rates' for colleges and universities.	The same figures may be used by funding providers.
Economy efficiency	Time taken to clean/polish a certain area of floor.	The same figures (if available) would be of use to potential tenderers.

Classification of PIs

PIs may be classified on a two by two matrix deriving from a dimension of intended audience (internal/external) and a distinction between indicators which are primarily cost related (economy/efficiency) and indicators which are primarily outcome quality related (effectiveness). Table C10.1 illustrates this.

Further examples of cost-related indicators include 'cost per dustbin emptied' (local government) or 'cost per patient-day' (NHS).

Further examples of output/outcome/client satisfaction indicators include 'number of errors or complaints per 1,000 transactions' (any part of the sector) or 'reported cases solved' (police service).

Comparative nature of PIs

Of its own a PI is meaningless. It must be placed in a comparative context if it is to have either meaning or potential as a tool for management. Three main comparisons may be made:

1. A comparison with a corresponding indicator from another similar organization, for example another local authority or school (local government), or another trust or department within a trust (NHS).
2. A comparison with the same indicator derived from within the same organization and covering a different time period, for example last year's figures or a run of figures over a five-year period.
3. A comparison with some norm or standard either accepted within a particular culture or encouraged/imposed by some higher authority. Thus teachers may have a feel for what are reasonable expectations with regard to the performance of sixteen year olds, doctors may have a feel for reasonable expectations for workload for themselves and their colleagues. The government may impose/encourage certain standards, as for example through the various 'charters' which now cover most of the public sector and many of which include some key indicators (such as waiting time) which raise public expectations regarding the performance of their servants.

There are two points to be made with regard to these comparisons. First, it is important in regard to 1 and 2 that there is strict comparability in the way that the figures have been collected and subsequent calculations made. Like must be compared with like, and it is often by no means certain that all data has been collected in the same way. For this reason, it is entirely legitimate to query methodology when any two ostensibly similar indicators show any serious degree of divergence. Second, it is important that those who are affected by any normative indicator should have a respect for the author of the norms. That is why indicators promulgated from within professions are so powerful: there is little room for argument with peers. Some normative indicators derive from 'best practice': these are powerful because they have roots in professional practice and, provided the methodology is accepted, cannot be denied in practical terms.

Specificity of PIs

There is an important tension underlying PIs between those which are tightly focused on relatively minor aspects of an organization's work (e.g. time per square metre for floor polishing), and those which are very general and cover a whole swathe of its activities (e.g. overall completion rates for colleges and universities). Both are relatively easy to obtain accurately, but the first sort has applicability to only a very small section of the organization and, even if 'owned' and improved, is unlikely to enhance the overall performance of the organization significantly. The second, however, while much more significant in organizational terms, may well not be owned by any group tightly focused enough to do anything about it!

It is thus necessary for managers to perform a delicate balancing act between specificity and generality: to ensure that indicators are specific enough to be owned by groups who can do something about them if necessary, while avoiding indicators (for public consumption) which are so specific that they can be tied to individuals. Such indicators have their uses, but in the context of reward (if positive) and discipline (if negative).

Finally, the job of producing indicators is often allocated to an 'information management section (or department)', very often staffed by experts in computers, statistics or both. It is imperative that the outputs of any such section should be intelligible, directed to the right people and interpreted by managers who can see the implications of the indicators.

Internal and external usage of PIs

Once the indicators have been calculated and made available to their target audiences, they can be used. Internally, they can be used to facilitate change. This is discussed in the following subsections. Externally they can be used as resource-claiming levers or as ways to attract potential clients/customers.

PIs for internal use tend to be at the economy and efficiency levels. PIs for external use tend to be at the efficiency and effectiveness levels. Put another way, internal PIs tend to be used more at the operational/middle management levels: PIs for external consumption are of more interest to the middle/strategic level.

The two main uses for PIs are as indicators of the success or otherwise of activities or as bargaining levers in discussions of resource allocation. The first of these has clear potential for leverage in the management processes. The second has clear potential as an argument based on previous good use of resources or as a statement of need for additional resources to meet output targets.

Usage at different levels of an organization

The strategic manager, located at or near the top of an organization and responsible to its funders and/or management board, is concerned with macro indicators to do with overall quantity and quality of output. The manager is also concerned that the organization is meeting its overall budgetary targets. The PIs of most concern to the strategic manager are those which quantify effectiveness, as they can be used in discussions with key personnel outside the organization. The strategic manager will also be concerned, however, with the way in which these strategic indicators are made up, not in great detail but in sufficient detail to know where the strengths and weaknesses of the organization lie and where there are needs to address the balance of the organization and the quality of its management.

For example, the director of a local authority cleansing department will be concerned with macro indicators such as:

- Net spending as a percentage of budgeted net spending, where 100 per cent represents the goal
- Total volume of complaints over a period as compared with some valid comparator figure, e.g. another similar department or the same department in a previous year
- Various subindicators such as cost per residence for refuse collection, again in relation to valid comparators

The middle manager uses indicators in two ways. Those generated at operational level are passed up the line, where appropriate, as evidence for the need for resources or reward. Those emanating from above are passed down the line as rewards or as motivators for change.

Therefore indicators such as volume of complaints or cost per residence are passed up the line. The middle manager will also be concerned with the performance of the various teams into which the service is organized and will have a grasp of whether the complaints are mainly about some teams or whether there are any indicators of absenteeism or undue use of overtime.

The supervisory manager is concerned with a limited range of indicators which have to do, on the whole, with economy and efficiency and the quality of that particular aspect of provision for which that manager is directly responsible. Such indicators are passed up the line to the middle manager.

PIs as levers for change

Whether passed up or down the line there are two sorts of change which PIs can be used to facilitate:

- Change in resource pattern
- Change in output/outcome pattern, as measured either by volume or by quality

To effect change of any sort there must be agreement by all relevant parties about the validity and accuracy of the indicators and any comparisons which are made. Once that agreement is reached the potency of PIs is enormous.

Good PIs can be passed up the line as evidence that further resource will not be wasted. They can be passed down the line as positive motivators. Poor PIs can be passed down the line as evidence that change is needed and, if the comparators are there, as evidence that change is possible. Poor PIs can also be passed up the line as evidence that some sort of remedial action, perhaps training or structural change or even provision of additional resource, should be taken by higher management.

Provided that the key understanding of PIs is present, i.e. that on their own they are of little use, accurate and validly compared PIs are effective levers for change. It is hard to deny the possibility of cost improvement if other organizations have already achieved it. It is hard to deny the possibility of quality improvement when other similar organizations have fewer complaints and better outcome indicators.

If a section, department or organization produces consistently good indicators, it can use them as evidence that further funding and expansion could and should take place.

EXAMPLE: MIDDLETON UNIVERSITY

The following data for three-year full-time degree completion figures is being considered by the academic registrar of Middleton University:

	Admitted 1992	Passed Year 1 1993	Passed Year 2 1994	Passed Year 3 1995
University	4,000	3,200	3,000	2,800
Dept A	100	60	50	40
Dept B	100	90	85	80

Required

1. Calculate appropriate performance indicators.
2. Suggest additional information which might help the registrar.

Solution to Middleton University

1. The required PIs are completion rates, both stage and overall. Two examples are worked, the others (worked in a similar manner) are presented in Table C10.2.

   University overall completion rate = 2,800/4000 × 100% = 70%
   Department B Year 2 completion rate = 85/90 × 100% = 94.44%

2. The following information would be helpful:
   (a) Figures (overall and for similar departments) for several other universities of comparable size.
   (b) Figures for previous cohorts of students over, say, a three-year period, i.e. entering in 1989, 1990 and 1991 and graduating in 1992, 1993 and 1994.
   (c) Commentary on the figures, within the time context mentioned in (b) if possible, from responsible persons within departments A and B. Such commentary might include information about entry standards or any particular 'one-off' matters.

Table C10.2 Middleton University: stage completion rates

	Year 1 %	Year 2 %	Year 3 %	Overall %
University	80	93.75	93.33	70
Dept A	60	83.33	80	40
Dept B	90	94.44	94.12	80

(d) Any statement of 'normal' expectations from authorities such as HEFCE (the funding body) or the professional bodies (if any) associated with the work of departments A and B.

EXAMPLE: POPPLETON HOSPITAL NHS TRUST

The chief executive is considering a set of figures relating to throughput in acute beds in various specialties. These figures cover best practice, normal practice and worst practice and include reference to length of stay and bed empty time. Thus a throughput of 26 patients per bed per year will be obtained if the average length of stay is 10 days and the average bed empty time is 4 days.

For a particular specialty the figures are as follows:

	Bed empty	*Length of stay*	*Throughput*
Best practice	1	6	52
Normal practice	3	8	33.1
Poppleton	4	10	26
Worst practice	5	12	21.4

1. Does the chief executive have sufficient evidence to instigate action?
2. What other evidence might be necessary/helpful to the chief executive?

Section to Poppleton NHS Trust

1. Immediate action in terms of asking the relevant clinical personnel to comment on the figures as a matter of urgency is justified. There is clear prima facie evidence that the specialty is underperforming significantly on national norms and spectacularly in terms of best practice. It is always advisable, however, to ask for an explanation from the people most closely concerned.
2. It would be helpful to have comparable figures for other specialties within the trust, particularly for 'bed empty' where clinical considerations are not usually important.

NOTE

1. This definition is due to the author. It was first published in 1995 in *Local Government Financial Management*, ICSA Publishing, p. 122. The structure of the present discussion follows that of pp. 122–126 of that book.

QUANTITATIVE EXERCISES AND CASE STUDIES

WHAT THIS SECTION IS ABOUT

This section provides exercises which are matched to the work covered in Articles C1 to C10.

In addition, there are six case studies which range more widely, covering the work of more than one article and also requiring insights gained from Articles B1 to B9.

If the exercises are worked through steadily, then the case studies should provide an opportunity for students to develop skills of deciding which techniques are appropriate in any case.

The ability merely to manipulate numbers/quantities does not make a financial manager: that requires additional understanding of the context in which those figures are placed. Thus the selection of relevant material from Section B is also important.

HOW TO USE THIS SECTION

For each technique discussed in Section C there are two exercises provided in this section. Students may find it helpful to use one of them as they study Section C for the first time and the other as a revision aid. Key answers are provided on pages 219–221.

The case studies are best tackled initially as group exercises. If you are in a class, your tutor can arrange this. Otherwise, you may find it helpful to get at least one friend to work with. The studies are not difficult, but they do require you to select which of the various techniques you have studied is/are the most appropriate to tackle any particular case.

You may also have to think about the appropriate action to take in any case and that will require you to have thought about the various topics covered in Section B. The cases are therefore best left until nearly the end of your course of study so that you have covered all the relevant material.

CASH FLOW

These exercises depend upon the work covered in Article C1.

EXERCISE D1.1

The following figures apply to the income and expenditure of a local authority outdoor tennis court area which is open during the hours of daylight throughout the year.

Expenditure forecast

Supervisor's wages	£900 per month all year round
Assistant's wages	£700 per month all year round
Casual wages	£600 per month April and May
	£800 per month June, July and August
	£400 per month September and October
Maintenance	£100 per month November to March
	£200 per month April and May
	£400 per month June to October

Income forecast

Court hire	£10 per day November to March
	£40 per day April and May
	£80 per day June to August
	£60 per day September and October
Profit from sales/hire	£5 per day November to March
	£20 per day April and May
	£40 per day June to August
	£30 per day September and October

Required

1. Using a 1 April to 31 March year set out a cash budget using these predictions.
2. Indicate the worst and the best predicted cash balances.
3. What is predicted to be the overall surplus/deficit for the year?
4. What financial advice might you offer the authority concerning this matter?

EXERCISE D1.2

A large local authority has total receipts from all sources as follows:

Council tax:
>   £60 million received in April
>   £60 million received in May
>   £120 million received in 10 equal instalments from April to January

Grants and national non-domestic rate
>   £240 million received in 12 equal instalments from April to March

Fees and charges
>   £180 million received in 12 equal monthly instalments
>   £60 million received in September at the start of the school year

Its outgoings amount to £720 million and may be regarded as having a totally 'flat' profile.

Required

1. Construct an April to March cash budget.
2. Indicate those months where there is a clear surplus.
3. On the assumption that the treasurer can invest such surpluses at 0.5 per cent per month, how much interest could be made by such investment (neglect compounding of interest)?
4. Advise the treasurer on this matter.

PROJECT CASH FLOWS/PAYBACK

These exercises depend upon the work covered in Article C2.

EXERCISE D2.1

A local authority car park is about to open. The capital cost of £350,000 will be met as follows: £50,000 has already been paid, before opening, and the remainder is to be paid in three equal instalments towards the end of years 1, 2 and 3, respectively. It is estimated that the cost of supervision will amount to £50,000 annually and that maintenance will cost nothing during the first year, but £10,000 per annum thereafter. Income is anticipated to average £300 per day for 300 days per year.

Required

1. Draw up a table showing the cash flows for fifteen full years.
2. Indicate the point at which the capital outlay will have been recovered.
3. Indicate the probable cumulative surplus/deficit after the fifteenth year.
4. Advise the local authority as to how they might recover their investment sooner.

EXERCISE D2.2

A management buy-out is being considered for a local bus firm. The management team are considering purchasing the garage buildings and offices with their redundancy payments and entering into a lease–buy scheme for the 100 vehicle bus fleet. The buildings are valued at £500,000 and would be paid for on the last day of year 0. The lease–buy scheme costs £10,000 per vehicle for ten years and a final 'option to purchase payment' of £5,000 per vehicle in year 11. The totality of running and operating costs are estimated at £40,000 per vehicle per year and the income from fares and grants are estimated to total £5.2 million annually.

Required

1. Draw up a table showing the cash flows for an appropriate period.
2. Indicate the point at which the cumulative deficit is turned into a cumulative surplus.
3. Indicate the point at which the buy-out team could recover their initial redundancy money investment.
4. What factors might make these predictions unreliable?

DISCOUNTED CASH FLOW

These exercises depend upon work covered in Article C3.

EXERCISE D3.1

An individual has £30,000 to invest and is offered a choice of three schemes.

The first requires paying the £30,000 in one lump and guarantees a lump sum of £50,000 after six years.

The second requires paying the £30,000 in three equal instalments of £10,000 at annual intervals starting with the deposit payment now and the others after one and two years, respectively. The guaranteed return is £50,000 after ten years.

The third scheme requires payment of the £30,000 in ten equal instalments of £3,000 at annual intervals and is guaranteed to yield £50,000 after ten years.

The investor is advised that interest rates are likely to remain stable at about 5 per cent. You may neglect any tax matters.

Required

1. Draw up tables of cash flow (discounted at 5 per cent) for each of the three schemes.
2. Advise the investor accordingly.

EXERCISE D3.2

A management buy-out is being considered for a local bus firm. The management team are considering purchasing the garage buildings and offices with their redundancy payments and entering into a lease–buy scheme for the 100 vehicle bus fleet. The buildings are valued at £500,000 and would be paid for on the last day of year 0. The lease–buy scheme costs £10,000 per vehicle for ten years and a final 'option to purchase payment' of £5,000 per vehicle in year 11. The totality of running and operating costs are estimated at £40,000 per vehicle per year and the income from fares and grants are estimated to total £5.2 million annually. A discounting factor of 5 per cent should be applied.

Required

1. Draw up a table showing the (discounted) cash flows for an appropriate period.

2. Indicate the point at which the cumulative deficit is turned into a cumulative surplus.
3. Indicate the point at which the buy-out team could recover their initial redundancy money investment.
4. What factors might make these predictions unreliable?

BREAK-EVENS

These exercises depend upon work covered in Article C4.

EXERCISE D4.1: HUTCHES LIMITED

A firm manufactures cages for small animals, each cage having variable costs totalling £8. The annual overheads of the factory amount to £40,000. Sales of 30,000 hutches annually are hoped for bringing in a sales total of £480,000.

Required

1. Calculate the unit sales price of the hutches and hence derive the contribution and the break-even sales figure.
2. What is the margin of safety expressed in terms of hutches sold?
3. Illustrate the calculation using a break-even chart.
4. What profit will be made by the firm if the sales figure of 30,000 hutches is achieved?
5. What profit will be made by the factory if 25,000 hutches are sold at the anticipated price, but the remaining 5,000 hutches are sold discounted at a sale price of £12?

EXERCISE D4.2: SMARTY DRESSES

A clothing firm manufactures dresses which on average cost £15 in labour and £10 in materials. They sell for £35 to wholesalers. It is hoped to sell 15,000 dresses at this price. The annual fixed costs of the clothing factory amount to £100,000.

Required

1. Calculate the contribution per dress and hence the break-even annual sales of dresses.
2. What is the hoped-for margin of safety?
3. Illustrate the calculation by means of a profit volume diagram.
4. Use this diagram to determine the profit which will be made if all 15,000 dresses are sold at the planned price of £35.
5. What profit will be made if the last 2,000 dresses are sold at £30?

COSTING

These exercises depend upon work covered in Article C5.

EXERCISE D5.1: AVOCET CATERING SERVICES

Avocet District Council has for many years run a range of in-house catering services. There has been some concern regarding the way in which the costing of the various activities has been performed and it has been decided to undertake a full-scale costing exercise.

The four main departments/cost centres have been identified as follows:

- Production departments: kitchen (K), counter (C)
- Service departments: stores (S), admin (A)

The current business plan identifies estimated costs as follows

	Dept K £	Dept C £	Dept S £	Dept A £	Total £
Total of direct costs	500,000	100,000	100,000	100,000	800,000
Indirect materials	5,000	5,000	–	5,000	15,000
Indirect labour	15,000	5,000	10,000	5,000	35,000
Central overheads					120,000
Power					80,000
Premises					120,000
Workwear					3,600

The following additional data is also supplied

	Dept K	Dept C	Dept S	Dept A	Total
Wattage, kW	45	10	35	10	100
Floor area, m^2	4,800	8,000	2,400	800	16,000
Employees	36	24	6	6	72
Usage of stores (%)	80	20	–	–	100
Usage of admin (%)	50	50	–	–	100

Required

1. Apportion the overhead costs for central overheads, power, premises and workwear to the four departments using appropriate criteria. (*Note*: central overheads are to be apportioned by employee.)
2. Reapportion the total costs for the service departments to the production departments using the appropriate usage rates.
3. Hence calculate the total of indirect costs and overhead costs for the two service departments.

Note: a pricing example based on this calculation is included in Exercise D6.1.

EXERCISE D5.2: MIDDLETON UNIVERSITY

The arts faculty of Middleton University has three teaching departments (English, History and Philosophy) and two service departments (Administration and Faculty Library). The university is undertaking a radical reappraisal of its costings.

Currently available information regarding costs is as follows:

	Dept E £	Dept H £	Dept P £	Dept A £	Dept FL £	Total £
Indirect labour	60,000	80,000	40,000	60,000	120,000	360,000
Indirect non-labour	35,000	35,000	25,000	25,000	60,000	180,000
Central overheads						720,000
Staff offices						180,000
Teaching rooms						360,000
Common space						240,000

Further information is also supplied:

Staff	30	40	20	40	50	180
Students	450	600	300	–	–	1350

The university has ruled that overheads shall be allocated/apportioned/reapportioned using the following ciriteria:

Central overheads	per capita, staff
Staff offices	per capita, staff
Teaching rooms	per capita, students
Common space	per capita, staff + students
Administration	per capita, students
Library	per capita, staff + students

Required

1. Make an initial apportionment of overhead costs to the five departments according to the criteria indicated. (In all these calculations round to the nearest £. There will be some small rounding errors.)

2. Reapportion the overhead costs of the two service departments to the three teaching departments according to the criteria indicated.
3. Hence, calculate the total overhead costs for the three teaching departments after apportionment and reapportionment.
4. Comment on the university's apportionment/reapportionment criteria.

Note: a pricing example based on this calculation is included in Exercise D6.2.

PRICING

These exercises depend upon work covered in Article C6 and refer back to the costing calculations performed in Exercises D5.1 and D5.2.

EXERCISE D6.1: AVOCET CATERING SERVICES

The annual direct and indirect costs for Avocet Catering services are given in, or can be calculated from, Exercise D5.1.

During the course of a year the total number of meals served is 800,000 and the total number of drinks served is 1,600,000.

The catering supervisor reckons that a drink takes about 10 per cent of the preparation and serving time as compared with a meal and that its material costs are also about 10 per cent.

Required

1. Calculate the total costs (direct and indirect) for the kitchen and counter separately.
2. Hence separate the costs for 800,000 meals and 1,600,000 drinks to each section.
3. Work out the total preparation and service cost for one meal and one drink separately.
4. Using a 20 per cent mark-up and rounding to the nearest 5p, what price should be charged for a meal and a drink, respectively?

An evening function consisting of 200 meals and drinks has been arranged where the preparation and cooking will be done in the kitchen, but an outside firm of caterers will provide wine, service and entertainment.

5. What charge should the kitchen make for 200 meals/drinks on the assumption that the price should be doubled to reflect quantity/quality improvement, but noting that the counter will not be involved?

EXERCISE D6.2: MIDDLETON UNIVERSITY

- The direct costs for the History department amount to £1.5 million.
- The division of the work of the department is reckoned at approximately 40 per cent undergraduate teaching, 30 per cent postgraduate teaching and 30 per cent staff research.
- Of the 600 students, 450 are undergraduates and 150 are postgraduates.
- Approximately 2,700 person-days are available annually for staff research.

Required

1. What is the annual cost to the History department of teaching one undergraduate?
2. What is the annual cost to the History department of teaching one postgraduate?
3. What is the cost to the History department of one person-day of research?
4. On the assumption of mark-ups of 10 per cent, 20 per cent and 30 per cent, respectively, what should be charged for teaching one undergraduate-year, one postgraduate-year and one person-day research?
5. The Administration and Faculty Library departments clearly have substantial direct costs, but these do not seem to be included in the available figures.
   (a) How could/should they be incorporated?
   (b) What general effect would their inclusion have on the prices/charges?

VARIANCE ANALYSIS

These exercises depend upon work covered in Article C7.

EXERCISE D7.1: FLOWERVILLE GARDENS

Flowerville Gardens is an in-house organization providing a planting, tending and maintenance service to Flowerville Community Trust's many flower beds. Its business plan has been constructed on the basis of the following assumptions:

- Each bed will require 600 plants over the course of a year at an average cost of 25p per plant.
- Each bed will require 100 hours of labour during the course of a year at an average labour rate (inclusive of all overheads) of £7 per hour.

In fact the first year's activity shows a different story!

- Each bed needed 680 plants which were obtained at an average cost of 22p each.
- Each bed required 96 hours of labour for which the actual labour rate (inclusive of all overheads) was £8.50 per hour.

Required

1. Calculate the total variance per bed and the variance for 500 flower beds stating clearly whether this is adverse or favourable.
2. Analyse the variance per bed into two variances, one due to labour variances and the other due to materials variances.
3. Analyse the labour variance into variances due to efficiency and rate.
4. Analyse the materials variance into variances due to quantity and price.
5. Comment on your findings.

EXERCISE D7.2: PIPETOWN GAS

Pipetown Gas is an organization set up to install gas central heating within the authority's many council dwellings. The financial outcomes of the first year of activity have produced some disquiet and the following figures have been produced.

The intended usage of copper pipe and labour, per dwelling, were as follows:

- Pipe: 40 metres at £1.50 per metre
- Labour: 40 hours at £9 per hour (inclusive)

The actual figures after one year of operation proved to be:

- Pipe: 45 metres at £1.75 per metre (much more wastage than anticipated)
- Labour: 45 hours at £11 per hour (a good deal of overtime worked)

Required

1. Calculate the total variance per dwelling.
2. Analyse this into labour and materials variances.
3. Analyse the labour variance into variances due to efficiency and rate.
4. Analyse the materials variance into variances due to usage and price.
5. What would the total variance be for 3,000 dwellings?
6. What measures might be taken to reduce the variances, i.e. to bring the figures more into line with the original intentions?

COST OF CAPITAL

These exercises depend upon work covered in Article C8.

EXERCISE D8.1: SCHOOL CRECHE

A grant-maintained secondary school has decided to investigate the cost of providing crèche facilities for its staff. A suitable building is available, but it needs renovation and redecoration which between them are estimated to cost £3,000. A bank is prepared to lend this money, repayable over a ten-year period at £60 per month. The committee considering the possibility has also been advised that £500 per year should be set aside for routine maintenance and redecoration.

Required

1. Calculate the total annual capital charge.
2. If the crèche is opened for 380 sessions per year and is attended by 20 children at each session, calculate the capital charge per child-session.

EXERCISE D8.2: MUDFORD CAR PARK

Mudford District Council is about to decide upon whether to go ahead with a new car park to be built in conjunction with an inner city supermarket. The total cost of the car park is estimated at £3,000,000 of which the supermarket will be responsible for 40 per cent, leaving the council responsible for the balance. Construction will take one year.

The cost of the car park will come in three tranches:

1996–97	10 per cent prebuild for design, etc.
1997–98	80 per cent paid in instalments while construction proceeds
1998–99	10 per cent retention to be paid when faults have been rectified

The cost of the capital to the council is £120 per year per £1,000 borrowed, payable from the first year after the borrowing.

Required

Calculate the cost of the capital to the council for each of the following years:

1. 1996–97
2. 1997–98
3. 1998–99
4. 1999–2000

FORECASTING

These exercises depend upon work covered in Article C9.

EXERCISE D9.1: MIDDLETON UNIVERSITY

The number of enrolments for the course in macromathematics with microbiology at Middleton University has followed the following pattern over the past eleven years:

1985–86	60	1986–87	61	1987–88	59
1988–89	55	1989–90	57	1990–91	53
1991–92	48	1992–93	50	1993–94	46
1994–95	44	1995–96	42		

The departmental staff feel that the students are most effectively taught in groups of 20.

Required

1. Use a simple graphical technique to estimate the likely enrolments for 1996–97.
2. Use a 3-year moving average technique, plotting your results graphically, to estimate the likely enrolments for 1996–97.
3. Should the department take the plunge and restrict enrolments to 40 students for the next few years?

EXERCISE D9.2: MUDFORD LEISURE CENTRE

The number of persons using the various facilities of Mudford Leisure Centre has been as follows over the past nine years.

1987–88	300,000	1988–89	320,000	1989–90	340,000
1990–91	380,000	1991–92	420,000	1992–93	460,000
1993–94	470,000	1994–95	480,000	1995–96	470,000

The centre was designed to cater for 500,000 users per year.

Required

1. Use a simple graphical technique to estimate the likely usage for 1996–97.
2. Use an exponential calculative technique based on α values of 0.3 or 0.7 to predict the usage for 1996–97, explaining your choice of α value.
3. Should the council be sympathetic to the centre staff's request for an extension to the centre?

PERFORMANCE INDICATORS

These exercises depend upon work covered in Article C10.

EXERCISE D10.1: MIDSHIRE CLEANSING DEPARTMENT

The director of the Midshire Cleansing Department is considering the performance of his street cleansing section and has some data from which PIs may be calculated. Also on his desk are a note from a friend who runs a comparable operation in Northshire and some figures from the Association of Street Cleansers.

The figures for Midshire are as follows:

	Kilometres of street swept	Person-hours (basic rate)	Person-hours (overtime)	Complaints from public
1994–95	12,000	16,650	3,350	600
1995–96	10,000	15,000	4,000	750

His Northshire friend states that her street cleansers cleanse about 1 kilometre per hour, and that they have 'two or three hundred complaints per year'. Overtime working has been held steady at about 5 per cent of basic rate working for several years.

The ASC figures suggest that the average for all districts is 0.8 kilometres per hour and that a zero complaint rate (taken as indicative of total quality) should be aimed for. It offers no figures regarding overtime.

Required

1. Calculate appropriate indicators for Midshire and draw attention to any comparisons or contrasts with other available PIs.
2. What action(s), in your opinion, should the director take?

EXERCISE D10.2: POPPLETON DGH CATERING

Poppleton DGH NHS trust runs a catering service which provides meals for patients delivered to the wards and meals for staff of all grades served in a staff dining room. There is some concern within the catering department regarding wastage which appears to take place both before food preparation (stock room) and after preparation (unused meals).

The following figures have been obtained by the service director:

	Intended meal production (000s)	Actual meal production (000s)	Actual meal consumption (000s)
1994–95	1,500	1,300	1,200
1995–96	1,400	1,200	1,100

Required

1. Calculate appropriate PIs for both years and comment on any apparent trends.
2. Discuss the nature of any further information which the service director should obtain before taking any managerial action.

CASE STUDY 1: SIDWELL SPORTS CENTRE[1]

Sidwell Sports Centre consists of a multifunction hall with appropriate changing rooms and shower facilities, an indoor swimming pool and a floodlit all-weather surface which is mostly used for football training. It is in its second year of operation and all the facilities and equipment are in good condition with no maintenance problems. The centre is on the same campus as a secondary school on the edge of a large city. Access by public transport is difficult although there is plenty of parking space and there are a couple of large housing estates—one private and one (mainly) council—within easy walking distance. The centre is open 15 hours per day for 364 days per year.

The manager of the centre is responsible for keeping the net expenditure within a cash limited budgeted allocation.

Permanent full-time staff consist of the following:

Grade	Gross costs	Overtime rate
Manager	£23,500 p.a.	n/a
Assistant A	£19,500 p.a.	n/a
Assistant B	£19,500 p.a.	n/a
Bath attendant (2)	£210 per week	£5 per hour
Changing supervisor (2)	£155 per week	£4 per hour
Hall attendant (2)	£210 per week	£5 per hour
Cashier (2 FTE)	£155 per week	£4 per hour
Caretaker	£210 per week (+ house)	£5 per hour

In addition there are part-time staff set on as follows:

Bath attendant (2)	£4 per hour, each does 20 hours per week
Hall attendant (2)	£4 per hour, each does 20 hours per week
Cashier (1)	£3.25 per hour, does 20 hours per week

All permanent staff work a nominal 40-hour week. The manager and the two assistants work a rota system which ensures that there is always a senior member of staff present. A short overlap period is built into the system.

The time is mid-July and the cumulative figures for the first three months of the year are on the manager's table (see Appendix 1). Also on the table are some notes that an assistant manager has put together from various documents she has found time to read (Appendix 2).

What is to be done?

Hints

1. Work out the maximum size of the financial problem over the full year assuming worst-case scenarios.
2. Consider each line of the budget report in the light of the notes and your understanding of the situation and thus devise strategies for:
   (a) Minimizing the overspend in 1995–96
   (b) Turning the situation round to achieve operation within cash limits for future years.

APPENDIX 1   TOTAL ACTIVITY REPORT

Sidwell Sports Centre   Manager: S. Laurel

Budget Report as at 30 June 1995

	Annual budget £	Profiled budget £	Actual £	Variance £
Expenditure				
Salaries (inc. on costs)	62,500	15,625	15,625	nil
Wages (inc. on costs)	120,000	30,000	33,300	3,300 adv.
Heating and lighting (Hall)	16,000	4,000	3,600	400 fav.
Heating and lighting (Pool)	40,000	10,000	10,800	800 adv.
Floodlight energy	4,800	1,200	nil	1,200 fav.
Repairs and maintenance	8,000	2,000	80	1,920 fav.
Rates	15,000	3,750	3,750	nil
Income				
Pool	32,000	8,000	6,000	2,000 adv.
Hall	32,000	8,000	6,000	2,000 adv.
Surface	12,000	3,000	1,200	1,800 adv.
Misc. sales and vending machines	4,000	1,000	1,400	400 fav.
Net expenditure	186,300	46,575	52,555	5,980 adv.

APPENDIX 2   NOTES CULLED FROM ASSISTANT MANAGER'S DESK

1. There is to be a general rise in the cost of energy of 5 per cent with effect from 1 September 1995.
2. There is to be an increase in the annual salaries of staff of 5 per cent backdated to 1 April 1995. Half of this is to be absorbed by the individual cost centres.
3. There is to be an increase in weekly wages and hourly rates (basic and overtime) of 6 per cent. This will be effective from 1 September 1995 and all must be absorbed by the individual cost centres.
4. A memo from the council's energy control officer suggests that installation of an energy saving system (supplied by O. Hardy and Co.) could save up to 15 per cent of the heating energy bill. The lease cost of this would be attributed to the cost centre and would be £4,000 p.a. for the pool and £1,300 p.a. for the hall. The equipment could be installed by 1 November 1995.

5. Owing to rapid deterioration in the fabric of the town hall, any unused cash allocations for repairs and maintenance must be returned to the treasury. This will be done by removing any favourable repairs and maintenance variances as at 30 September 1995 and consequently adjusting the budget.
6. The Famous Scot athletic support company has offered £1,500 sponsorship of a football coaching scheme. There seems to be a chance of free publicity not only for the surface but also for the pool and hall.
7. Flotation Garments wish to rent a small space at the rate of £28 per week in order to run a small swimming boutique. The income would be assured from 1 October 1995, but there would be a considerable reduction in the income from miscellaneous sales.

NOTE

1. This case study has been developed over a period of about seven years and used with managers from local authorities, with undergraduates on public sector management programmes and with MBA programme participants. Used as a group discussion and report back, it takes about two hours.

CASE STUDY 2: TARRANTO STREET HOSPITAL KITCHENS[1]

Tarranto Street Hospital combines both maternity and geriatric provision. The combination is not as strange as it sounds as for both care groups there is need for regular and structured clinic and advice work usually combined with relatively short periods of residence. The patients are normally mobile and emergencies per se are rare.

On the maternity side, about 100 women are resident at any given time: for the vast majority of these the stay is of a week or less, indeed usually only a couple of days. There are, however, several day clinics and support facilities involving group and individual work. The mothers-to-be/mothers often attend for a session involving lunch.

On the geriatric side, only about 100 old people are resident at any given time, but there are also many individual and group counselling sessions and these too involve lunch, partly as a therapeutic activity.

In round figures, there are 100 FTE nurses/auxiliaries, 20 FTE doctors/paramedics and 50 FTE other workers.

Colleen Hickson works as the catering manager. She is responsible for the provision of all meals to patients and staff. The staff have a dining room: the patients are fed on the wards or in special dining areas set apart for their use. Many nursing staff, unofficially, use patients' provisions (by overordering), and this practice has traditionally been ignored.

To assist her, Colleen has a deputy and two senior assistants who between them manage:

5 FTE cooks
2 FTE storekeepers
6 FTE serving-hands (all part-time)
5 FTE cleaners/washers-up (all part-time)

The actual number of people employed in the catering section is 36.

General guidance as to diet is provided by one of the consultants as a part of his duties, and in addition doctors may require special diets for individual patients as part of their treatment. Apart from these special cases (which amount to about 5 per cent of the workload) Colleen is expected to provide:

	On the wards	*In the canteen*
Breakfasts	200	100
Lunches	1,200	200
High teas	300	150

These are weekday figures. At weekends the volume is considerably reduced. In addition to these meals there is a continuously available supply of beverages in the canteen and a fairly heavy request for special buffets for meetings of various official bodies.

As a final piece of her workload, Colleen is in charge of the Spider's Web, a nicely fitted-out enclave of the main dining room which is available for private hire at evenings and weekends. This can provide high-quality waitress service food and Colleen regards it as a chance to show off her skills as well as being a source of additional income.

For the past five years the catering department has exceeded its cash limited budget by about 10 per cent. The Spider's Web has not caught the public imagination and its contribution to funds is negligible. The urgent pressure of considering contracts has brought about the need for radical reappraisal of the role and function of the department and the need to establish a proper financial basis.

Required

Work out a way of building up cost structures so as to arrive at:

1. A tender price (or set of prices) for the catering operation
2. The costs of the Spider's Web in order to facilitate a decision regarding its future.

Hints

1. A considerable degree of imagination and lateral thinking is required. It may be helpful to make estimates of the various contributory costs and think in numbers rather than in abstracts or algebraic formulae.
2. Use of a computer spreadsheet may be helpful in setting out models once the basic pattern has been established.
3. The overall costing model must be full absorption costing, but there is room for argument as to whether the Spider's Web could be costed at the margin and any income seen as beneficial.

NOTE

1. Tarranto Street Hospital is based on reality. The real-life hospital has now been closed. This case study, which is deliberately short on financial detail, is designed to develop understanding of the way in which financial managers have to work with limited information and sometimes make estimates, hopefully fairly sensible. Using groups of about four or five students, good results in terms of development can be obtained in about three hours.

CASE STUDY 3: UPCHESTER CAR PARK[1]

Upchester Borough Council wishes to build a 500 place car park on land which belongs to the council and which it has failed to sell over the past few years. It is hoped that the car park will be complete, fully operative and revenue earning by 1 October 1998.

CAPITAL COSTS

The total capital cost of £4,000,000 must be paid in three instalments. The first 10 per cent as a deposit in 1996–97 to cover initial planning and excavations. The second 80 per cent in 1997–98 to cover the bulk of the cost. The third 10 per cent in 1998–99 as a retention and released when all is satisfactory. All the capital cost is borrowed and charges at the rate of £120 per £1,000 borrowed are payable from revenue funds from the year after the capital transaction.

REVENUE COSTS

It is intended that the car park will be staffed by 2 persons on duty continuously for 24 hours per day. This implies employing 10 people who work shifts and cover holidays, etc. The annual wage and wage-related costs per person is £12,000.

There will, in addition, be maintenance costs at the rate of £20,000 in 1998–99 and £40,000 from 1999–2000 and thereafter.

USAGE

It is appreciated that there will be times, e.g. Saturday mornings and the period just before Christmas, when the car park will be absolutely full. On the other hand, there will be times, e.g. the early morning 'small hours', when the park will be virtually empty. The overall average usage may vary between 30 and 60 per cent.

CHARGES

There is disagreement between members of the highways committee as to whether the pricing policy should aim to break even or to make a surplus of, say £100,000 per year, or even more.

Required

Draft a report advising the members of the highways committee of the hourly charge to be made assuming different usage levels and different requirements regarding surplus or otherwise. Your report should identify any action to be taken in regard of predicting usage levels and any action which might be taken to reduce overall costs.

Hints

1. Start with the implications of the capital cost in revenue terms and add in the other revenue costs as they come on stream. Go on to consider the total annual costs for the different years from 1996–97 onwards. Do not forget the 'half year'.
2. Then move to consider income. Remember there will be no revenue income until 1998–99. Perform the calculation as a break-even and modify it for surplus as you feel appropriate. Again, do not forget the 'half year'.
3. Consider what forecasting technique might assist the committee.
4. Are there any radical changes which might bring costs down?

NOTE

1. This fairly limited case study is artificial in the sense that it is not based directly on any one particular council or car park. It is realistic, however, in that it is to some extent open-ended. The usage pattern cannot be accurately forecast and thus the fixing of price is to some extent a shot in the dark. HND classes take about an hour and a half over the calculations and another hour or so drafting the report which concludes the exercise.

CASE STUDY 4: VINDLEBRIDGE AMBULANCE STATION[1]

Vindlebridge Ambulance Service NHS trust includes a garage facility for the preparation, servicing and repair of the ambulance fleet. It has been noticed that there is spare capacity, i.e. the employees, equipment and space are not fully utilized, and it has been proposed that income could be generated by running a garage service, offering service, MOTs and repairs initially to employees of the trust, but later, possibly, to members of the public.

CAPITAL CHARGES

The garage and all equipment is charged at £20,000 annually to revenue.

REVENUE COSTS

The garage employs:

1. One manager/storekeeper at £18,000 p.a. She does not work on the floor of the garage but is entirely concerned with supervision.
2. Three mechanics at £15,000 p.a. each. It is reckoned that one of these is spare most of the time, although at peak periods all are usefully employed.
3. A secretary/administrator at £10,000 p.a. FTE. He works only half-time and is, by his own account, often underemployed.

Repair materials are bought as required by the manager using the garage's van which costs £2,000 per year to run. General items such as oil, antifreeze, filters, tyres and so on cost £10,000 annually.

LEVEL OF WORK

The ambulance fleet consists of 40 vehicles, each of which receives about 75 hours' attention during the course of the year.

Required

Draft a report advising the board of the NHS trust as to the situation with regard to the current practices in the garage and the desirability or otherwise of allowing it to develop a service.

If a service were developed, what would be an appropriate hourly charge? You should note that the local service station charges £15 per hour for its labour.

Are there any other solutions which might be adopted to solve the problem of overcapacity?

Hints

1. This is very straightforward provided you think logically about what is actually happening and make some estimates of actual hours worked by the personnel concerned.
2. The report might be scathing: use diplomatic language!

NOTE

1. This is based on a combination of the service sections of two real-life ambulance stations, happily both of them now transformed, one by streamlining, the other by taking on additional work! The calculation is very straightforward. The report needs some attention to diplomatic language. HND classes take about an hour on the calculation and a further hour on drafting a satisfactory report. Word-processing skills can be taught through report drafting and redrafting.

CASE STUDY 5: WESTSHIRE SCHOOL CLOSURE[1]

Westshire LEA is currently responsible for three rural schools, A, B and C, in a relatively compact area of the county. Falling rolls and the expansion of post-16 facilities at the local FE college have meant considerable overcapacity and it is thought inevitable that one of the schools should be closed. There is no obvious geographical preference and most other factors are very evenly balanced. It is thought that financial considerations are likely to weigh very heavily with the education committee.

BUILDINGS

The situation with regard to the premises is as follows:

	Capacity	Annual maintenance	Heat/light, cleaning	Capital needs
School A (19C buildings)	800	£21,000	£21,600	Refurbishing at cost of £750,000
School B (pre-1940 buildings)	600	£12,000	£12,000	New heating system cost £300,000
School C (post-1945 buildings)	600	£9,000	£10,000	No major need

PUPILS

The situation with regard to pupils is as follows:

	Currently on roll	Estimated 1998–99
School A	720	600
School B	500	400
School C	500	500

STAFFING

The current staffing situation is as follows:

	Head	Senior staff	Assistant teachers	Ancillaries
School A	1	4	38	6
School B	1	3	25	5
School C	1	4	30	7

The retirement situation has been investigated and is summed up as follows:

	Head	Senior staff	Assistant teachers	Ancillaries
School A	probable	2 probable	6 probable 3 possible	1 probable
School B		2 probable	5 probable 2 possible	1 probable
School C		1 probable	2 probable 5 possible	2 probable

EDUCATIONAL FACTORS

Other things being equal, the preferred size of school is between 600 and 800 pupils. The two remaining schools should be staffed according to the following model:

- One headteacher and an appropriate number of senior staff
- One assistant for every 20 pupils
- An appropriate number of ancillaries

COSTS OF RELOCATION

- Any redeployed teachers/ancillaries will cost £900 p.a. in travel.
- Any relocated pupils will cost £300 p.a. for bussing.

COSTS OF PROVIDING ADDITIONAL CLASSROOM ACCOMMODATION

Additional capacity can, if necessary, be provided on any site at the following cost:

For 100 extra pupils	£150,000
For 200 extra pupils	£270,000
For 300 extra pupils	£390,000

The necessary capital would be borrowed with total charges of £120 p.a. per £1,000 borrowed.

Other points

- The prices quoted are current, but inflation may be neglected.
- The costs of mothballing the school chosen for closure may be neglected.
- The capital receipts from the possible sale of the school chosen for closure may be neglected.

Required

1. A note to the chief education officer summarizing both the current staffing position and the needs in 1998–99. You should also state your opinion as to whether 'natural wastage' will be sufficient to solve any staffing problem revealed.
2. Calculations showing the costs of and savings made by closing each of the schools.
3. A report making a clear recommendation on financial grounds as to which school should be chosen for closure.

NOTE

1. I have been using a case study along these lines for over ten years at a number of different levels, although it has had to be adapted to suit changing times. It works very well provided that the need to examine each alternative is stressed. Group work is successful with subgroups separately trying their own ways of calculating the effects of closing each school before getting together to see which is the most effective method of calculation and ironing out errors.

   In today's circumstances, of course, league tables and the threat (from an LEA's point of view) of the school chosen for closure going 'grant maintained' are highly relevant and would certainly alter the tenor of the report. The underlying financial principles, however, are not invalidated. Allow about three hours for the case study.

CASE STUDY 6: EXHAMPTON HOSPITAL CONTRACTS[1]

Exhampton Hospital NHS trust has several clinical departments, one of which, cardiology, provides medical and surgical interventions to patients referred to them by local GPs. In respect of the surgical interventions about 80 per cent are planned, in the sense that the hospitalization is by appointment and the operation takes place after some time on a waiting list. The remaining 20 per cent are unplanned in the sense that the patient is in a critical condition and the hospitalization/operation takes place as an emergency.

Fund-holding GPs normally purchase only the planned 'cold surgery', but a planned trial is going on in which fund-holding GPs are also to be charged for unplanned interventions involving on their lists. It is thus necessary to separate the costing/pricing for planned and unplanned surgical interventions.

MEDICAL INFORMATION

The planned operations tend to be easier as measured in terms of both theatre time and postoperative use of technology. The consultant has offered her opinion that the difficulty ratio is something like planned : unplanned: 2 : 3.

There is also a difference in the length of time spent in hospital. For planned operations this averages 8.5 days. For unplanned operations the average is 13.5 days.

TREATMENT COST INFORMATION

- The total cost of cardiology theatre time is £18,000,000 (including all overheads).
- The total cost of postoperative technology, including special nursing/paramedical assistance is £4,500,000.
- The total cost per patient-day for 'hotel services' and basic nursing is £115.

PATIENT VOLUME

There are 1,250 cardiology surgical interventions in the course of a year.

Required

Calculate an approximate cost for both planned and unplanned interventions on the basis of the information and estimations given above.

Draft a report to the district health authority (as primary purchaser) indicating the price for each type of intervention which should be charged to fund-holding GPs.

Hints

1. The key to this lies in dividing up the three sorts of treatment cost in appropriate ways and reflecting this into the volume of cases.
2. The report should be straightforward.

NOTE

1. This case study is unproved: it has been written especially for the book and consequently I am not sure how it will go in the classroom. The main thrust is, of course, to do with apportionment of costs on non-obvious bases. I would guess that calculation and report would take, between them, about two hours in a group situation with HND students.

ANSWERS TO NUMERICAL
EXERCISES IN ARTICLES D1–D10

A booklet, intended for course tutors, containing full workings to these examples together with suggestions for the main points arising from the case studies in D11 to D16 is available on request from the publishers.

D1.1 2. Best £1,800 at end of September; worst (£4,975) at end of March

        3. Deficit for year £4,975

D1.2 2. All months except March

        3. £3.75 million

D2.1 2. During the twelfth year

        3. £110,000

D2.2 2. During the third year

        3. After five years

D3.1 2. Scheme 1 yields a net surplus of £5,250.
           Scheme 2 yields a net loss of £430.
           Scheme 3 yields a net surplus of £4,497.

D3.2 (This is the same as D2.2 in all respects except the inclusion of discounting.)

        2. During the third year

        3. During the seventh year

D4.1 1. P = £16, C = £8, BE = 5,000 hutches

        2. 25,000 hutches

        4. £200,000

        5. £180,000

D4.2   1. C = £10, BE = 10,000 dresses
      2. 5,000 dresses
      4. £50,000
      5. £40,000

D5.1   1. Central overheads: K £60,000, C £40,000, S £10,000, A £10,000
         Power: K £36,000, C £8,000, S £28,000, A £8,000
         Premises: K £36,000, C £60,000, S £18,000, A £6,000
         Workwear: K £1,800, C £ 1,200, S £300, A £300
      2. From S: to K £133,040, to C £33,260. From A: to K £67,150, to C £67,150
      3. K £353,990, C £219,610

D5.2   1. Central overheads: E £120K, H £160K, P £80K, A £160K, FL £200K
         Staff offices: E £30K, H £40K, P £20K, A £40K, FL £50K
         Teaching rooms: E £120K, H £160K, P £80K
         Common space: E £75,295, H £100,392, P £50,196, A £6,275, FL £7,843
      2. From A: to E £97,092, to H £129,456, to P £64,728
         From FL: to E £145,948, to H £194,597, to P £97,298
      3. E £683,385, H £899,455, P £457,222

D6.1   (This depends upon the calculations for D5.1.)
      1. K £853,990, C £319,610
      2. Drinks: K £170,798, C £63,922. Meals: K £683,192. Drinks: £255,688
      3. Meal 117.36p, Drink 14.67p
      4. Meal £1.40, Drink 20p
      5. £460

D6.2   (This depends upon the calculations for D5.2.)
      1. £2,133
      2. £4,800
      3. £267 per person-day
      4. UG £2,346, PG £5,760, R £347

D7.1   1. £115.60 adverse per bed, £57,800 adverse for 500 beds
      2. Labour £116 adverse, materials 40p favourable
      3. LEV £28 favourable, LRV £144 adverse
      4. MUV £20 adverse, MPV £20.40 favourable

D7.2   1. £153.75 adverse per dwelling
      2. Labour £135 adverse, materials £18.75 adverse
      3. LEV £45 adverse, LRV £90 adverse
      4. MUV £7.50 adverse, MPV £11.25 adverse
      5. £461,250

D8.1   1. £1,220
      2. 16p

D8.2 1. 0
      2. 1997–98 £14,400
      3. 1998–99 £129,600
      4. 1999–2000 £144,000

D9.1 1. About 40
      2. 44, but note that the graph lags the actual
      3. Probably worth reducing planned intake to 40

D9.2 1. Just over 480,000 but probably not 500,000
      2. Using 0.3, then 444,837, note high degree of smoothing
         Using 0.7, then 471,374, note more geared to recency
      3. Even allowing for the lag of smoothing, the centre does not need expansion

D10.1 1. 1994–95 0.6 km per person-hour, overtime/standard time 20 per cent, complaints 600
         1995–96 0.53 km per person hour, overtime/standard time 26 per cent, complaints 750
         All PIs compare adversely with others and trend is downhill.

D10.2 1. 1994–95 pre-preparation wastage 13.3 per cent, post-preparation wastage 7.7 per cent
         1995–96 pre-preparation wastage 14.3 per cent, post-preparation wastage 8.3 per cent

GLOSSARY

Audit   The process of checking that the published account statements of an organization[1] represent a 'true and fair' summary of its operations. Whether carried out internally or externally, the process can reveal weaknesses in financial reporting systems which can, in turn, lead to the possibility of improper use of financial resource and/or fraud. There is a legal requirement that published accounts should be certified as representing a true and fair account. The search for deliberate deception is sometimes known as 'probity audit'. 'Value for money audit' is a term used in the public sector to describe the checking that financial resources are applied with an eye to achieving economy, efficiency and effectiveness (q.v.)[2].

(The) Audit Commission   (The Audit Commission for Local Government in England and Wales and the National Health Service) This is the body statutorily charged with the external audit of these parts of the public sector and, in particular, to encourage the search for value for money (q.v.). The Audit Commission uses local accountancy firms to undertake some of its work.

Break-even   A point, usually stated in volume terms, where the receipts from sales of a good or service match the sum of the fixed costs (q.v.) and variable costs (q.v.) of producing it. Associated concepts are payback (q.v.) and contribution (q.v.). Once the break-even point is reached sales income contributes towards a genuine profit.

Budget (The Budget)   A budget is a more or less detailed expenditure plan covering a specified period, usually a year. It represents the limits of spending under various headings. The Budget usually refers to the annual announcement by the Chancellor of the Exchequer of the national plans for raising money (mostly through taxation). Since 1993 this has been moved from March to November to coincide with the announcement of the spending plans.

(The) business plan   In its narrower sense, a document which demonstrates to outside financial agents (e.g. potential lenders or investors) that the intentions of an organization are soundly based and realistic and that the organization is therefore a 'good risk'. There is a wider, and in the public sector, more common usage which is a more general statement of the objectives of the organization in volume terms and how the available resources will be used to achieve those objectives. Some public sector business plans make little if any direct reference to finance.

Business rate   The tax on local businesses based on the rental value of their property. The tax is collected by local authorities on the basis of a centrally determined rate, passed back to the government and reallocated to local authorities on the basis of a centrally determined formula.

Capital (budget) Financial resources over and above revenue (q.v.) which are used to purchase long-lasting assets such as vehicles, buildings and equipment. The capital budget, including any necessary borrowing, has to be agreed by the council as a whole and must conform to rules set by central government. Nearly all capital expenditure, even where immediately financed by borrowing, is ultimately financed by revenue income, as the interest payments and the capital repayments come out of revenue sources. The exceptions to this rule are capital expenditure financed by the selling of assets or by capital grant.

Capital receipts Monies raised from the selling of previously acquired capital assets, for example land or buildings, in order to finance new ventures. *See* capital.

Capping The limitation by central government of an activity of local government. Thus expenditure capping stipulates the maximum expenditure of a local authority and council tax capping stipulates the maximum tax which can be levied.

Cash flow The general term used for the movement of money flowing into and out of an organization over a period. Cash flows can be represented diagrammatically or in tabular form. Negative cash flows, i.e. more money flowing out than in, are costly as money has to be borrowed to 'bridge the gap' in continuing to finance operations. They may also be the symptom of serious problems in the organization. Where cash flow over a long period is predicted (for example as part of a business planning or project appraisal process) it is customary to use a discounted cash flow (q.v.) technique.

CIPFA Chartered Institute of Public Finance and Accountancy, a professional body for public sector accountancy.

Client See purchaser.

Collectivism A belief that a community is more than the sum of its individuals and that therefore individuals ought to be regarded as a part of the community. One of its key concepts is co-operation. See individualism.

(Compulsory) competitive tendering (CCT) The putting out of contracts for the supply of goods or services to a bidding process which should result in the contract being awarded to the cheapest bidder (consistent with quality). This process had been practised in some local authorities for some services for many years but, for certain services, was made compulsory in various stages in the late 1980s and early 1990s.

Contract In law, an agreement (which need not be written) between two parties one of which supplies the other with a good or service in return for a 'consideration'. In the context of local government, all contracts are written, the quantity and quality of goods and services, on the one hand, are clearly stipulated and the 'consideration', i.e. price, on the other hand, is clearly defined. There are usually clauses dealing with failure to meet the contract conditions (penalty clauses) and clauses dealing with possible minor ongoing amendments (variation clauses).

Contractor See provider.

Contribution Used in pricing to describe the 'profit' on the sale of any item of good or service which can be set against the fixed costs of running the organization. The initial aim of any organization is to recover all its fixed costs from these contributions (it has then 'broken even') before moving into a genuine profit situation with the individual contributions then counting towards the overall profit.

Corporate management   A way of organizing the management of an organization which seeks to enhance the articulation and realization of goals covering the whole organization rather than its constituent parts. In large organizations there is usually a tension between the goals of the individual departments/directorates, which are often mainly service oriented, and the overall goals of the organization, which have perforce to respond to wider economic and political constraints. Corporate management is one way of attempting to maximize the creativity of this tension.

Cost centre   A division of an organization's budgetary framework which corresponds to some organizational division (e.g. department or section) or activity (e.g. service A, service B). Typically, the cost centres of complex organizations are not tidily organized and may reflect both aspects.

Costing   A branch of management accountancy which is concerned with calculating the cost to an organization of the goods and services which it either consumes internally or sells to customers. Although there are different costing models, some key concepts in most such models include direct cost and indirect costs or overheads. The last may in turn be divided into product-related overhead and organization-related overhead.

Council tax   The popular name for the tax, introduced with effect from 1993–94, on local residents charged according to the value of the property they occupy/own.

Demographic   To do with the composition and balance of the various groups (e.g. children, elderly people) which combine to make the whole population.

Denationalization   The process of returning a publicly owned enterprise to the private sector. This process was used widely by the Conservative administrations of the 1980s and early 1990s which, for example, sold the state-owned water, gas and electricity industries to private concerns. It was one of the methods of privatization which formed a key part of Conservative belief at the time. *See* nationalization, privatization.

Depreciation   The 'writing down' of the value of an asset to the balance sheet of an organization over a period of years. The initial book value is the price paid. The final book value is usually reckoned as zero or some notional amount. The length of period of depreciation is a period of years, e.g. 5 years for vehicles or 60 years for buildings. Depreciation may be linear (equal instalments) or percentage (e.g. 10 per cent per year). There were problems in the 1980s due to rapid appreciation of the value of buildings.

Direct cost   Used in management accountancy to describe those costs of an activity (e.g. production of a good or service) which are clearly and directly necessary to that activity. They normally include, at a minimum, labour and materials.

Discounted cash flow (DCF)   A technique which allows for the interest costs associated with future income and expenditure. Present money is worth more in the future because it can earn interest. Conversely, future money is worth less today and can thus be discounted. It should be noted that this concept is entirely based on interest charges. It has nothing whatever to do with inflation. Associated concepts net present value (q.v.) and test discount rate (q.v.).

Economy   Attained when cash resource is turned to non-cash resource, e.g. labour or materials, at minimum possible cost, i.e. labour is bought cheaply and materials at minimum price. *See* value for money.

Effectiveness   The achievement of needed and worthwhile service outcomes. There is certainly a 'quality' dimension to effectiveness and, arguably, an 'equity' dimension, i.e. an aspect to do with making sure the service is targeted where it is needed. *See* value for money.

Efficiency   The conversion of non-cash resource into the maximum possible service outputs. *See* value for money.

(The) enabling authority   A term which gained currency in the late 1980s to describe a model of local government which did not itself provide services but provided the frameworks of decision, regulation and payment which enabled outside organizations to provide the services. Thus an enabling authority might decide on the quantity and quality of refuse collection, arrange for tenders and contracts, monitor performance and pay the contractor (using money from local and central sources) without itself actually performing the service. The same model, although not the same name, was used in the late 1980s and the early 1990s for civil service departments which entrusted executive action to agencies, private or public.

Exchange rates   Measures of the purchasing power of one currency in terms of another/others, for example the purchasing power of the pound (£) against the dollar ($) or Deutschmark (DM). They are important to the management of public finance because: (a) at the strategic level of national government it is usually seen as desirable to maintain a strong national currency, and (b) at subnational level the efforts of the state to achieve this may have considerable knock-on effects in terms of interest rates, anti-inflationary policies and so on.

Exponential smoothing   A technique used in forecasting based on the analysis of time series (q.v.). It enables the user to place less reliance on older figures. A constant (between 0 and 1) is chosen. The smaller the constant, the greater the smoothing. The greater the constant, the more sensitive the analysis is to recent figures. A sensible compromise figure is 0.7.

External audit   *See* audit.

Financial management   (1) The narrower, more specialist, meaning is to do with the maximization of financial resource through such devices as the management of investments or cash flow and debtor control. (2) The wider, more general meaning, is to do with the financial aspects of good management practice.

Fiscal   To do with public revenue, especially the nature and balance of taxation.

Fixed cost   A cost of production of a good or service which is independent of the volume produced. Examples would be the rent of a building or the loan charges on capital borrowed for the purchase of machinery. Associated concept variable cost (q.v.).

Forecasting   The estimation of some future numerical value, for example sales, income or clients. Major forecasting techniques depend on history (i.e. what has happened in the past), survey and questionnaire (i.e. what people say they will do) and observation (i.e. what people are actually doing elsewhere). Historical data sets in the form of time series (q.v.) are often used in financial forecasting. It is often felt desirable to smooth the past data in some way so as to obtain a clearer impression of trend. Techniques used for such smoothing include moving averages (q.v.) and exponential smoothing (q.v.).

Functional analysis   An alternative name for objective analysis (q.v.).

General grant   A sum of money made available to a local authority by central government which can, in principle, be spent on anything. In practice, the calculation of the amount is done in such a way as to leave the local authority little discretion. This is because many factors (e.g. demographic and geographical) are taken into account.

Gross budget/expenditure   A statement of the total spending of an organization. It is greater than the net budget/expenditure (q.v.) by the amount financed from fee income and charges.

Ideology   A set of more or less consistent beliefs which can be used to explain or justify actions. Liberal democracy and Marxism are examples of political ideologies.

Incremental budgeting   This methodology, sometimes known as roll-forward budgeting, uses the budget for the current time period as a starting point for determining the budget for the next time period. Typically, any heading will be modified upwards by inflation and downwards by planned efficiency savings. Any other changes will be deliberate growth or cut-back in the heading in question. Associated concepts include zero-based budgeting (q.v.) and priority-based budgeting (q.v.).

Individualism   A belief that individuals ought to be treated as such, bearing responsibility for their own actions, and not merely as part of a community. A key concept of individualism is competition. *See* collectivism.

Inflation   The reduction in the purchasing power of a unit of currency over a period of time. Inflation rates are conventionally measured in terms of percentage per year and for stable states are usually well under 10 per cent per year, typically much lower and often in line with economic growth rate. In Britain in the 1980s, relatively high inflation rates were reduced by application of the theory of monetarism which, among other features, argued that a reduction in the money supply would result in a curbing of inflation. This was and is important to the management of public finance since many public spending cuts were and are justified in terms of a need to reduce/stabilize inflation.

Interest rates   The annual percentage rates at which money can be lent or borrowed. In any state there is a range of such rates which vary according to the lender, the status of the borrower, the sum borrowed and the period of the loan. The range, however, depends in all cases on the base lending rate determined by the state's central bank. In Britain this is the Bank of England. There is an ongoing debate as to how independent such banks should be. The matter is important to the management of public finance because: (a) the government is an important borrower and (b) public bodies are becoming increasingly aware of the costs of their existing and new capital investments.

Internal audit   *See* audit.

Internal market   An arrangement whereby the different divisions of an organization buy and sell goods and services from each other at clearly defined prices and levels of activity/quality. When the levels of price and quality are comparable to those obtaining in the external environment, i.e. the world outside the organization, then the conditions for (compulsory) competitive tendering (q.v.) exist.

LAFIS   Local Authority Financial Information System, a computerized system for comparing actual and planned income and expenditure on a regular basis and passing on the information generated, in accessible form, to the relevant mangers.

Levy   *See* precept.

LGMB   The Local Government Management Board is a Quango (q.v.) charged with training and educational responsibilities in the field of management development for local government officers and members.

Local financial management (LFM)   *See* local management of schools.

Local management of schools (LMS)   The delegation, from a local education authority to the governors of a school, of the responsibility for a high proportion of its budget, including the cost of teaching staff. All LEA secondary schools and most LEA primary schools had such delegated authority by late 1993.

Marginal opportunity analysis (MOA)   A device for prioritizing budgetary decisions by comparing potential cut-backs in one area with potential developments of equal cost in another.

(The) market   A concept of economic theory used to describe the interplay of forces of supply and demand which influence level(s) of price and (quality) of goods and services. In a free market the influence amounts to complete determination, i.e. where there are no artificial restrictions 'the market defines price'.

Market testing   The process of requiring civil service departments and agencies to submit the non-policy dimensions of their activities to tender. The consequences have so far been either the slimming of the organization concerned (where it has retained the work) or its contracting out to an external agency. It is the central government equivalent of compulsory competitive tendering (q.v.).

Moving average   A technique used in forecasting based on the analysis of time series (q.v.). Successive groups of raw data are averaged, e.g. months 1, 2, 3; months 2, 3, 4; months 3, 4, 5 ... The averages so obtained usually have the effect of ironing out any short-term trends and yielding (often for graphical presentation) a good impression of overall trend.

Nationalization   The process of bringing some activity into the public sector and either directly or indirectly into government control. Nationalization was practised extensively by the post-war Labour governments from 1945–50 and 1950–51 when private industries such as coal, railways, iron and steel and road transport were nationalized. Nationalization had previously been practised by both Liberal (Port of London Authority) and Conservative (BBC and British Airways) governments. *See* denationalization, privatization.

Net budget/expenditure   A statement of the spending of an organization after income from fees and charges has been allowed for. It is smaller than the gross budget/expenditure (q.v.) by the amount of these charges.

Net present value (NPV)   The value of a future transaction at today's date. It is less than the current value of the transaction because of discounting due to the cost of borrowing money. Spreadsheet-like tables of NPVs are available with rows of timescale and columns of interest rates. The cells are then factors (e.g. 0.975) which when multiplied by the cash value of the future transaction give its NPV. Associated concepts are discounted cash flow (q.v.) and test discount rate (q.v.).

Objective analysis   The analysis of organizational expenditure under headings corresponding to the purposes or objectives of the spending, e.g. education, leisure, housing. Such an analysis will often correspond to departmental structure. A related concept is subjective analysis (q.v.).

One-line budget   The principle of giving more freedom by passing a manager's spending authority on in the form of a simple statement of the maximum permitted spending, without specifying subheadings.

Overhead   Used in management accountancy to describe a cost which is not directly associated with the front-line production of a good or service. Such overheads may, however, be fairly closely associated (e.g. within the same department or section) or more distantly related (e.g. at head office). Ultimately, all overheads must be built (along with the direct costs (q.v.)) into the full cost(s) of the goods and/or services provided by the organization.

Payback period   The time in which it is predicted that a capital-based venture (e.g. the installation of an efficient heating system) will recover its initial costs (e.g. by reductions in the cost of energy). Payback calculations are often done using discounted cash flow (q.v.) techniques.

Performance indicator   A figure which can be used either inside or outside an organization as a comparative measure of success. Some indicators are closely related to costs, others to volume and yet others to measures of quality and/or customer satisfaction. Many public authorities are required to publish a range of performance indicators annually which, where possible, should be accompanied by comparative figures from a family cluster of other similar public authorities. Performance indicators are useful as devices for negotiating resource allocation and as levers for change.

PESC   The Public Expenditure Survey Committee is responsible for overseeing the Public Expenditure Survey process. Basically, although it was intended to provide a longer term planning process free from short-term bargaining, it has developed into a mechanism for adjudicating between the competing claims of government spending departments.

Planning, programming and budgeting (systems) PPB(S)   Systems which attempt to construct budgets in the light of the objectives of an organization, e.g. provision for elderly people, as seen across departmental boundaries so as to reduce duplication and institutional resource waste. They are thus clearly linked to ideas of corporate management (q.v.). There is also a dimension of timeliness about PPB(S), i.e. when the expenditure on a particular activity will be required. The concept of objective analysis (q.v.) is relevant.

Precept   A sum of money collected by a local authority on behalf of another authority and subsequently passed on. District authorities, for example, pass on a precept to the relevant county and also to any parishes within their boundaries. Some precepts are, for historic reasons, known as levies.

Pricing   The methodology used to determine the price to customers of goods and services provided by an organization. The three key methodologies (often used in combination) are cost plus, awareness of competition, and awareness of what the market will bear. The notion of contribution (q.v.) is also relevant.

Priority-based budgeting   A device for allocating scarce resources across departments/directorates by requesting each department to prioritize its spending needs. A line is then drawn giving each department 'equal misery', i.e. the same proportion of funding.

Privatization   The process of removing public services from direct political control. It was a major feature of 'rolling back the frontiers of the state' as practised by the Conservative governments led by Margaret Thatcher and later John Major. Denationalization was one form, but others included the granting of corporate status to polytechnics and FE colleges, the compulsory competitive tendering (q.v.)/market testing (q.v.) of various services offered direct to the public (e.g. running local authority leisure centres) or within organizations (e.g. local authority computer or legal sections) or within authorities on behalf of the public (e.g. public works departments or hospital cleaning). *See* nationalization, denationalization.

Probity audit   *See* audit.

Provider   One of the key terms of the purchaser–provider arrangement which characterizes internal markets (q.v.). The provider must meet a defined level of service (service-level agreement (q.v.)) at a defined price. If the provider cannot do this and the purchaser has 'real money' then the provider stands the risk of losing the contract with consequent loss of income and staff. The concept is the same as 'contractor' in 'client–contractor'.

Public expenditure survey committee   *See* PESC.

Purchaser   One of the key terms of the purchaser–provider arrangement which characterizes internal markets (q.v.). An important question to be asked is whether the purchaser has 'real money' which could be spent outside the organization, or whether the money is notional, i.e. just a paper transfer. The concept is the same as 'client' in 'client–contractor'.

Quango   Quasi-autonomous national (non in USA) governmental organization, an agency of the state which performs a role which does not, usually, need direct political control and is therefore not under the day-to-day control of a minister. Employees are not normally classed as civil servants.

Revenue (budget)   The routine annual income and expenditure (plan) covering the day-to-day operation of an organization.

Revenue consequences of capital schemes (RCCS)   Used to express the notion that all capital expenditure (q.v.) has direct consequences for the revenue budget (q.v.). The four important cost aspects are depreciation (q.v.), maintenance, utilization and loan charges (interest and debt repayment).

Revenue support grant   Sums of money made available to local authorities from the government in the form of general grants (q.v.) and specific grants (q.v.). For most local authorities the revenue support grant is the single largest source of income.

Service-level agreement (SLA)   A detailed account of the quantity and quality of service to be provided by a provider to a purchaser over a defined timescale in a market or quasi-market situation. Where the market is an internal market (q.v.) the SLA is a proxy for one part of a contract. Where an organization goes to an outside supplier for a good or service an SLA is inappropriate and a genuine contract should be drawn up.

Specific grant   A sum of money made available to a local authority for a particular purpose, e.g. public transport or policing, on which it must be spent.

Standing financial instructions (SFIs)   The rules by which an authority and its employees must abide with respect to all financial transactions. CIPFA (q.v.) provides model SFIs as part of its financial information service.

Subjective analysis   The analysis of organizational expenditure under categories of spending such as staff, premises, materials, etc., rather than by organizational division. *See* objective analysis.

Taxation   The process by which a government raises revenue by levying charges on individuals and organizations over which it has jurisdiction. Typical taxes include charges on income or profits, charges based on the price of purchases/transactions, special duties on such items as tobacco and alcohol, residence charges (often based on the value of property), capital gains charges levied on items which when sold show substantial appreciation and inheritance taxes/ death duties payable on the capital possessions of deceased persons.

Tender   A document which formalizes an offer to supply goods and/or services to a defined level of quantity and quality for a price. A potential purchaser invites tenders and sets the specifications. Potential suppliers then define the price at which they are willing to supply. The purchaser is then in a position to choose which tender best meets their needs of which one of the most important will be low relative price.

Test discount rate   A notional figure, expressed as a percentage and currently 5 per cent, which is the rate stipulated by government to be used by public authorities when performing discounted cash flow calculations. Associated concepts are discounted cash flow (q.v.) and net present value (q.v.).

Time series   Any record of level of activity, e.g. sales, clients, income, over a period. The time series is usually available as a tabulation. Its uses are mainly as an aid to the analysis of the past or as a guide to projections for the future. Most time series are more easily understood if they are produced as a graph rather than as a table. An associated concept is forecasting (q.v.).

Transfer payment   A payment made to an individual or organization for which there is no corresponding service received. Examples include child benefit, student grants, unemployment benefit and state pensions.

Ultra vires   A doctrine which places limits on the authorized powers of an organization or an individual. No-one should 'go beyond' (*ultra*) their 'powers' (*vires*). This doctrine is of great importance in the public sector, particularly local government.

Unitary state   A description applied to a state where the national government is clearly and constitutionally superior to any tier of local or regional government. The United Kingdom is such a state as local government derives its powers entirely from central government. Other states such as the United States of America and Germany are, however, not unitary as their constitutions specifically reserve some powers to a regional tier ('states' or 'Länder').

Value for money (VFM)   The combination of the 'three Es': economy, efficiency and effectiveness (q.v.), so that cash resource is economically turned into maximum non-cash resource which is in turn converted efficiently into maximum service output. If this service output is effective (needed and worth while) then VFM has been achieved.

Variable cost   A cost of production of a good or service which varies with the volume produced. Examples include the cost of materials used and of the labour involved. An associated concept is fixed cost (q.v.).

Variance   A difference between planned and actual spending. Variances are detected through budgetary control systems such as LAFIS (q.v.) and passed onto managers as part of regular budgetary information statements. One major financial skill required by managers is to appreciate the significance of variances. Another is to understand techniques of dealing with them where necessary.

Variance analysis   A technique for breaking up a total variance into the various factors of which it is composed. The two most important factors are those due to labour and materials and these may in turn be divided into variances due to changes in the price and efficiency of labour or the cost and utilization of materials. Another important variance depends on changes in overhead rates, and this too can be subdivided.

Virement   The power to move spending power from one head of budget to another, e.g. to spend 'stationary budget' on travel, 'capital budget' on revenue, etc. The power to vire is a useful tool for the manager. It is often used retrospectively to offset overspending on one budget head by underspending on another.

Welfare state   The concept of government provision or support for the essentials of life such as housing, education, health, employment and social security/pensions. No modern state has total state provision of such essentials (although Sweden might be cited as having come nearest). No modern state has zero provision of such essentials, although the United States might be cited as among the most minimal in this respect. Britain's welfare state grew primarily from the 1870s but was consolidated through a series of measures passed between 1944 and 1948 by the wartime coalition government (Churchill) and the post-war Labour government (Attlee) in the light of the remarkable consensus produced by the Beveridge Report. The chief features of debate have been: what welfare areas should be included; to what extent should the state be responsible; to what extent should individuals be responsible for making their own provision; and how might the state most effectively 'target' individuals or groups which cannot/will not make adequate provision for themselves.

The 1980s and early 1990s saw a marked shift in housing (reduction in local authority housing) and employment (a set of important changes in the pattern of employment) and the beginnings of a shift in terms of health (the growth of private medicine) and education (reduction of the power of local education authorities and vastly increased access to further and higher education). The issue of social security and pensions targeting is likely to provide a focus for debate for some years to come: the demographic shifts are relevant to this.

Zero-based budgeting (ZBB)   A system of making a budget which, in principle, starts from scratch each year.

NOTES

1. The term 'organization' has frequently been used. This could refer a public authority, e.g. local authority, or NHS trust or one of its departments/directorates, to a civil service department or government agency or to a private sector company. Many of the concepts of financial management apply across sector boundaries.
2. This glossary occasionally refers the reader to other kindred terms with the letters (q.v.). These stand for *quod vide*, the Latin for 'which see'.

BASIC PRINCIPLES OF ACCOUNTING AS APPLIED TO PUBLIC AUTHORITIES[1]

Note: This appendix is written as if all accounting were done manually using books and pens and rulers! In practice, of course, accounting systems are computerized. This makes no difference whatever to the theory.

FINANCIAL ACCOUNTING AND MANAGEMENT ACCOUNTING

Financial accounting and its audiences

The main objective of a financial accounting system is to provide an historical record of the use of an organization's financial resources over a given period, usually a year. This information will be used by different interested parties for a variety of reasons.

Typical audiences for private sector organizations include:

- Directors and shareholders who need to know what has been done with their money and how much 'dividend' is to be paid
- Her Majesty's Inspectors of Taxes, who will use the accounts as a basis for their calculations

For public authorities the chief audiences are:

- Departments of government, who use information from the accounts for calculating such things as future funding arrangements
- Politicians, especially at local level, and NHS trust board and health authority members, who will wish to know levels of spending on particular activities as a basis for making decisions on future resource allocations
- Electors, who, at least in principle, have a concern for the financial performance of the state and their local authority
- Lending institutions, who will wish to gauge the security of loans made and the financial strength of an organization as a basis for future lending

The main thrust of this appendix is concerned with the principles of financial accounting.

Management accounting and its audiences

The main objective of management accounting is to produce regular and relatively frequent financial data and related performance indicators so that audiences inside the organization can have the information required to assist them in managing the organization on a day-to-day basis.

For both private sector and public sector the main audiences are managers at different levels who need to know how they and their teams are performing in relation to agreed budgetary targets and non-financial objectives.

The main thrust of the book as a whole has been managerial.

THE OUTPUT DOCUMENTS OF FINANCIAL ACCOUNTING

The two main documents produced as a result of the processes of financial accounting operating on the transactions of an organization are as follows:

1. The *balance sheet* which summarizes the overall financial standing of the organization at a particular date in terms of:
   (a) What it owns (assets)
   (b) What it owes (creditors)
   (c) What it is owed (debtors)
   and its accrued balances resulting from profits and provisions over a period of time.
2. The *trading and profit and loss account* which summarizes the main financial transactions of the year which relate to normal activity. For some 'not for profit' organizations trading accounts are inappropriate and are replaced by *income and expenditure accounts*, sometimes known as *revenue accounts*.

    This is true for the public sector as a whole, but there are divisions of local authorities, e.g. direct labour organizations, and some contracting NHS organizations for which genuine trading accounts must be kept.

There is a connection between the two final outcomes so far discussed in that:

The balance sheet for year x operated on by the outcomes of the trading over a year becomes the balance sheet for year $x + 1$.

It should also be noted that the balance sheet is not strictly an account but a statement of the outcomes of accounts!

THE BASIC BOOKS OF RECORD

In principle, there is only one book of record for an organization, known as the 'ledger'. In practice the ledger consists of a 'cash book' and a number of 'subledgers' which refer to various activities of the organization.

Obvious subledgers could be:

- Debtors/sales/income
- Creditors/purchases/expenditure
- Assets/liabilities/capital

All these accounts could be replicated for every department of the organization and brought together annually for the organization as a whole.

THE BASIC SYSTEM: DOUBLE ENTRY

The basic system used is that of 'double entry bookkeeping' in which every transaction is recorded in two accounts: as a *credit* (to give/value given) in one and a *debit* (to receive/value received) in the other. Convention dictates that the debits are recorded on the left and the credits on the right.

THE RECORDING OF TRANSACTIONS

Every transaction is recorded twice. This is because public authorities use double entry bookkeeping in line with the conventions indicated above and standard practice elsewhere:

1. If a transaction involves a transfer of money from the organization, e.g. a purchase or a wage payment, it is recorded:
   (a) as a credit in the cash book; and
   (b) as a debit in the appropriate ledger.
2. If the transaction involves a transfer of money to the organization, e.g. a payment of council tax, a payment for a contracted service or a government grant, it is recorded:
   (a) as a debit in the cash book; and
   (b) as a credit in the appropriate ledger.

The above principles are true with regard to any public organization. Different practices have grown up, however, within the different branches of the public sector and the notes below outline some of the features of accounting for local authorities, the NHS and central government.

ACCOUNTS FOR LOCAL AUTHORITIES

The main funds

The financial transactions of a local authority are by law reflected in only two funds: the *collection fund* and the *general fund*.

For each fund an *annual revenue account* is prepared and the excess of income over expenditure or expenditure over income in the year added to the respective opening balances on the funds. This thus provides the closing, i.e. year end, fund balances.

The collection fund records as income[2]:

1. Business rates (levied on owners or occupiers of industrial or commercial properties)
2. Council tax (from individual householders)

The collection fund records as expenditure:

1. Payment of business rates (to the government).
2. Levies precepted by certain bodies, e.g. fire and police authorities.
3. The amount levied at the beginning of each financial year by an authority's general fund to cover expenditure on the cost of services not financed by fees, charges and other income.

   The amount which an authority may levy in this way for use within its general fund is controlled by central government using a device known as 'expenditure capping'.

All the income and expenditure of a local authority not recorded in the collection fund is recorded in its general fund. However, separate revenue accounts may be maintained for individual services and there is a statutory requirement to record separately the financial transactions relating to council housing and direct service organizations, e.g. repairs and maintenance, grounds maintenance or cleaning of buildings, which are required to achieve a statutorily set annual rate of return.

In fact, local authorities maintain separate revenue accounts covering major services such as housing, education, social services, leisure, direct service organizations, etc. In preparing its annual accounts, the transactions on these individual revenue accounts are aggregated to provide the overall general fund revenue account.

The balance sheet of a local authority, as with any other organization, summarizes its overall financial standing at a particular date. Care must, however, be taken in using information contained in the balance sheet because fixed assets, e.g. land and buildings, are normally included at historical cost (i.e. what was paid for them) rather than current value (i.e. what they would fetch on the open market).

Capital accounting

The requirement of the 1980 Planning and Land Act that Direct Labour Organizations (DLO) should produce a return of 5 per cent on capital threw into prominence the differences between:

- local authority revenue accounting and the trading accounting of private sector businesses; and
- the different bases of capital valuation in the two sectors.

During the 1980s CIPFA worked on these problems and produced a provisional code of practice (*Compulsory Competition: Meeting the Challenge Part VI*)[3] in 1988 as well as a set of *Guidance Notes*[4] in the same year.

The 1988 Local Government Act, which introduced CCT for a wider range of services, made subtle differences to the original 1980 wording which imply that the CIPFA guidelines and code of practice have, in effect, the force of law.

In performing the rate of return calculations it is necessary to modify traditional local authority presentation of figures in line with the two points made above:

1. The apparent surplus should be increased by 'add-backs' covering interest charges, principal repayments and renewals fund contributions, and reduced by 'deductions' covering depreciation and stock adjustment.
2. The capital employed consists in effect of four parts:
   (a) Depot land, which is assumed all to be related to direct service provision, and is valued at the mid-year average
   (b) Stores land, which is assumed to be 67 per cent directed to direct service provision, and is valued at the mid-year average
   (c) Buildings, vehicles and plant, which are valued on a market basis (rather than historically as previously)
   (d) Stock

The effect of the modifications at 1 is usually to increase the surplus (thus making it easier to achieve the required rate of return), while 2 will usually increase the total capital value (thus making it harder to achieve the required rate of return!).

There is a fuller discussion of this point and a very clearly set out example in Chapter 6 of Henley *et al.* (1995).

ACCOUNTS FOR THE NHS

The required financial statements for the various components of the NHS mainly consist of:

- An income and expenditure account for the financial year, 1 April to 31 March
- A balance sheet for the year end, 31 March
- A cash flow statement for the financial year showing the increase/decrease in cash and cash equivalents

Additionally, where relevant, the remuneration of board members must be detailed.

There are no particular peculiarities in the construction or presentation of these statements. However, it is worth summarizing the constraints under which the various authorities/trusts work and their relationship to one another. .

(District) health authorities

The (district) health authorities are the primary purchasers of services and receive an annual grant which is cash limited by statute. Although health authorities provide some services themselves, the majority of services are provided through contracts with NHS trusts and other agencies. Income and expenditure accounts reflect this with the bulk of expenditure being on contracts.

The cash limit is taken very seriously by the chief executive who is the 'accountable officer'. In practice, overspending is a thing of the past. Underspends may be carried forward, but clearly large underspends might result in the imposition of a lower cash limit. In practice, the level of underspend is in the region of 0–1 per cent on a budget which might vary from £200 million upwards.

The main significance of the balance sheet is only in relation to current assets and liabilities as (district) health authorities have relatively little in the way of fixed assets. Likewise, the capital–revenue distinction is not of such significance as it was before.

NHS trusts

There are three important requirements laid upon trusts:

1. They are expected to break even on their income and expenditure account.
2. They are expected to keep within their external financing limit (EFL).
3. They are expected to show a rate of return (currently 6 per cent) on their capital employed.

In practice, any anticipated surplus on the income and expenditure account may be reinvested as capital. The main control/regulator for capital is the EFL. The return on the employed capital is calculated by dividing the adjusted operating surplus by the average value of the capital assets.

Trusts own a good deal of capital stock, thus the balance sheet is of more than passing interest! Fixed assets (land and buildings) are valued triennially by the district valuer with indexation. They are thus subject to current cost accounting, which may be contrasted with the way in which the private sector is moving, i.e. away from current cost accounting and back towards the historic cost concept. Other assets are depreciated over suitable periods in the usual way. When trusts are formed it is necessary to create an item akin to share capital in order to balance the balance sheet. This item is made up partly of interest bearing loans and partly of public dividend capital.

Trusts have two financial flexibilities which were not present under the previous directly managed arrangements. They can invest surplus funds within certain limitations and the revenue–capital distinction is of less significance than before.

GP fundholders

The actual financial freedom of GP fundholders is not great. In the first place, only a proportion of the total service is funded through fund-holding arrangements, mainly non-urgent elective surgery, and second, the income and expenditure account for each fundholder forms a part of the (cash limited) income and expenditure account of the relevant health authority.

Fundholders are not cash limited as such: only one has had its fund-holding status withdrawn, and there were other factors involved in that case. The implication is that health authorities must cover overspending by fundholders. Underspending, on the other hand, may be carried forward for up to four years, a factor which again could put pressure on a health authority.

In practice, health authorities try to work closely with fundholders in an attempt to manage the situation for mutual benefit.

Regional health authorities

The 8 (previously 14) regions were abolished with effect from 1 April 1996. Their offices and officers became part of the NHS executive. The regional directors are financially accountable to the chief executive of the NHS.

Regions pose no special accounting difficulties, but their abolition does imply that some authority has to be responsible for administering their closing assets and liabilities. In some cases neighbouring districts will take over these assets and liabilities.

ACCOUNTS FOR CENTRAL GOVERNMENT

From 1999–2000 accounts published and laid before Parliament will be in accordance with accruals accounting procedures and will separate capital from revenue items. These practices will also apply to the annual Public Expenditure Survey with effect from 2000. The changes, so baldly stated, are in fact fundamental and held by the Chancellor who announced them, Kenneth Clarke, to be highly significant.

The changes have come about and will be implemented as a result of a long process of deliberation and benchmarking—the observation of best practice in other countries. The usual phrase which covers the change is 'resource accounting', more fully resource accounting and budgeting, 'a set of accruals accounting techniques for reporting on the expenditure of UK central government' and 'a framework for analysing expenditure by departmental objective, relating this to outputs wherever possible'[5].

The chief proposals, which will undoubtedly be implemented as they are all widely accepted within the civil service and there are no matters of party contention, are as follows:

1. A change from cash accounting to accruals accounting.
2. The introduction of a distinction between expenditure of revenue and capital items in both budgeting and accounting.
3. A requirement for all government departments, executive agencies and trading funds to produce:

    (a) An annual income and expenditure account (alternatively known as an operating cost statement or revenue account)

    (b) An annual balance sheet covering all fixed and current assets and liabilities, and

    (c) A cash flow statement which will reconcile net operating cost to cash spend.

4. A requirement to supplement these formal accounts with:

    (a) An analysis of revenue and capital spending by 'main objective', and

    (b) An output and performance analysis, comparing actual outputs with targets expressed in both financial and non-financial terms and presented by 'main objective'.

5. Conformity with generally accepted accounting practice, in particular relevant companies legislation and approved accounting standards.

6. Parliamentary approval on the basis of accruals rather than cash.

7. Presentation of expenditure plans in accordance with accruals rather than cash. This last requirement brings depreciation and the cost of capital finance within the control total.

The change to accruals accounting and the separation of revenue from capital expenditure together will bring central government into line with local government and the NHS. The required analyses and performance figures are, of course, not financial accounting requirements as such, but will stimulate management accounting and encourage the continued search for value for money within all parts of the public sector.

NOTES

1. The preparation of this appendix owes much to the encouragement and help of Trevor Gee, formerly Financial Services Manager with Sheffield MDC, who checked a first draft, prevented several glaring errors and omissions and suggested some important improvements. John Brassington, Director of Finance for Trent Region was particularly helpful in matters concerning the NHS and made several valuable suggestions for improving the draft. The section on central government accounting owes much to the paper *Resource Accounting and Budgeting in Government* written by Martin Evans and published in 1995 by the Public Finance Foundation under the auspices of CIPFA. Any errors are the responsibility of the author.

2. This statement is in accordance with the 1994 CIPFA Accounting Code of Practice. Previously the RSG, now recorded in the general fund, was also paid into the collection fund.

3. CIPFA (1988) *Compulsory Competition: Meeting the Challenge Part VI*. Chartered Institute of Public Finance and Accountancy, London.

4. CIPFA (1988) *Guidance Notes*. Chartered Institute of Public Finance and Accountancy, London.

5. Green Paper, *Better Accounting for Taxpayer's Money: Resources Accounting and Budgeting in Government* (Cm 2626, July 1994).

SOURCES OF INFORMATION AND FURTHER READING

For readers wishing to compare the contents of this book with other general works on public finance and public sector financial management, the following books may be recommended:

Coombs, H.M. and D.E. Jenkins (1991) *Public Sector Financial Management*, Chapman & Hall, London.

Glynn, J.G. (1993) *Public Sector Financial Control and Accounting*, 2nd edn, Blackwell, Oxford.

Henley, Sir D. *et al.* (1995) *Public Sector Accounting and Financial Control*, 5th edn, CIPFA/ Van Nostrand Rheinhold, London.

Pendlebury, M.W. (ed.) (1989) *Management Accounting in the Public Sector*, CIMA/ Heinemann, Oxford.

An important series of updating books is published by the PFF an adjunct of CIPFA. This useful series of books produced by the Public Finance Foundation (recently in association with Chapman & Hall) and adopted by The Open University as set texts, is published annually. Each covers the events of the previous year dealing with general issues and contemporary matters and with an emphasis on financial affairs. The five most recent currently to hand are:

Terry, F. and H. Roberts (eds) (1991) *Public Domain 1991*, Public Finance Foundation, London.

Terry, F. and P. Jackson (eds) (1992) *Public Domain 1992: the Public Services Yearbook*, PFF/ Chapman & Hall, London.

Trinder, C. and P. Jackson (eds) (1993) *The Public Services Yearbook 1993*, PFF/Chapman & Hall, London.

Jackson, P. and M. Lavender (eds) (1994) *The Public Services Yearbook 1994*, CIPFA/ Chapman & Hall, London.

Jackson, P. and M. Lavender (eds) (1995) *The Public Services Yearbook 1995/96*, CIPFA/ Chapman & Hall, London.

A further PFF series with an important financial dimension are the Readers, each of which contains a number of contributions from acknowledged experts in their fields. So far published or announced are:

Flynn, N. (ed.) (1994) *Change in the Civil Service*

Jackson, P.M. (ed.) (1995) *Measures for Success in the Public Sector*

Terry, F. (ed.) (1994) *Towards Restructuring: The Dimensions of Change in Local Government* (*transport*) due 1996
(*higher education*) due 1996

The various aspects of the finance/financial management of the public sector produce a specialist literature. Especially well developed is the local government area. Here CIPFA plays a leading role. The most complete and up-to-date account of the current position with regard to all aspects of the financing of local government is, without doubt, the *Financial Information Service* provided by CIPFA. This consists of a number of loose-leaf volumes subscribed to by most (if not all) local authorities and located (usually) in the treasurer's department.

These volumes are regularly updated with new sheets from CIPFA and contain basic information applicable to all departments together with a number of volumes dealing with specific services, e.g. housing, education and so on. They are very big—being so comprehensive—and can appear quite off-putting: it is worth while getting a bit of help from a member of treasury staff on the first occasion of use!

The Institute of Chartered Secretaries and Administrators (ICSA) publishes a useful series *LG Agenda* which includes updating on financial and other matters.

Bernard M. Jones (1995) *Local Government Financial Management*, ICSA Publishing, deals with the topic in a way which has been described as 'clear and easy to understand'.

Roger Buttery and Robert K. Simpson (1989) *Audit in the Public Sector*, 2nd edn, Woodhead-Faulkner/CIPFA, is a useful specialist book on this topic although, of course, not covering the extension of the work of the Audit Commission to the NHS.

In this connection the various publications of the Audit Commission which cover both local government and the NHS are well worth studying.

On the more technical financial accounting aspect, M. Rogers (1995) *Public Sector Accounting*, Stanley Thornes, is to be recommended.

Journals and magazines

Two magazines which provide regular updating on matters of local government finance, usually in the form of short articles applied to various practical problems, are *Municipal Journal* and *Local Government Chronicle*. They are also useful in that they provide frequent case studies of good practice.

Health Services Management published by the Institute of Health Services Management (IHSM) has regular features regarding financial and related matters.

Two more general journals which are published less frquently are *Public Money* and *Public Finance and Accountancy*. These are addressed much more to longer term and theoretical issues and the general tone is more reflective and analytical.

The Economist is a weekly publication which covers a wide range of topics. There is a regular and important section on British affairs including informed and critical discussion of British public finance. The great strength is the immediacy of the comment: the weakness is that the theoretical perspective is sometimes lacking or biased.

Serious newspapers such as the *Daily Telegraph*, the *Financial Times*, the *Guardian*, the *Independent* and *The Times* frequently carry useful reports and analyses of current financial matters.

INDEX